BUSINESS
Superbrands

AN INSIGHT INTO SOME OF BRITAIN'S STRONGEST B2B BRANDS 2007

www.superbrands.uk.com

Chief Executive
Ben Hudson

Brand Liaison Directors
Fiona Maxwell
Liz Silvester

PR & Marketing Manager
Hannah Paul

Events & Joint Ventures Manager
Rachel Springate

Head of Accounts
Will Carnochan

Managing Editor
Angela Cooper

Author
James Curtis

Designers
Chris Harris
Laura Hill

Other publications from Superbrands (UK) Ltd:
Superbrands 2006/07 ISBN: 0-905652-02-X
CoolBrands 2006/07 ISBN: 1-905652-03-8

To order these books, email brands@superbrands.uk.com
or call 01825 873133.

Published by Superbrands (UK) Ltd.
44 Charlotte Street
London
WIT 2NR

© 2007 Superbrands (UK) Ltd published under licence
from Superbrands Ltd.

www.superbrands.uk.com

Printed in Italy

ISBN: 978-0-9554784-0-6

Contents

Endorsements

John Noble
Director
British Brands
Group

In these pages is all the evidence anyone might need to demonstrate the diversity of sectors to which the principles of branding can be applied – construction, banking, recruitment, logistics, transport, business services and more.

Furthermore the companies showcased are fine examples of the art – superior performance rooted in a deep understanding of their customers, combined with an engagement with their audience that sets them apart from their competitors. Most have been practicing this art for decades, resulting in trust and loyalty amongst their users and an ever wider reputation for excellence.

To build such brands requires vision, understanding, long term investment and discipline. The rewards are reaped by the companies certainly but also by their customers and the business community more generally, as a result of the ideas, choice, trust and diversity they bring to the market.

Paul Gostick
International Chairman
The Chartered Institute
of Marketing (CIM)

The Chartered Institute of Marketing (CIM) is pleased to endorse publications that promote best practice in branding, and CIM has endorsed the Superbrands publications over a number of years. We are now delighted that the independent council have included CIM this year as a Business Superbrand.

CIM works tirelessly to raise awareness and understanding of marketing within business – specifically the value that marketing creates, and the impact that it has on the bottom line. Including CIM in the list of Business Superbrands is clear recognition of marketing's place at the heart of business and CIM's leadership role in representing the marketing profession.

Branding is not just for consumer goods, it has an important part to play for business and service brands too. Most business to business and services relationships are built on trust and in reading this book, you will gain insight into how the featured companies build trust into their brands.

About Superbrands

The Superbrands organisation presents expert and consumer opinion on branding. This publication – our fifth Business Superbrands volume – forms part of a wider programme that pays tribute to the UK's strongest business to business brands. Using the comprehensive selection process, experts and consumers, in this case business professionals, identify the country's strongest B2B brands; these are the only brands eligible to join the programme. Through identifying these brands and providing their case histories, the organisation hopes that people will gain a greater appreciation of the discipline of branding and a greater admiration for the brands themselves.

Full details on Superbrands in the UK can be found at www.superbrands.uk.com.

The Business Superbrands Stamp

The brands that have been awarded Business Superbrand status and participate in the programme, are entitled to use the Business Superbrands Stamp. This powerful endorsement provides evidence to existing and potential consumers, media, employees and investors of the exceptional standing that these Business Superbrands have achieved.

Member brands use the stamp on marketing materials, including product packaging, advertising, websites, annual reports as well as other external and internal communication channels.

Business Superbrands Selection Process

Independent researchers use a wide range of sources to compile a list of the UK's leading B2B brands. From the thousands of brands initially considered, a list of between 1,200-1,500 brands is forwarded to the Business Superbrands Council.

The independent and voluntary Business Superbrands Council considers the list and members individually award each brand a score from 1-10. Council members are not allowed to score brands with which they have a direct association or are in direct competition to. The lowest-scoring brands (approximately 50 per cent) are eliminated at this stage.

A panel of approximately 1,500 individual business professionals are surveyed by YouGov plc, the UK's most accurate online research agency. These individuals are asked to vote on the surviving brands.

These brands are then ranked based on the combined score of the Business Superbrands Council (50 per cent) and the panel of business professionals (50 per cent). The lowest-scoring brands are eliminated and the leading 500 brands are awarded 'Business Superbrand' status and are invited to join the Business Superbrands programme.

Business Superbrands
Council 2007

Anthony Carlisle
Executive Director
Citigate Dewe Rogerson

Russell Clarke
Ex Global Head of Marketing
Hemscott plc

Steve Cooke
Marketing Director
BMRB

Jonathan Cummings
Marketing Director
Institute of Directors

Cherry DeGeer
Global Practice Leader – Communications
Rio Tinto

Marc Edney
Group Marketing Manager
BSI Group

Gary Groenheim
Head of Marketing
CNBC Europe

Simon Gruselle
Corporate Marketing Director
Datamonitor

John Mathers
CEO
Enterprise IG, UK

David Mitchell
Ex Head of Brand Communication EMEA
Intel

Ruth Mortimer
Editor
Brand Strategy

Marc Nohr
Managing Partner
Kitcatt Nohr Alexander Shaw

Daniel Rogers
Editor
PRWeek

Graham Spencer
Director of Marketing, Europe
Towers Perrin

Simon Woodroffe
Founder
YO!Company

Simon Wylie
Founding Partner & Managing Director
Xtreme Information

Jean Wyllie
Managing Director
Porter Novelli

Stephen Cheliotis
Chairman
Superbrands Councils UK

Foreword

Angela Cooper, Managing Editor

 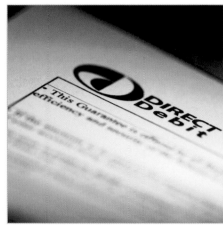 

It gives me great pleasure to introduce this, the fifth edition of Business Superbrands.

Several key developments have taken place since the previous volume of this publication. Principally, Superbrands in the UK has become an independent entity, Superbrands (UK) Ltd, under licence from Superbrands Ltd. This corporate change has freed up the local team to make the changes to our operations that we have been keen to implement.

The methodology process and the transparency of our results have been developed to ensure that we remain in tune with the current business environment. The Business Superbrands selection process now encompasses the opinions of both the Business Superbrands Council – an independent and voluntary expert panel – and the opinions of some 1,420 business professionals. This element of the process was conducted by the research agency YouGov plc. Full details of both the council voting process and consumer election can be found in this publication.

In addition to this, the look, feel and content of this book have been reassessed. A complete redesign was undertaken as a result of feedback on the previous edition from both the Business Superbrands Council and our member brands. You will also find that a number of new features have been incorporated. This includes a comprehensive explanation of the Business Superbrands selection process as well as in-depth insights into the involvement of both the council and YouGov plc Online Election. Furthermore, for the first time, a full list of the 500 qualifying Business Superbrands is included at the back of this publication.

You will also find a section dedicated to some of the charities supported by our member brands. Superbrands (UK) Ltd has chosen to support Cancer Research UK as our first 'charity of the year' and are very proud to be supporting this cause. This charity is also featured in this section.

For our Business Superbrands 2007 programme, we have entered into a partnership with The Telegraph Group to produce a brand-focused supplement, which coincides with the launch of the book, featuring the full results of our Business Superbrands research.

The Superbrands website (www.superbrands.uk.com) has also been redesigned and features the Business Superbrands case studies as well as further information about the organisation and our other programmes.

Finally, I hope that the following case studies aid the appreciation and understanding of the investment, endurance and marketing finesse required to become a Business Superbrand.

QUALITY

RELIABILITY

DISTINCTION

AccountancyAge

Accountancy Age has been the leading weekly newspaper for accountants since its launch 37 years ago. Over that period it has grown into one of the most influential and respected business titles in the UK, serving the needs of its audience week in week out. In the last five years it has grown into a fully integrated, cross-media title delivering news, information and advice in print, through electronic media and at face-to-face events.

PRINT • BRIEFINGS • CAREERS

EXHIBITIONS • EVENTS • CONFERENCES

ONLINE • ELECTRONIC EDITIONS • JOBS

Market

Accountancy Age is the only weekly newspaper in the sector – many others have launched against it but none has survived.

Nevertheless there is no shortage of other competitors. In terms of recruitment advertising, which has always been the bedrock of Accountancy Age, its most significant competitor is the Financial Times. Editorially the FT is also Accountancy Age's closest competitor, though it competes against all the national papers' business pages, several websites and, to a lesser extent, the monthly membership magazines published by each of the five main UK institutes. These are more significant in terms of the display advertising market, along with a handful of other monthlies and a growing number of online start-ups.

Achievements

In the last five years alone, Accountancy Age's journalists have won or been shortlisted for more than 40 major publishing awards.

In 2005 the title secured the first cross-media audit certificate issued by magazine auditor ABCe, reflecting its pioneering work in producing digital editions that complement the title's existing print offerings.

In its coverage of the Enron and Worldcom scandals it was one of the first publications to suggest that the fallout could cause the collapse of its auditor Andersen, then one of the biggest accounting firms around.

Its fears were well founded and this and other aspects of the title's influential coverage saw it become the favoured commentator by the likes of the BBC, CNN, CNBC, Bloomberg and others. Accountancy Age has led on other issues since – from football's financial problems to corporate governance reform – and remains an active commentator for other media.

Readers spend an average of 26 minutes reading each issue, according to NOP research published in 2005. Accountancy Age is also ranked highest by readers for being an 'enjoyable and interesting' read and number one for jobs.

Sir David Tweedie, who, as chairman of the International Accounting Standards Board, has been one of the most influential UK accountants

1969	1980
Accountancy Age is launched as 'the voice of the profession' by Michael Heseltine. He describes the circumstances leading up to the launch as his 'best stroke of luck'.	VNU acquires Accountancy Age from Haymarket.

of the last 20 years, has described Accountancy Age as being 'a great force for good' which, 'unlike many national papers actually tries to analyse the issues to determine who is right rather than merely report on disputes'. Praise indeed from such a respected industry figure.

Product

For its first 30 years, Accountancy Age was an extremely successful print weekly servicing the needs of UK qualified accountants. Over the last several years it has grown into one of the most pioneering B2B titles in the UK.

First came the launch, in 1999, of AccountancyAge.com. This online offering has grown significantly from its early days. So much so that it now attracts more than 220,000 readers a month and more than one million pages impressions. In addition, its comprehensive daily newswire offering covers everything from tax to technology, practice to business as well as general news.

Accountancy Age also stages face-to-face events, including Softworld, the UK's premier accounting and finance technology show since its launch 18 years ago, and the Accountancy Age conference, which was launched in 2006.

Accountancy Age TV launched in autumn 2006. The main programming is a weekly magazine discussion show, The Big Question. It features senior members of the editorial team discussing the most important of the week's news events as well as an interview with a senior figure from the profession. The weekly web conference, the Insider Business Club, also comes under the Accountancy Age TV umbrella alongside special broadcasts from Accountancy Age's annual awards and other events.

Recent Developments

Accountancy Age has recently developed a suite of digital editions. Its most successful is called Young Professional. Launched in 2006 and incorporating audio and video, the product was created to serve the needs of part and newly qualified accountants and grow the next generation of Accountancy Age readers.

Over the last 12 months it has also refined its virtual conference and round table offerings. The Accountancy Age Talent Esymposium replaced a live careers fair, reflecting market changes. For example, it has become much more difficult to attract young accountants to a real event. The symposium format enables potential visitors to 'attend' a virtual conference and hear from expert speakers and interact with employers.

Accountancy Age has also launched the Insider Business Club, a weekly web conferencing club for finance directors and senior members of their teams. Members manage their profiles online, including providing details of events they are interested in. In addition, members can listen to – and participate in – a round table panel discussion on subjects that affect senior financial decision-makers in business. Each event, which is covered in print each week, is available live and on demand through iTunes.

Promotion

The weekly newspaper remains Accountancy Age's most effective promotion vehicle. However it also works with many of the accountancy institutes that train students to promote Accountancy Age and uses on and offline advertising campaigns to promote its products.

Accountancy Age journalists also contribute to other media – print, radio and television – as industry experts.

In addition, its annual awards are attended by more than 1,200 of the most senior industry players and have grown into the premier annual event for accountants.

Brand Values

Accountancy Age is a weekly newspaper that sets out to equip its professional readers – from the most senior finance directors and partners to newly qualified accountants – with all they need for their next meeting or indeed their next job.

Accountancy Age is the only independent title dedicated to keeping accountants – in practice, business as well as the public and voluntary sectors – up-to-date with financial and accountancy news as it happens and in the most appropriate format. This may be in print, online, via digital editions or through regular careers guides, management briefings and live events.

Coverage is every bit as broad as the diverse roles in which the audience works. It covers business, practice and the public and voluntary sectors as well as tax, audit, corporate finance, business recovery and consultancy.

At times Accountancy Age may be considered as the irksome, independent voice of the profession and at others, its conscience. Always, however, it aims to mirror the industry in which it operates.

www.accountancyage.com

Things you didn't know about Accountancy Age

In the last five years alone, Accountancy Age journalists have won or been shortlisted for more than 40 major publishing awards.

AccountancyAge.com now attracts almost 220,000 unique visitors each month – almost equivalent to the number of qualified accountants in the UK.

Accountancy Age is willing to poke fun at its readers. This is done on a regular basis via Colin, its cartoon accountant – one of the most popular finance professionals around.

In 2005 Accountancy Age became the first publication in the UK to receive a cross-media audit certificate from magazine auditor ABCe, reflecting its pioneering work in producing digital editions that complement the title's existing print offerings.

1995	1999	2004	2006
The Accountancy Age Awards are launched.	AccountancyAge.com is launched.	Digital editions – including regional and specialist ebooks – are launched; Best Practice, a title serving the needs of high street advisers, becomes a monthly spin-off.	A comprehensive redesign of the print edition takes place. In addition, the launch of a pioneering ebook titled Young Professional takes place as well as the launch of a weekly web conference – Insider Business Club.

better work, better life

Adecco, formerly known in the UK as Alfred Marks, is the world's largest recruitment company, with 6,600 offices in 70 countries and 33,000 employees supporting a network of over 150,000 clients.

Market

The global labour market is changing dramatically. Longer life expectancy means that people are staying in work for longer, and low birth rates mean there are fewer young adults entering the workforce. In this environment, skills are becoming increasingly scarce, creating strong demand from employers to find the workers they need.

In addition, the globalised economy is making labour an internationally mobile resource. The influx of workers into the UK from the new EU accession countries demonstrates this. Around 1.5 per cent of the European Union's working population are employed through staffing companies, largely on short-term contracts ranging from a day to a year (Source: International Confederation of Private Employment Agencies).

In the UK, the recruitment market was worth £23.5 billion in 2004/05 (Source: Annual Recruitment Industry Survey). Although the industry has grown by nearly 40 per cent since 1999, the recruitment market is closely linked to the health of the economy. This meant that a slight fall in UK economic growth was mirrored by a four per cent fall in recruitment industry growth during 2005.

Temporary and contract recruitment services is the biggest sector for the recruitment industry, generating over 80 per cent of revenue.

Adecco is the market leader in the global market for general staffing, the third biggest player in the professional staffing and services

sector and second biggest in providing career development consultancy.

Globally, the recruitment industry generates around US$400 billion in revenues. Temporary staffing accounts for US$140 billion of this with independent contractors generating over US$200 billion in revenue.

Achievements

Adecco has built an enviable position of strength in the global recruitment industry, and, in the UK, was recently ranked second in the 2005 Top 100 Report by Recruitment International.

In addition, Adecco is ranked first or second in 11 of the world's top 13 staffing markets, which account for 95 per cent of total industry revenue.

Adecco has the highest market share, revenue, cash flow and market capitalisation in the industry. With sales of 18.3 billion euros in 2005, and net income of 453 million euros, the company is ranked 265th in the Fortune Global 500 list of the world's biggest companies.

The company's increased focus on professional services has boosted Adecco's business even further, with second-quarter profits in 2006 leaping by 37 per cent to 191 million euros. The figure beat

analysts' expectations of 125 million euros. In 2005, its annual net profits were also up by 37 per cent year on year.

On any given day, Adecco serves some 150,000 clients, and over 250,000 per year. Helping millions of people find work, Adecco payrolls 700,000 people daily.

The company takes its role as a good corporate citizen very seriously, with membership to Business in the Community, Investors in People, the Employers Forum on Disability, Race for Opportunity and the Third Age Employment Network.

Product

Adecco's services encompass short-term and contract staffing, career services, outsourcing, permanent recruitment, outplacement, training and consulting.

The group recently restructured itself around six global business lines, to further focus itself around professional services. These specialisation areas are: Finance & Legal; Engineering & Technical; Information Technology; Medical & Science; Sales, Marketing & Events; and Human Capital Solutions.

Adecco specialises in offering clients flexible staffing solutions that help them operate more

Whether you are looking for your next career step, have a potential vacancy that needs to be filled or are thinking about a career change talk to Adecco first.

With over 350 branches nationwide and a network of branches throughout the midlands. We have relationships with companies that are always looking for talented individuals to work in permanent or short term roles, contact us or pop into your local branch for an informal chat.

Adecco Recruitment Solutions
Suite 30, East Wing, Third Floor, 21- 25 Newdegate Street, Nuneaton CV11 4EJ
Contact Simon or Louisa on: 02476 385551

better work, better life   adecco.co.uk

1919	**1957**	**1964**	**1977**
Alfred Marks, Adecco's original trading name is the first recruitment agency to be formed in the UK.	The ADIA Group is founded in Switzerland. The recruitment firm grew rapidly, expanding into France, Austria and the US.	ECCO is founded in France, quickly becoming the country's largest provider of temporary employment. By 1996, it would become Europe's largest personnel company.	Alfred Marks joins the ADIA group.

efficiently and productively, providing the people it places with rewarding short-term assignments or careers.

Recent Developments
In August 2006, Adecco announced the appointment of a new chief executive officer, Dieter Scheiff. Taking over from Klaus J Jacobs, who is now Group Chairman, Mr Scheiff was previously CEO of DIS AG, Germany's leading professional staffing company.

A major development at the group is the global rebranding of the Adecco visual identity. After an extensive period of design development the company is implementing new brand guidelines, and has begun a programme of complete branch refurbishments. The new branding reflects the company's increased focus on professional services as well as its 'better work, better life' goal.

Other new developments at the group include the introduction of new Adecco Career Centres. The first of these opened in June 2006 in Brussels. Career Centres aim to offer, for the first time, the full scope of work and career-related services and offerings under one roof and from a single source. The concept also allows job-seekers to benefit from other services, including skills assessment and career planning, customised training and job placement services. For companies, the service offering includes selection and recruitment, contracting and outsourcing, interim management and outplacement.

Promotion
Adecco is well known for its investment in employment research, and has completed three valuable studies in the past year. Research studies illustrate Adecco's commitment to driving business insight and development; whilst also supplying a suitable platform for B2B promotion.

The Call Centre Census was completed following a nationwide survey of Call Centre Operatives (CCOs). Its objective was to better understand employee perceptions, thus improving both client and candidate experience in the recruitment and

retention of CCOs. The results challenged some commonly held perceptions of call centre working. It also disclosed some interesting findings surrounding skills and development, as well as employee views on motivation, stress, benefits and incentives.

By understanding the needs of call centre employees, Adecco is better placed to service clients in the areas of recruitment and retention. In addition to this, Call Centre management can take the findings and apply them to their own requirements for maintaining and improving levels of employee performance, motivation levels and customer service.

In a separate study Adecco teamed up with the Chartered Management Institute for the first time to examine 'Business Energy'. Motivation Matters was designed to assess the motivation levels of UK managers, as well as contributory factors.

The report provided a stark picture of the extent to which motivation matters in driving the productivity of employees, and highlighted key areas to be addressed to help improve and maintain motivation levels.

As the world's largest recruiter, Adecco interacts daily with thousands of businesses, helping to provide innovative solutions to a variety of HR challenges. The research findings enable the company to better assist and advise its clients in this regard.

A third report, conducted in partnership with the Institute of Directors (IoD), investigates how SMEs are approaching employee management and recruiting. The Small Business Recruitment and Retention Survey focuses on key HR challenges in the context of current economic trends.

Human resources accounts for approximately half of UK Small to Medium Enterprise (SME) expenditure in the UK, making it the largest collective cost for UK small businesses. With some 20 million people employed in the sector, it seems obvious that human resources and recruitment should sit at the heart of directorial and commercial interest.

The survey describes the UK HR landscape in the SME sector as one trying to balance the evident

value of robust HR and recruitment processes with the significant time and resource investment required to maintain such an environment. It also goes some way to outline directors' attitudes towards major trends in UK employment, such as flexibility, recent legislative change and the network of organisations that support HR in the SME space.

Brand Values
Adecco is the world expert in connecting people both globally and locally with the talent they need and the work that they want.

The company encapsulates its vision and brand positioning around a clear goal: 'better work, better life'. Adecco believes that a person's motivation to improve their work experience will create opportunities to improve all parts of their lives. As such, the company is devoted to helping its colleagues and clients to achieve this goal.

www.adecco.co.uk

Things you didn't know about Adecco

Around the world, Adecco employs some 312 people every minute.

The company's roots lie with the original trading name of Alfred Marks, the first ever recruitment agency in the UK that was formed in 1919.

Adecco co-ordinated the recruitment, training and management of 10,000 volunteers for the 2002 Commonwealth Games in Manchester which was the largest volunteer force assembled since World War II.

700,000 people are paid by Adecco on any given day with approximately three million having worked during the year.

1996	1997	2000	2005
ADIA and ECCO merge, forming ADECCO. The combined operation comprises 2,500 branches around the world.	The Adecco name first appears on the UK high street.	Adecco acquires Olsten Staffing, becoming the biggest recruitment company in the US.	After a strategy review, Adecco makes a commitment to realign itself across six professional service business lines.

ALLEN & OVERY

Allen & Overy is an international legal practice with approximately 5,000 staff, including some 450 partners working in 24 major centres worldwide. It is a multi-disciplinary firm, offering expertise in areas including banking, corporate, employment, pensions and incentives, international capital markets, litigation, private client, projects, real estate and tax.

Market

Responding to the global scale of clients, the globalisation of capital markets and the boom in cross-border mergers and acquisitions, law firms are adopting an increasingly global focus. The liberalisation of economies and rapid growth in emerging markets in Asia, Eastern Europe and the Middle East is also driving change in the legal sector, requiring firms to respond and innovate quickly to serve client needs. Allen & Overy believes the strongest national firms can survive in this globalised market, but only if they can convince clients that they have partnerships that offer a credible cross-border alternative to the networks of the international firms.

Allen & Overy is one of the world's top international legal practices – an elite group of law firms, by their size and global reach. Four other such firms are Clifford Chance, Slaughter and May, Freshfields Bruckhaus Deringer and Linklaters.

According to Thomson Financial 2005, Allen & Overy is the leading adviser, acting for the managers, in the international debt market and, according to Mergermarket 2005, it advised on more M&A deals than any other law firm in the European telecommunications, media and technology (TMT) sector. In 2005, it was also ranked first by Dealogic for global projects, by volume and value.

Achievements

Allen & Overy had a stellar year in 2006, increasing its revenue from £666 million to £736 million. This strong billing performance was driven by its buoyant core markets of M&A, finance and litigation and also by the strength of its international network and the value it provides to the firm's global clients.

The firm's reputation as an international specialist was strengthened by some landmark projects, such as handling China's largest-ever initial public offering (IPO). The Bank of China's IPO on the Hong Kong Stock Exchange in June 2006, the largest

Insights into a full service law practice

WE PRACTISE LAW AT THE HIGHEST LEVEL LOCALLY AND INTERNATIONALLY

global listing for six years, raising over US$11 billion, was the largest equity offering in China's history.

Allen & Overy advised and worked alongside BOCI Asia, Goldman Sachs and UBS as joint global co-ordinator and joint lead manager on the IPO and listing, which highlighted the increasing importance of Chinese companies and financial institutions on the world markets.

This wasn't the only headline-grabbing deal in which Allen & Overy recently played a pivotal role. Late 2005 saw the conclusion of one of the largest-ever cases held in the English Commercial Court, involving an original claim of £3.9 billion being made against the former directors of Equitable Life. Allen & Overy defended the reputations of six non-executive directors involved, who had been accused of breach of duty of care and negligence. To ensure these individuals had representation in court, Allen & Overy agreed to act on a no-win, no-fee basis. Equitable Life withdrew its claim and agreed to settle with a £5.2 million payment to the six Allen & Overy clients.

Successes like this have led Allen & Overy to win a host of industry awards and accolades. These have included Finance Team of the Year (Capital Markets/Structured Finance) in the Lawyer Awards 2006, Derivatives Law Firm of the Year in the Derivatives Week Awards 2005, Project Finance Team of the Year in the 2005 and 2006 IFLR Asian

Awards and International Law Firm of the Year in the 2005 Which Lawyer? Awards.

Small wonder as only the best talent (see Senior Associates Conference, pictured bottom left) is recruited and developed.

Product

Allen & Overy provides a full range of legal services, acting for private and public companies, international conglomerates, governmental agencies, banks and other financial and commercial institutions. With 24 offices on three continents, the firm has lawyers speaking 39 different languages.

The firm's areas of expertise span many areas. Its Banking practice advises clients on all types of international finance, including global loans, project finance, restructurings, leveraged finance, regulatory and asset finance.

1930	1959
Allen & Overy is founded by George Allen and Thomas Overy. Its reputation is made as a result of George Allen's role as advisor to King Edward VIII during the abdication crisis of 1936.	Allen & Overy advises on the first ever hostile takeover in the City of London.

Allen & Overy's global Corporate practice employs over 600 qualified lawyers worldwide, acting for many of the world's leading corporates, investment banks and financial institutions. The firm specialises in complex, high value, cross border work, advising on deals ranging from public takeovers to IPOs and demergers.

The firm's Employment, Pensions and Incentives practice is one of its fastest growing areas of speciality, with an international team advising clients on all aspects of employment, pensions and employee benefits law.

The International Capital Markets practice works in another fast-changing sector, advising clients including financial institutions, corporates, governments and trustees of debt and equity related securities. This is a highly complex area, with the firm's expertise covering the most innovative highly-structured products in this sector.

Allen & Overy's Litigation and Dispute Resolution practice has an international reputation for dealing with all forms of commercial disputes. As well as specialising in large and complex litigation, the practice is becoming increasingly focused on providing risk management advice to major clients, often at board level, to help them spot potential areas for risk and, if possible, avoid disputes entirely.

The Private Client practice acts for private clients, including wealthy individuals, trust companies, charities and entrepreneurs.

In Project Finance Allen & Overy acts for lenders, project owners and sponsors, governments, public authorities, contractors, developers and investors on various projects, from roads to airports, all over the world.

Recognised by clients and the industry as providing a holistic approach to real estate services, Allen & Overy's Real Estate practice is highly ranked in Legal 500 for numerous real estate categories including commercial property, real estate finance, construction, planning and litigation.

Allen & Overy's Tax practice provides a comprehensive business tax advisory service to clients, emphasising tax-efficient structures and tax planning.

Recent Developments
To help make the most of the skills and enthusiasm of the majority of the people who comprise the

Allen & Overy brand, Allen & Overy regularly holds gatherings for associates and other staff. At these events, participants share experience and best practice and help to map their own careers – as well as the future of the international legal practice.

In late June 2006, for example, senior associates from around the world gathered in Brighton on England's south coast to discuss their role in the practice. Joining them, by invitation of the associates themselves, were selected Allen & Overy partners and directors.

By the end of the conference, the associates had not only challenged the traditional partner role but also suggested greater senior associate participation in the daily operations of the practice. As a result, Allen & Overy is exploring ways in which its associates can bring a different perspective to management decisions.

Allen & Overy's move to its new Bishops Square building in London has given it the opportunity to create a workplace that reflects what it is – and what it wants to be – a global practice dedicated to client service. Building features include a more welcoming and efficient reception area, state-of-the-art meeting and dining facilities with panoramic views, a world-class 300-seat auditorium and, throughout the structure, décor inspired by the continents where it operates.

Promotion
To keep employees up to date and engaged with the firm's latest activities, the important communications tools of a daily-updated intranet news service, a comprehensive webcasting programme and regular face-to-face management presentations are used. Alongside this Allen & Overy publishes a newsletter, A&O News, which is distributed to all staff.

Sponsorship is another valuable tool for connecting with external stakeholders, and dovetails with the firm's extensive community-

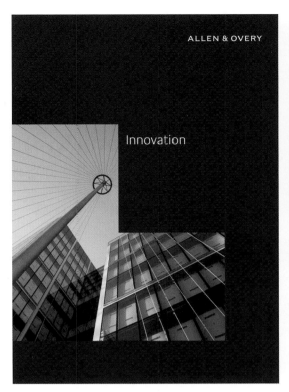

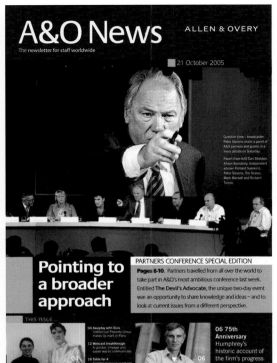

related activities. In the UK, for example, Allen & Overy sponsors Artbeat, based on a model developed by the New York and Hong Kong offices. This initiative for young artists was launched in 2003, in partnership with secondary schools in Tower Hamlets and with the assistance of Workplace Art Consultancy. Allen & Overy sponsors professional artists to design and lead workshops for young people in the borough, challenging and guiding them to create artwork for display in the firm's London offices.

Brand Values
Allen & Overy's brand is built on its ability to combine global scale with local expertise. This is encapsulated in its statement: 'We practise law at the highest level, locally and internationally'.

It prides itself on having fresh innovative ideas and insights, helping clients to find new and more cost-efficient ways to get legal information and advice. It helps to put ideas into practice, with a can-do culture that creates practical solutions for the most complex scenarios.

As is evidenced by its extensive pro bono work, valued at £12 million for the year 2005/06, Allen & Overy is also committed to serving the community, believing that access to justice is a universal right, not just the preserve of those who can afford it.

www.allenovery.com

Things you didn't know about Allen & Overy

In Allen & Overy's multinational teams the number of fluent English speakers, whose native language is not English, outnumbers the number of native English speakers.

One of Allen & Overy's oldest pro bono relationships stretches back to 1991, when it began working with the Battersea Legal Advice Centre. Every Tuesday evening Allen & Overy volunteers provide free legal advice to local people.

Allen & Overy was recently ranked top in a survey by the legal industry news site, www.rollonfriday.com, as the best international legal practice to work for, with the best rates of pay.

1963	1978	1985	2002
Allen & Overy helps draft the first ever Eurobond.	Allen & Overy opens its first international office.	Allen & Overy opens an office in New York.	Allen & Overy Shanghai opens, the third office in China.

Allied Irish Bank (GB)
Our business is business banking.

The Allied Irish Bank (GB) brand is described as an 'evolving aspiration' that relies on understanding and engagement with customers. Listening, and continuously responding to customer needs, combined with relevant innovation has built the brand in to what it is today. Allied Irish Bank (GB)'s business is business banking.

Market

Allied Irish Bank (GB) is a specialist business bank offering a full range of products and services for growing and expanding mid-corporate business and professional customers.

The Bank has a broad spectrum of business customers and has developed specialist teams in its key sectors which include accountancy and legal practices, healthcare, education, hotels and leisure, public sector and charities as well as recently developing expertise in the environmental services sector.

The Bank continues to establish itself as first choice for growing businesses and professionals and a serious alternative to the traditional British banks. It aims to achieve these goals through a personalised service and a continued commitment to its key business principals of: providing a tailored service and adjusting this as customers' requirements develop and change; developing long term relationships with customers; local bankers who are interested, knowledgeable, experienced and fully involved with all decisions; short lines of communication and speedy decision making; having a management team which works closely with centralised specialists.

In Private Banking, there is no mistaking the mark of quality.

Allied Irish Bank (GB)

People you can bank on.

Entrust your business to Allied Irish Bank (GB) – voted 'Britain's Best Business Bank' six times in a row.

Ascot
Allied Irish Bank (GB)
Founding Partner

Allied Irish Bank (GB)
Our business is business banking.

Achievements

Allied Irish Bank (GB) has had the unprecedented success of being awarded the title of 'Britain's Best Business Bank' in an independent survey by the Forum of Private Business on each consecutive occasion since 1994. This impressive accolade recognises the Bank's ability to consistently deliver superior customer service to its customers and is testimony to the longstanding commitment from the Bank and its people to delivering true relationship banking.

On an annual basis, the Bank is in touch with its customers' views using a detailed customer satisfaction survey. The latest results showed that 90.5 per cent of respondents said they are likely or very likely to be using Allied Irish Bank (GB) in two years time and 81 per cent of customers have personally recommended the Bank on one or

more occasion. Furthermore, the Bank was placed in the top quartile of suppliers, with a score of 84.3 per cent, in the Satisfaction Index™ and 74.3 per cent of respondents thought that Allied Irish Bank (GB) was the best or better than most other business banks.

It is a testament to the Bank's longstanding commitment to staff development that it has achieved the recognition of the Investors in People Standard across its office network since 1995, exceeding 90 per cent of the measures set down by the new IiP national benchmark. Continuing investment in staff development has been the key to its success in not only retaining employees, but also in aiming to provide exceptional service to its customers.

Product

In Business Banking, Allied Irish Bank (GB) is committed to tailoring products and services to meet customers' specific needs – with capabilities at every level the Bank strives to provide continuity and ingenuity in adapting these products as business requirements change. All managers are decision-makers, developing long term relationships with their customers in providing day-to-day banking and are closely involved with their local business community.

Traditional banking continues to be at the core of Allied Irish Bank (GB)'s Private Banking service, which provides comprehensive wealth management advice for business customers of the Bank and has offices in Edinburgh, Manchester, Birmingham and London.

Over the last two years, the Bank has expanded its business banking services to include:

Merchant Services – the increasing trend towards the use of payment cards continues, which is why the Bank has introduced cost effective card payment solutions that are secure, efficient and easy to use.

iBusiness Banking – whilst the Bank remains focused on personal service, many customers also appreciate the ability to manage their accounts online. iBusiness Banking customers can conduct

1825	1970s
The Bank's first London office opens in Throgmorton Avenue.	AIB Group grows to create a strong branch network in Britain.

Allied Irish Bank (GB)
Our business is business banking.

Working with top-flight businesses throughout the country.

Charity, London

College, East Anglia

Media group, North Wales

transactions and financial management at their convenience, enhancing the level of service they receive from the Bank.

In Corporate Banking, Allied Irish Bank (GB) has specialist corporate banking teams which work closely with branches to provide a seamless service in its key sectors, underpinned by a solid understanding of the complexities of corporate and institutional business. The Bank's strategy is to deliver a first class service through business innovation, knowledgeable staff and short lines of communication.

Recent Developments
In line with the Bank's mid-corporate business positioning, branches have been restyled away from the traditional British bank, with its rows of tellers, to reflect the needs of modern day business banking customers with meeting rooms and open office space. With 33 full service branches and nine business development offices, the Bank has invested heavily in key business areas, opening a new office in Birmingham City, relocating two London offices to Hampstead and Gray's Inn Road as well as creating a new corporate office in Manchester.

Performance remains strong and Allied Irish Bank (GB) was assigned a standalone credit rating by Standard & Poors, with a positive outlook. The Long-Term rating was subsequently raised from an A to an A+ in May 2005. The Short-Term rating

maintained a healthy A-1. This rating reflects the Bank's sound financial profile and its status as a core group subsidiary of Allied Irish Banks plc.

Promotion
With an objective of achieving growth, the Bank recognises the need to continue raising its profile. The Bank has taken an integrated approach to this and has created strong national, regional and specialist advertising campaigns. Engaging with the media on a daily basis, building relationships and providing expert opinions on key business topics has been the underlying focus of the communication plan.

Business sponsorship is a key part of the Bank's promotional activity and it actively seeks opportunities to work with business organisations and professional bodies. In 2006 the Bank sponsored several high-profile awards including the Accountancy Age Awards, attended by over 1,300 guests, and the CBI Growing Business Awards.

Proving that business and the arts can also successfully work together, the Bank continued its partnership with LAMDA in their annual Communication and Performance Awards.

A major undertaking by the Bank's parent, Allied Irish Banks plc, was the official sponsorship of the Ryder Cup in 2006, providing the trip of a lifetime to a staggering 8,000 customers. Allied Irish Bank (GB) entertained 400 of its own customers and at the same time achieved invaluable levels of publicity.

Allied Irish Bank (GB) has a strong horse racing heritage and is a leading provider to the racing industry – 25 of the 59 racecourses in Britain bank with Allied Irish Bank (GB). A natural progression for the Bank was to become the first Founding Partner of Ascot Racecourse, an agreement that will see the Bank partner the racecourse until 2010.

The Bank has recently refreshed the creative for one of the UK's largest 'poster' sites. This is situated at Heathrow Airport, alongside the travelator, taking hundreds of thousands of passengers to and from the Republic of Ireland every year. The site is just over a third of a kilometre in length.

Brand Values
The Bank has a strong commitment to upholding its core brand values – Dependable, Engaging and Pioneering.

As part of AIB Group, the Code of Business Ethics for all employees reaffirms the general principles that govern how the Bank conducts its affairs. It recognises that maintaining the trust and confidence of customers, staff, shareholders and other stakeholders by acting with integrity and professionalism, as well as behaving with prudence and skill, is crucial to the continued growth and success of the Bank.

www.aibgb.co.uk

Seven times winner of 'Britain's Best Business Bank'.

Going the extra furlong for Ascot.

Things you didn't know about Allied Irish Bank (GB)

AIB Group is Ireland's leading banking and financial services organisation. It operates principally in Ireland, Britain, Poland and the US. It employs more than 24,000 people worldwide in more than 750 offices.

Allied Irish Bank (GB) has been voted 'Britain's Best Business Bank' on seven consecutive occasions since 1994.

In 2006, 23 staff celebrated 25 years of service with the Bank.

Allied Irish Bank (GB) banks one in eight higher education institutions and 25 of the 59 racecourses in Britain.

1980s	1996	2006	
International success brings about Group investment in branches in the US.	In October, AIB's retail operations in Great Britain and Northern Ireland are incorporated as AIB Group (UK) plc trading in Great Britain as Allied Irish Bank (GB).	Allied Irish Bank (GB) reports a significant profit growth of 27 per cent to 103 million euros.	AIB Group assets total 144 billion euros – a good reflection of the Group's growth since 1966 when AIB's aggregate assets were equivalent to 323.8 million euros.

AVIS

Avis has provided a seamless service to the corporate traveller since 1946 and is now the largest rental company in Europe – a position achieved by listening to its customers and continuing to deliver the 'We try harder.' promise.

Market

Avis leads the European car rental market with a 16.5 per cent share (Source: Euromonitor 2004), with approximately 25 per cent of its rentals to the corporate market. Together, rentals in France, Germany, Italy, Spain and the UK account for around 80 per cent of Avis Europe's revenues.

Achievements

At the heart of Avis' recent achievements is the introduction of its revolutionary 'Inspired Change' programme. Seen as the most radical change for the rental industry in the past 20 years, it followed research undertaken by Avis with nearly 13,000 customers across Europe to find out exactly what they want from a car rental company.

Avis has been recognised by the travel and fleet industries, receiving numerous awards which have recently included: Best Overall Car Rental Company by the British Airport Authority's customers; Best Car Rental Company Worldwide by Business Traveller magazine readers; Best Business Car Rental Company by Business Travel World magazine; and Best Car Hire Company at the Telegraph Travel Awards. The judges commented that Avis' focus on customer satisfaction and investment in account management differentiated it from its industry competitors.

Avis is ranked 60th in The Sunday Times '100 Best Companies to Work For' survey, positively reflecting the views of Avis employees, and demonstrating that Avis understands that having a happy, satisfied and fulfilled team is

fundamental to being able to deliver its 'We try harder.' message every day.

Product

Avis is committed to understanding and offering its customers what they want – transparency and fairness in pricing and products, and an unrivalled service worldwide.

THE SUNDAY TIMES
100
BEST COMPANIES TO WORK FOR
2005

Product offerings are focused on the needs of business travellers. Avis Preferred is designed for frequent travellers, minimising paperwork and queues, so they can

be on the road in minutes. Small businesses can benefit from the competitive rates, loyalty points and free rentals offered by Avis Advance. For rentals longer than a month, there is MaxiRent – a value-for-money, flexible alternative to traditional leasing.

Avis works closely with its corporate customers, developing tailored solutions for their staff and customers to help them achieve their business goals. In a market where fleet costs are rising, Avis offers a 'total cost' strategy to help companies reduce costs and improve efficiencies.

Avis is committed to corporate social responsibility. It offsets carbon emissions through its partnership with The CarbonNeutral Company and has an above-industry-average 'A' rating from the Safety and Environmental Risk Management Rating Agency.

1946	1963	1972	1973
Warren Avis founds Avis Airlines Rent a Car Systems at Willow Run Airport, Detroit – the world's first airport car rental operation.	Avis launches its 'We're only No.2. We try harder.' campaign, the very essence of the company's culture.	Avis introduces 'Wizard' – the first real-time rental reservation system.	Avis achieves market leadership in Europe, Africa and the Middle East, just eight years after Avis Europe was founded.

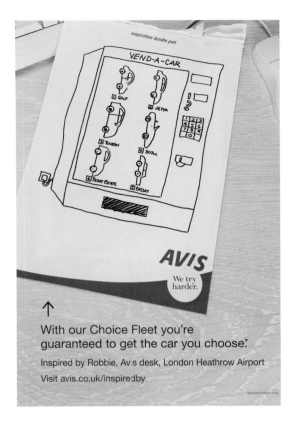

With our Choice Fleet you're guaranteed to get the car you choose.*
Inspired by Robbie, Avis desk, London Heathrow Airport
Visit avis.co.uk/inspiredby

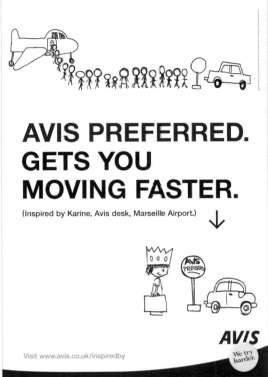

AVIS PREFERRED. GETS YOU MOVING FASTER.
(Inspired by Karine, Avis desk, Marseille Airport.)
Visit www.avis.co.uk/inspiredby

AVIS RAPID RETURN. DROP OFF YOUR CAR AND GO IN 60 SECONDS.
(Inspired by Giovanna, Avis desk, Catania Airport.)
Visit www.avis.co.uk/inspiredby

Furthermore, Avis employees are actively involved in fundraising and charity initiatives to support their local communities and their selected national charity, Macmillan Cancer Relief.

Recent Developments
In 2006, as part of its 'Inspired Change' programme – which was based on research from nearly 13,000 customers across Europe – Avis introduced a range of groundbreaking initiatives that have transformed the clarity and speed of its corporate rental and business travel offerings.

Firstly, a new transparent and easy-to-read Rental Agreement addressing the major issue for customers of perceived 'hidden charges'. The new agreement gives price clarity to the cost of the

rental, detailing any insurance options taken, a fuel reading and damage report all on a single piece of paper.

Avis has also introduced a clearer guide to car types and now simply offers Small, Medium or Large cars with a choice of Manual or Automatic, Petrol or Diesel. Further to this, drivers can now guarantee the exact make and model of car they rent, thanks to the new Avis Choice Fleet which is available at major UK airports. This is a first in the industry.

A new Fuel Up Front service has also been launched to give customers a fair and convenient refuelling option. Customers can choose to pre-pay for a full tank of fuel when they collect their car meaning they can return it empty, without worrying about paying over the odds for the service.

The new Avis Insurance Guide is designed to spell out in a straightforward and jargon-free language exactly what options are available and the relevant charges involved.

Finally, Rapid Return enables the customer to return their car in as little as 60 seconds. A member of staff is able to check the vehicle and print a receipt on-the-spot. Rapid Return is available at 125 Avis locations across Europe with more being added continually.

Promotion
Some 53 years ago, Avis was the second largest car rental company in the US and was already expanding overseas. However, by 1963 it was struggling with a 10 per cent share of the US market, compared to 75 per cent held by Hertz.

Avis managed to use this to its advantage by launching an advertising campaign that was to prove to be crucial in turning its fortunes around and indeed went down in advertising history. The slogan 'We're No. 2. We try

harder.' emphasised its commitment to customer service and fundamentally remains at the core of Avis' brand today.

This is reflected in the current 'Inspired By' pan-European advertising campaign which focuses on how the innovations the company is making will improve the customer's car rental experience.

Brand Values
The Avis 'We try harder.' philosophy was born in the 1960s as an impassioned pledge by Avis people to be open, honest and to 'give a little extra'. It's still as strong today, as the company stays closely aligned with changing values. For the future, listening to customers, making change happen, and living 'We try harder.' remain priorities for Avis – a company that is pioneering, passionate and truly in touch.

www.avis.co.uk

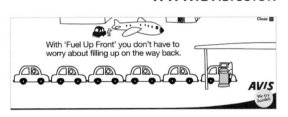

With 'Fuel Up Front' you don't have to worry about filling up on the way back.

Avis can't afford not to be nice.

Or not give you a new car like a lively, super-torque Ford, or not know a pastrami-on-rye place in Duluth. Why?
When you're not the biggest in rent a cars, you have to try harder.
We do. We're only No.2.

1986
Avis Europe becomes the first car rental company to successfully float on the London Stock Exchange.

1996
The launch of the Avis website – www.avis.co.uk – takes place and is the first car rental website.

2005
A prototype 'speed-rental' location at Avis Gatwick is unveiled.

The Rapid Return service is launched across UK airports.

2006
Avis' new easy-to-use, transparent Rental Agreement is launched.

Avis becomes the first car rental company to offer a 'Choice Fleet'.

BACS Payment Schemes Limited (BACS) has been at the forefront of delivering efficient reliable and secure electronic funds transfers between banks, consumers and businesses for almost 40 years. Its products generate over five billion transactions from over 100,000 business users in a single year, with over 80 million payments being processed on a peak day.

Direct Debit is the best way to submit and collect bill payments...

- It's secure
- It's convenient
- Reliable
- Hassle free
- No missed payments
- Can manage finances
- Don't have to queue.

...and remember to

- Have the Direct Debit Instruction form on mailing literature
- Include the Direct Debit Guarantee
- Reassure your customers by using the Advance Notice
- Ensure your database is kept up-to-date
- Update staff regularly on new Direct Debit products.

www.directdebit.co.uk

Market

Ever since BACS pioneered the industry almost 40 years ago, the use of automated payments via Direct Debit and BACS Direct Credit has mushroomed – total transactions for 2006 are projected to be worth over £3.4 trillion.

As the leading provider of automated payment services, BACS has an unsurpassed market profile. According to independent brand recognition research conducted amongst corporates across various industry sectors, BACS has a 100 per cent prompted awareness as a company providing payment services.

BACS serves a diverse market. The UK businesses that use its payment services are one substantial sector, with approximately 115,000 users, both as originators of Direct Debit and users of BACS Direct Credit. Outside of this business audience, BACS also has a relationship with millions of UK adults who use Direct Debits to pay their bills or receive their wages or salaries by BACS Direct Credit. The UK Government is another key constituent in the BACS sphere, as it is the single largest originator of BACS Direct Credits.

Achievements

The importance of BACS to the UK economy cannot be underestimated. It is responsible for processing 90 per cent of all UK salaries and a wide range of Government payments, including benefit and inland revenue tax credits. It is so important that it is classed as being part of the UK's Critical National Infrastructure (CNI), defined as those assets, services and systems that support the economic, political and social life of the UK.

Since 1968, BACS payments have transformed the way organisations manage their cashflow and the way consumers pay bills. Conceived in the 1960s, Direct Debit is used today by over 70 per cent of the UK population.

BACS had a record breaking year in 2006. Each day it was responsible for processing on average 15 million transactions, rising to 80 million

transactions in a single day, and has done so with zero failures.

The company has a strong track record of ground-breaking innovation, a notable example of which is the ultra-secure and award-winning BACSTEL-IP, launched in 2002. This allows customers to submit and monitor payments using Internet Protocol (IP) technology and is designed to be more reliable, more secure and faster than the old system.

In late 2005, BACS successfully completed the migration of all 100,000 plus corporate customers to the new service – one of the largest ever electronic banking projects of its type. For three years BACS worked in close partnership with the UK's leading banks and some 25 approved software providers on the migration to the unique IP payments channel.

During 2006, an IT project of critical national importance took place behind the scenes at BACS. All key stages of the programme were completed successfully including the transfer of all the UK's banks and major corporations to a new payments engine. This is now one of the most advanced automated payment infrastructures in the world.

Product

BACS is a membership-based industry body wholly owned by some of the UK and Europe's leading banks and building societies. Its role is to own, develop, enhance and preserve the integrity of automated payment and payment-related

1968	1971	1975	1982
Electronic transfer of funds between banks is introduced in the UK – christened the Inter-Bank Computer Bureau. Prior to this, it was all done on paper.	The service is renamed Bankers Automated Clearing Services (BACS).	BACS introduces one of the largest and most powerful transaction engines in the world. Data for the new machine is read from large magnetic tapes, delivered by motorcycle couriers.	Transaction data begins to be sent by telephone, via the new BACSTEL system. The speed of data delivery rises again and further levels of security are added to payment processing.

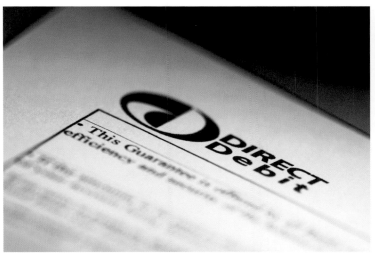

services. BACS advocates best practice amongst those companies who offer payment services and is responsible for the associated payment clearing and settlement services.

Its principal products are Direct Debit, BACS Direct Credit, and Standing Orders.

Direct Debit has become an intrinsic part of business and consumer life. The total volume of Direct Debits processed is now over 2.7 billion per year.

Approximately 15,000 UK organisations use Direct Debit for collecting a variety of regular and occasional bills, including utility payments, insurance, council tax, mortgages, loans and subscriptions.

In addition to this, BACS Direct Credit allows organisations to pay individuals and businesses directly into their bank accounts.

Direct Credit can also be used for a wide variety of other applications. Over 100,000 organisations use Direct Credit for supplier payments, pensions, employee expenses, insurance settlements, dividends and refunds.

Recent Developments

An important initiative in late 2006, undertaken by the company's in-house marketing and design team, was to introduce a refreshed brand positioning. The BACS logo has been in existence for nearly 40 years and in this time has been through a number of changes. However, the

essence of the brand as trusted, reliable and dependable has been retained.

This new look and feel retains the established logo whilst incorporating a new brand element – the BACS colour band – aiding BACS positioning as a dynamic and inspiring thought leader.

Promotion

BACS's in-house marketing and design team ensure the consistent communication of the visual identity, based around the BACS corporate colours, the BACS colour band, together with its brand values.

To communicate with its broad audience, BACS invests in a number of marketing tools, including public relations, direct marketing, online marketing, relationship management, events and awards.

In a decision driven by environmental concern the company has made a move away from sending direct mail, increasingly using e-marketing for communications, such as newsletters.

PR is highly effective for BACS and its PR team help it to achieve widespread coverage in industry-focused trade publications, including Insight and Third Sector, and also across broader news publications such as The Financial Times, Business Week and online with The Daily Telegraph.

Industry trade events targeting local authorities, charities and contact centres are also used as a means to raise awareness of BACS involvement at Government level as an advocate and campaigner

for improvement in payment services throughout the UK.

Brand Values

In line with the 2006 brand refresh, its values and strengths reflect its strong heritage, but also aim to inspire the organisation moving forward. The updated brand values were defined as: 'Inspiring'; 'Authoritative'; 'Thought Leader'; 'Diplomat'; 'Dependable'; and 'Constructively Challenging'.

BACS is recognised throughout the UK as a trusted professional body and the authoritative voice on automated payments. For almost 40 years it has led the UK's payments industry in improving quality and raising standards, delivering new and enhanced services, improving business efficiencies and consumer experience.

www.bacs.co.uk

Things you didn't know about BACS

For over 30 years, BACS was run from the De Havilland aircraft factory, from where Amy Johnson originally set off on her ill-fated trip around the world.

The BACS service desk manages over 95,000 customer calls per annum, with a call closure rate in excess of 95 per cent on first call.

The number of Direct Debits processed each year has contributed to a general decline in cheque usage; 2006 saw a seven per cent fall in the number of cheques, saving millions of pounds in cheque production and reducing environmental impact.

The BACS service is part of the UK Critical National Infrastructure.

Mid 1990s	2002	2003	2006
Enough secure telephone connections take place to stop using magnetic tapes. BACS invests in new technologies, launching the Replacement Electronic Funds Transfer (REFT) system.	BACS processing moves to a secure site shared with the Bank of England. The ultra-secure BACSTEL-IP is launched, allowing customers to submit and monitor payments.	The company is split; BACS becomes the system operator, responsible for the promotion and integrity of the payment schemes, whilst Voca is given ownership of the infrastructure that payment schemes can run on.	BACS takes on its first non-UK bank member – Danske Bank – and completes one of the largest electronic banking customer migration projects ever seen.

BASF
The Chemical Company

BASF, the world's leading chemical company, is a major supplier to the chemical, automotive, energy and construction industries worldwide. Headquartered in Germany, BASF posted sales of more than 42.7 billion euros in 2005, has production sites in 41 countries, and employs approximately 94,000 people.

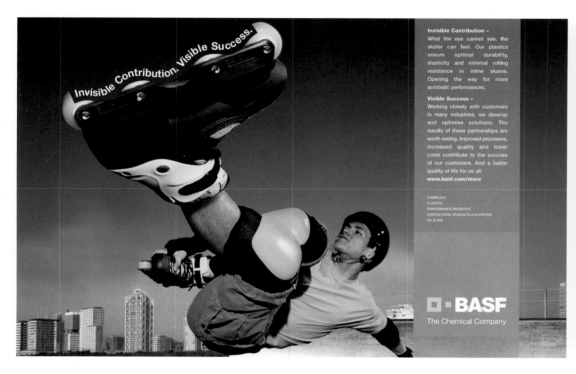

Market

BASF competes across an extraordinarily wide canvas, with customers in practically every industry. Its most important markets are chemicals and energy, the automotive industry, agriculture and construction. The electrical/electronics, packaging, furniture, health, paper, cosmetics, detergents, textiles and leather industries are also major users of BASF products.

As a result, BASF is one of the few corporations with processes and products along the entire chemical value-adding chain.

The European Chemical Industry Council (CEFIC) predicts growth of 2.3 per cent for the chemical industry in 2006. BASF sales in the first half of the year were more than 20 per cent up on the first half of 2005.

Achievements

BASF's original site in Ludwigshafen, Germany, is today the world's largest chemical complex. All 350 plants are connected to others by at least one product or process stage. Starting with a few raw materials, this highly efficient process give rise to approximately 8,000 different products.

The company has a history of scientific innovation. It produced the first synthetic dyes, including the indigo used to colour jeans, the first polystyrene and the first magnetic recording tape. A BASF employee won a Nobel Prize for helping to develop the process for synthesising ammonia, which led to synthetic production of nitrogen fertilisers.

Today BASF is also a world leader in biotechnology and nanotechnology.

Innovations remain a decisive tool for BASF, investing over £1 billion annually in research and development. Furthermore, BASF is among the top five companies in Europe for patent applications.

Product

BASF's range comprises Chemicals, Plastics, Performance Products, Agricultural Products & Nutrition, and Oil & Gas. BASF is one of the leading global producers of styrenics (hard, impact-resistant plastics), engineering plastics and polyurethanes. Its broad range of Performance Products includes high-value performance chemicals and coatings as well as functional polymers for the automotive, oil, paper, packaging, textile, sanitary care, construction, coatings, printing and leather industries.

In addition, BASF is a major supplier of agricultural products as well as fine chemicals for the farming, food processing, animal and human nutrition and personal care industries.

In plant biotechnology, the company is developing plants that are less sensitive to drought or are more nutritious. A BASF subsidiary explores and produces crude oil and natural gas. Together with a Russian partner it markets, distributes and trades natural gas in Europe.

1865	**1901**	**1929**	**1935**
Badische Anilin & Soda-Fabrik is founded in Germany to produce coal tar dyes. Soaring population growth leads to strong demand for dyes, and BASF becomes a world-leading supplier.	BASF pioneers lightfast and washfast indanthrene dyes, which soon take over the supremacy of indigo in dyeing and printing.	BASF pioneers the first polystyrene, ushering in the 'plastics age'.	'Magnetophon', the magnetic audio tape developed together with AEG, is born.

Recent Developments

In 2006, BASF acquired the construction chemicals business of Degussa AG, the technology leader and largest supplier of construction chemical products. By combining its own chemical expertise and Degussa's know-how in construction chemicals, BASF can offer a greater range of innovative products and help customers to be more successful in the competitive construction sector. The acquisition boosted BASF's size with a further 7,400 employees, located at production sites and sales centres in over 50 countries.

Another important recent move was BASF's acquisition of Engelhard Corporation, a leading supplier in the fast growing market for catalysts, and Johnson Polymer, which provides BASF with a range of water-based resins that complements its products for the coatings and paints industry.

BASF is also expanding geographically, with a particular focus on the Asian Pacific. By 2010, BASF has the ambitious target of generating 20 per cent of its global sales and earnings from the region. BASF inaugurated its new Verbund site in Nanjing, China in 2005 – the largest individual investment in BASF's 140-year history. BASF and its partner, the China Petroleum & Chemical Corporation (SINOPEC Corp.), have already announced plans for further expansion of the site.

Promotion

In 2004, BASF introduced a new corporate design and logo. Calling itself 'BASF The Chemical Company', clearly states what it is and what it wants to remain – the world's leading chemical company.

The rebranding process has given a new and brighter look to BASF's literature and advertising. In Europe, where the company has been running corporate advertising since 2001, a new campaign was launched using the slogan, 'Invisible contribution. Visible success.'

The campaign focuses on customer needs and on the benefits provided by the company's products and services. Ads have appeared frequently in the national press in the UK and also on posters on the London Underground.

In 2005 and 2006 TV was added to the UK campaign, with ads on Channel 4 and digital channels.

For more than 30 years the company has been a sponsor of Manchester's Hallé Orchestra. It also sponsors the energy gallery at the Science Museum and an award for environmental initiatives in the plastics industry.

Brand Values

BASF's mission is to be of value to people – to create value for the company, its customers, shareholders, employees, and the countries in which it operates. It helps shape the future successfully and sustainability by means of intelligent solutions.

BASF is committed to sustainable development, balancing business development with environmental protection as well as social responsibility. BASF has committed itself to pursuing improvements in environmental protection, health and safety as well as customer satisfaction.

As a founding member of the United Nations' Global Compact initiative, BASF is committed to promoting and implementing Compact's nine principles concerning the safeguarding of human rights, labour and environmental standards. BASF carries out partnership projects with public sector organisations as well as Non-Government Organisations.

www.basf.com

Things you didn't know about BASF

BASF has a 30-year partnership with adidas. The latest development from this partnership is a new generation of sports shoes with a revolutionary impact absorption system.

BASF's Belmadur® technology protects the environment by making European softwoods so resistant and durable that they can be used just like tropical hardwoods.

BASF has developed an innovative gypsum wallboard containing paraffin wax which melts as temperatures rise. Absorbing large amounts of heat from the environment, it prevents the room temperature from rising further. At night, when outside temperatures fall, the heat is released when the wax solidifies.

1965	1995	2005	2006
BASF acquires Glasurit, one of the largest companies in the European coatings industry.	BASF acquisitions include the worldwide pharmaceutical business of UK-based Boots. Two years later, BASF rationalisation leads to the sale of its tapes business.	The global electronic chemicals business of Merck is aquired, plugging BASF into the semi-conductor and flat screen industries.	BASF acquires Degussa's construction chemicals business and the US catalyst manufacturer, Engelhard Corporation.

Basildon Bond

Basildon Bond has become a 'generic name' for quality stationery. With nearly 100 years of heritage, it has reinvented itself for the 21st century. Best known as a range of writing paper and matching envelopes, the brand has also diversified into business envelopes and CD sleeves. New for 2007 is a range of stationery featuring 100 per cent recycled paper.

Market

The revolution in personal and business communication over the last few years has had wide-ranging effects on the market for paper-based products. The medium of paper has both suffered and benefited from changes in usage. Postal traffic continues to grow year on year, and the consumption of paper in offices and homes is also rising. However, within these figures there are winners and losers, as consumers continually change the way they use paper. Responding to the evolving marketplace, Basildon Bond stationery products have been designed for use in both the office and home environments.

Basildon Bond has retained its dominance in the personal stationery market and kept pace with consumers' changing needs by diversifying into business envelopes, children's stationery and even CD sleeves.

Achievements

Basildon Bond is a quintessentially English brand and one that is internationally recognised by name. Its heritage appeals to end users who are looking to send letters with style. The brand actively champions the art of letter writing and it recognises the benefits letter writing can bring in expressing personal feelings, style and business professionalism. Millions of Basildon Bond writing pads and envelopes are sold every year and the brand is available in thousands of corner shops as well as being stocked by the large stationery retailers.

Product

Basildon Bond is best known as a range of branded personal stationery, with matching writing pads and envelopes, featuring high quality watermarked paper.

In a market that has experienced a tremendous growth in own label products, Basildon Bond is the dominant player to the detriment of other brands. The demographic trends, as letter writing becomes less widespread and a less frequent activity, weigh against personal stationery, but in fact this is boosting Basildon Bond's market position. There is growing evidence that consumers care that their letters stand out when they are sent, and for the stationery to reflect the attention and effort involved in the letter writing process. Therefore, using a quality watermarked paper for this

1911	1918	1932	1939–45	1950s	1960s/70s
The brand is established and manufacturing begins at Millingtons in Tottenham.	Basildon Bond is acquired by John Dickinson Stationery and production moves to Apsley, near Hemel Hempstead.	Basildon Bond is established as the best-selling notepaper in the UK.	World War II sees letter-writing reach record levels.	The Basildon Bond range expands into Notelets and Gift Sets.	The brand sustains consumer advertising campaigns.

purpose is more important than ever, and Basildon Bond meets this need. The Basildon Bond personal stationery pads and envelopes incorporate an iconic cover design, instantly recognisable from childhood memory, featuring a coloured square on the front.

In early 2004, this design was re-introduced and subtly updated, achieving a balance of contemporary style, history and nostalgia.

Yet, it is in the business market that recent growth has taken place as the brand has established a reputation for innovation and growth beyond the personal stationery arena.

One of the successful new products has been a range of paper CD sleeves. The range has quickly established itself as the leading brand in this product area, stocked by many high street retailers, and listed in several commercial stationery catalogues.

Basildon Bond business envelopes have been available for a few years, but have now been completely revamped and relaunched as a range of 100 per cent recycled paper envelopes in both white and manilla.

Recent Developments

After gathering clear evidence that office consumers increasingly look for recycled paper products, Basildon Bond recently launched a range of business envelopes using 100 per cent recycled paper, which still delivers the quality required to project a professional image. The white envelopes all use a 100gsm paper that is exceptionally smooth and white, and the manilla use 90gsm paper. In addition the window film, while perfectly clear, is 100 per cent biodegradable, made, remarkably, from corn not petrochemicals. This also means that even the window envelopes in the range can be included in any paper recycling.

Another innovation is the Envelopad which comprises 50 DL envelopes, in a pad. Envelopes can be peeled off as required with no gum residue left on the envelope edge. The wraparound cover keeps them protected when carried around or stored in a desk drawer. There is also a slot in the back cover for storing a book of stamps.

In the Personal Stationery range, a recycled paper option has also been introduced, available as a 'Duke' size pad with matching envelopes, featuring 100gsm white paper. In addition,

personal stationery is also available in a pink paper option, complete with a charity donation to Breakthrough Breast Cancer.

There is also a new range of children's stationery, Basildon Bee, featuring a cartoon bee character, aimed to appeal to parents and grandparents who know and trust the Basildon Bond brand. There are four lines in the range – a Scribble Pad, a Story Pad, a Scrap Book and an Art Pad.

Promotion

Personal stationery products are widely available on the high street, from outlets such as WH Smith, and are regularly promoted by various stockists.

The brand supports major charities in two ways across different products.

In 2007, Basildon Bond is continuing its support of the NSPCC for the fourth year running, with a donation being made to this charity for every box of Basildon Bond business envelopes purchased. The target is to raise £50,000 during 2007, bringing the total raised to over £200,000 since this campaign began. As a result John Dickinson Stationery has been awarded Patron status by the NSPCC.

With every Basildon Bond pink writing pad and pack of pink envelopes sold until the end of 2007,

John Dickinson Stationery is donating 10p to Breakthrough, one of the country's leading breast cancer charities. The aim is to raise £20,000 to help support the charity's vital research and education work. All pink pads contain a full sheet of information on the charity's activities.

These products have formed part of the promotional activity centred around Breast Cancer Awareness month in October each year.

Brand Values

Basildon Bond provides stationery that combines value with style, as it is pitched at the middle of the market in terms of price, giving consumers branded, watermarked stationery at an attractive price. After some years of under-investment in the brand in the 1980s and early 1990s, under new ownership, John Dickinson Stationery has revitalised and reinvented the brand, so that it is ready to be developed further as a range of products relevant to the needs of the modern stationery user. With concerns about the environment now top of the agenda, the move into environmentally friendly recycled paper stationery is particularly timely.

www.basildonbond.com

Things you didn't know about Basildon Bond

The brand name derives from Basildon Park in Berkshire, a country house where a meeting was held to decide on a new range of paper, back in 1911.

Basildon Park is now a National Trust property, made famous as a key location in the 2005 feature film version of Pride and Prejudice.

Basildon Bond became a Russ Abbot spoof secret agent character in the 1980s on his popular BBC TV series The Russ Abbot Show and has since inspired a computer game, 'The adventures of Bond... Basildon Bond', and a comic book Bond-like hero, Charles Basildon.

There is also a rose named Basildon Bond.

The Basildon Bond clock at Apsley is a well-known local landmark and hangs from one the original mill buildings, acquired by John Dickinson in 1804.

1990s	**2005**	**2006**	**2007**
Diversification into business envelopes and CD sleeves takes place.	The brand is first awarded Business Superbrand status.	The children's range, Basildon Bee, is launched.	Basildon Bond's Recycled Paper stationery range is launched.

. . . .

BBH is a full service agency which produces creatively-driven communications that build brands. The Agency develops long, mutually-rewarding relationships with its clients and still works with two of its founding clients – Audi and Levi's – 25 years on. Majority privately-owned, BBH is admired and respected by its peers, the industry and clients alike for its integrity and relentless pursuit of creative excellence.

Market

Since it was founded in 1982, BBH has demonstrated consistently strong year on year growth despite fluctuating market conditions and has grown from one office in London to six offices, based in New York, Singapore, Tokyo, São Paulo and Shanghai, with global billings of US$1.5 billion. BBH London will see a 33 per cent increase in revenues through 2005 new business wins from, amongst other brands, Google, Vodafone, British Airways and OMO (Persil). This growth was in contrast to the general industry's slow growth rate in 2005, which saw a decline of 3.9 per cent compared with the previous year (Source: warc.com).

Achievements

BBH has produced some of the most talked about advertising campaigns in Europe. Its work for Levi's

'The Original Jean' began in 1982 and has included early TV ads such as Launderette, featuring Nick Kamen famously removing his Levi's 501s. In the 1990s, the Agency was an early adopter of the value of the internet. A series of films about Flat Eric, a cool yellow puppet, were sent out virally and unbranded. After building intrigue amongst the target audience, the films were launched across Europe on TV. The Flat Eric campaign (and Flat Eric himself) became a cultural phenomenon, including appearances in various media and on magazine covers. The soundtrack to the ad even kept Eminem off the top of the charts.

Since 2000, BBH has produced campaigns such as Levi's Twist, which won a coveted black D&AD pencil and Levi's Odyssey which became one of the most parodied commercials of all time.

BBH's 'Axe Effect', launched in 1996, helped Axe's business more than double in size between 2000 and 2005 with phenomenon-creating campaigns including 2002's Pulse, with its famous dance, and 2006's Click campaign, which included a Ben Affleck TV spot and actual 'clickers'.

BBH also masterminded the endline 'Vorsprung durch Technik' for Audi in 1982. In 2005, the brand outsold Mercedes for the first time and became the world's first car manufacturer channel with the launch of the Audi Channel – developed by BBH.

One of BBH's most famous international campaigns is 'Keep Walking' for Johnnie Walker. The campaign runs in 125 countries and with its various executions, including Android, has resulted in an extra US$1 billion in value for Diageo since 2000.

Over the years BBH has won 34 IPA Effectiveness Awards, in each case demonstrating the contribution of advertising to its clients' businesses. In 2002, BBH won the IPA Grand Prix award for its work with children's charity Barnardo's, as well as the coveted IPA Effectiveness Agency of the Year Award. In addition, in 2003 BBH won two Marketing Society Awards, for marketing excellence on its Lynx and Olivio accounts and since 1993 has won 19 APG Strategy Awards which recognise the importance of the development of brand strategy. BBH has twice

1982	**1986**	**1993**	**1994**	**1996**	**1998**
BBH is founded by John Bartle, Nigel Bogle and John Hegarty in London, with the objective of producing truly outstanding work for like-minded clients.	BBH is voted Campaign magazine's Agency of the Year, and goes on to win the title again in 1993, 2003, 2004 and 2005.	BBH becomes the Cannes Advertising Festival's very first Agency of the Year by winning more awards than any other agency.	BBH again wins the Cannes Advertising Festival's Agency of the Year award.	BBH's first non-UK office opens in Singapore.	BBH New York opens, followed the next year by an office in Tokyo.

won the Queen's Award for Export for outstanding achievements in overseas earnings by a business in the UK.

Since 2000, the Agency has won 14 Agency of the Year titles, awarded by various publications. In 2005, BBH became the first advertising agency to be awarded Agency of the Year for three consecutive years by Campaign magazine. The Agency also picked up the award from Marketing magazine in the UK in 2001, 2003 and 2005, and AdAsia in 2004 and 2005. In 2005, the global group won the first Network of the Year award from Campaign and Advertising Age's Network of the Year in the US.

Product

BBH is an advertising agency structured to deliver through-the-line communications campaigns locally, internationally and globally. BBH aims to create fame for its clients' brands and to lead the world in creating shared noise and excitement around those brands. In essence, the Agency strives to create big brand ideas that drive hard business results.

BBH is not a typical agency network. There are six offices in five key regional centres: Europe, North America, Asia Pacific, China and Latin America. These regional hubs work collectively or independently, depending on the needs of the individual client. This micro-network structure allows BBH the reach and operational efficiency and, importantly, flexibility to develop international or pan-regional tailored communication solutions for brands.

Currently 79 per cent of the Group's income derives from work that runs in more than one country.

Recent Developments

With the future of the advertising and communications industries in mind, BBH has implemented a number of initiatives to take the Agency into the next era of advertising, an era where consumers are ever more difficult to reach and where brands must engage and entertain rather than interrupt media consumption.

In 2003, BBH launched a music publishing arm, Leap Music, which increases revenue for clients through ownership of music tracks featured in their ads.

BBH's rapidly-growing Content department, launched in 2003, develops cutting-edge advertiser-funded initiatives, different and tailor-made ways for brands to engage with their consumers. Examples of work include Google Space, a lab at Heathrow airport where travellers could raise their awareness of Google offerings; the Audi Channel, the world's first branded entertainment channel; Vodafone and Audi mobile phone campaigns; and recently, BBH Second Life, the Agency's virtual office.

The Agency is also embracing the changing landscapes of advertising by launching a brand invention business, Zag, in 2005. BBH has also created a fourth discipline to sit alongside Account Management, Account Planning and Creative: Engagement Planning, which brings media thinking back in-house and upfront in the creative development process.

Brand Values

The first ad created by BBH was for the European launch of Black Levi's 501s at a time when white jeans were all the rage. The print execution featured a flock of white sheep walking in one direction with one black sheep facing the opposite way and bore the strapline, 'When the World Zigs, Zag', encouraging individuals to think differently and to be aware that the obvious choice is not necessarily the best. For 25 years this strapline has been BBH's mantra and ensures the Agency commits to forging a different path to that of others. BBH zags in the way it approaches its own business, but most importantly, it employs this philosophy in its approach to its clients' businesses, and this has helped BBH produce category-changing brand ideas and advertising.

At the heart of BBH, and etched in steel on a wall in all BBH offices, is a set of 10 beliefs that sum up the way the Agency does business: The power of creativity and the primacy of the idea; Encouraging ideas from any source; The right of everyone to be listened to; The fundamental importance of effectiveness and accountability; Processes that liberate creativity; Client relationships that encourage equal status, allowing best advice; An organisation without politics; Providing opportunity, stimulation and consideration to all who work with us; The need for honesty, decency and integrity in all that we do; The obligations these beliefs place upon us.

www.bartleboglehegarty.com

2003
BBH partners with Brazilian agency, Neogama, creating NeogamaBBH.

2004
BBH's pioneering global network model wins Campaign magazine's first ever Global Network of the Year award.

2005
BBH picks up the Advertising Age Network of the Year award.

2006
BBH Shanghai opens.

Things you didn't know about BBH

BBH is the only advertising agency to win Campaign's Agency of the Year award three years running, namely 2003, 2004, 2005.

The BBH-created Audi Channel is the world's first end-to-end digital channel; Audi is also the world's first to promote a brand via a TV channel.

BBH has had nine number one hits in the UK with music from its ads and is the first agency to have launched a music publishing business.

BBH has won 14 Agency of the Year awards since 2000.

BBH is the first advertising agency in the world to have an office in Second Life.

BDO Stoy Hayward

BDO Stoy Hayward employs some 3,000 partners and staff operating from 15 business centres nationwide. It is the UK Member Firm of BDO International, the world's fifth largest accountancy network, with some 30,000 people and 600 offices in over 100 countries. With a market-leading employment proposition and the highest growth in its sector, it was the first accountancy firm to win 'Global Firm of the Year' in 2006.

Market

The UK accountancy market is in good health. Key Note research suggests £17.73 billion was spent on accountancy and related services in 2005, 10.7 per cent more than the year before, and this rate of growth continued in 2006.

Several factors are fuelling demand: economic conditions remain benign and changes to financial reporting and corporate governance regulations on both sides of the Atlantic have increased the requirement for accounting services and advice.

In the UK, the accountancy market has traditionally been dominated by the Big Four. These firms – PricewaterhouseCoopers, Deloitte, KPMG and Ernst & Young – currently audit all FTSE 100 companies, and the majority of the top 350.

However, this domination has become the subject of intense debate in the accountancy industry – BDO Stoy Hayward is at the forefront of the discussion. As the leading firm outside the Big Four, BDO Stoy Hayward argues that there is a worrying lack of open competition and choice for the largest audit assignments. For example, a recent report by the Financial Reporting Council revealed that 70 per cent of FTSE 100 companies have not put audit work up for tender for 15 years.

BDO Stoy Hayward has the largest number of FTSE 350 audit clients outside the Big Four.

Achievements

BDO Stoy Hayward is fast establishing itself as the firm that offers companies – and talented people – an alternative that is successful, relevant and refreshingly different.

The firm has substantially increased its share of the accountancy market. Since 2003 turnover has grown by 70 per cent, a rate far ahead of its competitors', average growth standing at 31 per cent.

This was recognised in the 2006 Accountancy Age Awards, with BDO Stoy Hayward being named 'Global Firm of the Year'. This was the first year that the firm has competed directly with the Big Four for the same award.

BDO Stoy Hayward's managing partner, Jeremy Newman, also received a personal honour – 'Personality of the Year'.

The firm has been recognised in a series of awards for its performance as an employer. It moved up 72 places to be named 19th in The Sunday Times 2006 '100 Best Companies to Work For' – and was the only accountancy firm to be included in the main category.

The firm was also voted Accountancy Age 'Employer of the Year' for an unprecedented two consecutive years and included in The Times 'Top 50 Places Where Women Want to Work' in 2006.

The firm's reputation has enabled it to attract the best quality employees – it has grown by more than one additional person each working day throughout 2006 – and it has one of the industry's lowest turnover rates. The latest staff survey, 'Pulse', conducted by leading independent research company ISR, found that over 90 per cent of employees support the firm's values and would recommend it as a good place to work.

BDO Stoy Hayward is helping to challenge many of the prevailing assumptions about the accountancy market, most particularly that the Big Four's size is a promise of superior quality and service and that only they can service larger companies.

Product

Understanding clients' business sectors and markets is key to ensuring the best possible advice and quality of work. Accordingly BDO Stoy Hayward continues to invest in building sector-specialist teams and now has groups focused on

1903	**1919**	**1952**	**1988**	**1992**	**1994**
A F (Fred) Stoy founds Stoy & Co.	R J (Jack) Hayward joins the firm.	Originally based in the City of London, the firm moves to the West End to be closer to the firm's new entrepreneurial client base.	The firm changes its name to Stoy Hayward.	Stoy Hayward merges with another medium-sized firm of chartered accountants, Finnie & Co.	The firm extends its national network through a union with 13 BDO Binder Hamlyn offices, and changes its name to BDO Stoy Hayward becoming the UK Member Firm of BDO International.

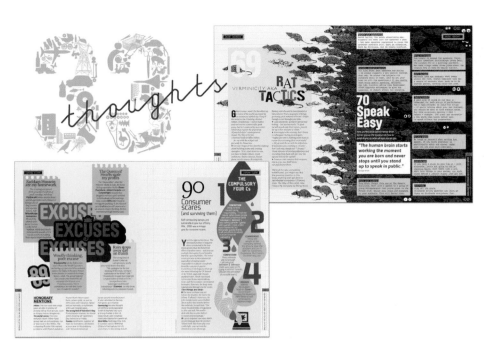

eight key sectors: business services; financial services; leisure and hospitality; manufacturing; professional services; real estate and construction; retail; and technology, media and telecoms. In addition the firm regularly operates in a wide range of other sectors including natural resources and 'not for profit' (charities, education and registered social landlords).

The firm offers a full range of services, including business assurance, business restructuring, corporate finance, forensic accounting, tax and investment management. It also offers market-leading services in areas such as Alternative Investment Market, IFRS conversion, risk assurance, restraint and confiscation, and tax solutions.

Recent Developments

BDO Stoy Hayward's national turnover increased by 27 per cent to £288 million in 2006 with an operating profit of £70 million, up by 16 per cent. This remarkable rate of financial growth has been achieved through the attraction and retention of the best quality people in the business, resulting in new business wins 28 per cent higher than in the previous 12 months.

Perhaps the most important advance has been the continual enhancement of the firm's employment proposition; over the past 12 months new and leading policies have been developed in areas ranging from Flexible Working to Corporate Social Responsibility (CSR champions have been appointed in every business unit to communicate and stimulate CSR activity around the firm) and an increased focus on diversity.

The firm's sustained strong growth has resulted in a number of offices relocating to larger premises, including investment in a substantially larger London office in Baker Street.

Developments such as these are enabling the firm to employ more high quality people, add new service lines and handle an ever wider range of clients and assignments.

Promotion

BDO Stoy Hayward uses all communication media to build its brand, including PR, events and seminars, direct mail, the internet and print advertising.

The firm continues to have great success with its high-profile magazine '33 thoughts' – which offers ideas, observations, advice and comment. It has won a number of awards including 'Launch of the Year' at the 2005 APA Awards and 'Editor of the Year' at the 2006 BSME awards.

In the spring of 2007 the firm launches a national brand advertising campaign. The main aim of the campaign is to raise awareness of BDO Stoy Hayward's capabilities as the credible and alternative accountancy services provider to larger companies and will primarily feature poster and press advertising.

BDO Stoy Hayward runs numerous high profile events, a recent example being a series of roadshows in Chinese cities about access to UK capital markets plus seminars in the UK on how to do business in China.

The firm also gains valuable brand awareness from its specialist reports – Industry Watch, the Private Company Price Index and FraudTrack to name but a few, and its website continues to be a highly effective communication tool.

Brand Values

'Being Successfully Different' is the vision underpinning the BDO Stoy Hayward brand. The firm is seen as 'high quality, straight-talking, pragmatic and human' and strives to be seen as 'the positive credible alternative', and certainly not just a 'Big Fifth' in the accountancy market.

It is successfully different because of its attitude towards its people – who are at the heart of how the business thinks and acts. The firm's success is centred on having an industry-leading employment offering.

The firm takes pride in being the 'challenger brand' in the industry, and prizes its reputation for fresh, innovative thinking and liberating and empowering its people. Its status as one of the best employers in the country is viewed as hugely important and the fulfilment and motivation of its staff has a major influence on its outward-facing character.

For BDO Stoy Hayward, no two clients are the same, nor any two employees, respecting people's differences is central to its values which makes a valuable and tangible difference for their clients too.

www.bdo.co.uk

Things you didn't know about BDO Stoy Hayward

BDO Stoy Hayward is the only accountancy firm to be listed in The Sunday Times '100 Best Companies to Work For'.

BDO Stoy Hayward has more clients in the FTSE 350 than any firm outside the Big Four.

BDO Stoy Hayward offers employees six days per year for carrying out volunteer work.

91 per cent of BDO Stoy Hayward clients would recommend them to other companies.

BDO Stoy Hayward joined with 89 BDO International Member Firms in a successful bid to provide services for a UK-based global technology, media and telecoms business.

BDO Stoy Hayward is the first accountancy firm to be named 'Global Firm of the Year' and the only accountancy firm to be voted Accountancy Age 'Employer of the Year' in two consecutive years.

2002

BDO Stoy Hayward achieves its goal of becoming a single national partnership with an associated firm in Belfast.

2005

BDO Stoy Hayward becomes the first firm outside the Big Four to audit a FTSE 100 company.

2006

BDO SH becomes the fifth largest accountancy firm in the UK.

Also in 2006, BDO Stoy Hayward is the first firm to be awarded Accountancy Age 'Global Firm of the Year'.

It is often said that 'Knowledge is Power'. But to be effective, that knowledge must be reliable, accurate and timely – and independent market research aims to deliver exactly that. The better informed we are about our markets, our customers, our staff and our competitors, the better the decisions we are likely to make. The BMRB name has been synonymous with quality, reliability and integrity in market research for over 70 years.

Market

Market research has seen a huge growth in demand in a number of key areas. The size of the UK research market has more than doubled in the last 10 years and according to the Market Research Society (MRS) was worth an estimated £1.3 billion in 2005. As one of the largest market research agencies in the UK, BMRB has been at the forefront of this growth.

Achievements

BMRB's achievements run across all areas of the business, and its commitment to quality, its staff, and its clients.

BMRB won two of the four BMRA Research Business Effectiveness Awards for 2005, the Award for Best Agency and the Award for Quality & Service

Excellence. BMRB was also short-listed for the Award for People Management.

BMRB was one of the first market research companies to have professionally recognised training programmes for both research and operations executives.

Very high standards of client satisfaction are consistently achieved. In 2006, 96 per cent of clients gave the company an overall performance rating of 'excellent', 'very good' or 'good'.

Product

BMRB offers market-leading research services in: Brand owner insight – Enlightenment (offered in

partnership with Millward Brown) harnesses the power of in-house and other data sources and applies these to a range of applications. The service provides answers to all types of marketing questions, quickly and flexibly.

Business to business research – BMRB offers a broad range of services, encompassing qualitative, quantitative and omnibus research. The team conducts telephone, face-to-face and online methodologies, in Great Britain and internationally.

Employee and customer research – BMRB Stakeholder is a specialist unit dedicated to understanding customer loyalty and employee

1925	**1933**	**1934**	**1939**	**1969**	**1987**
The research department of JWT reports on its first survey – 'Report of Investigation on Pears Soap Consumers, United Kingdom'.	The British Market Research Bureau is set up, marking its place as the longest established research agency in Britain.	One of the earliest and largest studies on newspaper readership for the Daily Herald is carried out.	BMRB becomes one of the first agencies to conduct major surveys for Government, including a survey for the Ministry of Food to monitor war-time rationing and the Board of Trade to investigate clothing coupons.	BMRB develops the Target Group Index (TGI) which has since become a standard trading currency for the UK media sector.	BMRB joins WPP Group plc.

engagement. It helps organisations measure and respond to the needs of their customers, employees and other key stakeholders to improve their business performance. BMRB Stakeholder is also the only licensed provider in the UK of Walker Loyalty Solutions – effective business tools for measuring and managing critical relationships developed by Walker Information, a world leader in customer and loyalty measurement.

Environmental and climate change research – BMRB offers a wealth of research resource and data on a wide range of issues relating to the environment. It conducts tailored qualitative and quantitative research amongst the general public, organisations and special interest groups.

Media research – BMRB Media works with the leading media owners and advertising agencies. It offers research expertise across all media and regularly provides insight into work relating to mixed media. BMRB aims to provide creative solutions and excellent client service for media buyers, sellers, advertisers and regulators alike.

Omnibus surveys – fast, accurate and cost effective, BMRB Omnibus is a leader in face-to-face, telephone, online and global omnibus surveys. Its broad portfolio of services offers flexible schedules and methodologies to suit wide-ranging research requirements.

Over 50s research – BMRB offers a range of research solutions for marketers targeting the over 50s as a consumer group, for policy makers measuring the impact of the over 50s on public policy and expenditure, and for employers realising the potential of the over 50s workforce.

Social policy and public sector research – BMRB Social Research is one of the largest providers of public policy research in the UK with a team of over 70 dedicated social researchers. Its reputation for quality, technical excellence and creative solutions is second to none. BMRB regularly conducts prestigious national projects such as the British Crime Survey.

Sports research – BMRB Sport offers effective research solutions for all Sports sectors, from professional sports through to grassroots participation and active leisure. Its tools and techniques, designed to help the drive towards participation, are built around the principles of getting people to start, stay and succeed in Sport. For the professional Sport sector, BMRB offers research to identify and grow revenue streams from media and sponsorship rights, and from the fan base.

Syndicated marketing and media surveys – Target Group Index (TGI) is the world's leading single-source measurement of consumers' product and brand usage, media consumption and attitudes. Originally developed in Britain by BMRB, TGI now operates in over 50 countries and is used by advertisers, media owners and agencies to provide worldwide consumer insight.

Travel and transport research – BMRB offers tailored research and insight for this diverse field. Its experience ranges from public policy research to commercial research for private travel operators and tourist boards.

Recent Developments

In 2006, BMRB launched new specialist areas of research including business to business; environmental & climate change; the over 50s; sports; and travel & transport. Each was established in response to emerging client needs.

BMRB are working towards being accredited to ISO 20252 in April 2007. This new international standard sets a common level of quality for market research globally.

Promotion

BMRB uses a comprehensive range of marketing communications tools to raise awareness and develop business for the products and services it specialises in.

BMRB's integrated marketing approach utilises advertising, PR, direct mail, website, email, delivering conference papers and sponsoring industry events. In addition, it regularly publishes a wide range of paper-based and online newsletters which focus on Social, TGI and Media research issues.

BMRB's findings and thinking are regularly published in the research and marketing trade press and beyond. Coverage has been achieved in publications such as Research Magazine, SRA News, Marketing, Campaign, the FT, The Times, Guardian, BBC Online and The Business.

Its Stakeholder Solutions division annually conducts the National

Employee Benchmark Survey which provides an insight into the attitudes and loyalty of Britain's workforce. Findings have been given coverage in the FT, Personnel Today and BBC Breakfast News.

BMRB's Centre for Excellence seminar programme plays an active role in helping clients better understand all aspects of the research process. BMRB runs over 100 seminars and workshops per year for clients.

BMRB organises seminars which each attract 80-120 delegates to discuss research relating to specific topics. Recent topics have included Healthy Eating and Marketing to an Ageing Population.

Brand Values

By providing unimpeachable information, BMRB empowers clients to make better business decisions. An important contributory factor in maintaining BMRB's high standards is the quality of the company's staff training programmes – regarded as some of the best in the industry.

BMRB consciously avoids being a 'jack of all trades'. The company's established excellence in specific research sectors, reinforced by its comprehensive operational resources, enables it to be flexible and creative in meeting client needs. BMRB's core values are encapsulated in the words 'high quality tailored research solutions'.

www.bmrb.co.uk

Things you didn't know about BMRB

When BMRB launched TGI in 1969 it researched 25,000 respondents. By 2005 TGI had grown to over 700,000 respondents annually worldwide.

Over the last five years BMRB has conducted over 150,000 interviews for the British Crime Survey.

From 1969 to 1983 BMRB, backed by the music industry and the BBC, produced the Record Charts (the 'Top 20').

Jay K, lead singer of the band Jamiroquai, once worked as a research interviewer in BMRB's telephone unit in Ealing.

1997
It is the first to conduct Multi-Media Computer Aided Personal Interviewing (MM CAPI) nationally.

Also in 1997 BMRB conducts its first web-based research project; a readership survey for The Lancet.

1998
The KMR Group is formed to create an international platform for integrated research, information and software provision.

2005
BMRB wins two of the four BMRA Research Business Effectiveness Awards for 2005.

Also in 2005, the Scottish office in Edinburgh is opened.

bp

BP is one of the world's largest energy companies. Its distinctive products and services provide heat, light and mobility to millions of people around the globe. With a portfolio of master brands encompassing Aral, ARCO, ampm and Castrol, BP's brands are present in more than 100 countries, serving more than 13 million customers daily.

Market

BP's specific areas of business include exploration for and production of crude oil and natural gas; refining and marketing of oil products; manufacturing and marketing of petrochemicals; and integrated supply and trading. BP is also an increasingly significant player in alternative energy and biofuels.

The relaunch of the BP brand in July 2000 proved to be a watershed in the company's history, and that of the entire energy sector. Since unveiling its new 'Helios' mark, BP has striven to establish itself as an environmentally conscious brand, developing sustainable ways to meet the world's growing energy demands.

Its success has not gone unnoticed, and investment in this category has increased as many of BP's competitors try to develop similar reputations. Shell, Total and Chevron have all instigated high-profile communications campaigns highlighting their efforts to meet both current and future energy demands. GE, too, has launched Ecomagination, which aims to provide technology for generating low-carbon power.

Combined with a recent upsurge in media interest, these moves by high-profile companies into 'green' schemes signal a tipping point in the perception of environmental concerns, from a social responsibility issue to a viable business proposition.

Achievements

For the sixth consecutive year, Business Week and Interbrand have jointly published their ranking of the 100 Top Global Brands by dollar value. As in every previous year, the BP brand's growth has outpaced industry competition. It grew by five per cent in 2006 (against four per cent in 2005), and remains the survey's top oil brand, with a value of just over US$4 billion.

Another recent achievement has come by way of a brand extension, in the form of BP's new renewable business division, Alternative Energy.

An old form of energy.
A new way to catch it.

alternativenergy
Powered by BP

In November 2005, BP announced plans to invest US$8 billion over 10 years in this new business, which aims to lead the market in low carbon power generated from the sun, wind, natural gas and hydrogen.

A number of factors in today's carbon-constrained world – the security of supply, the environmental impact of energy, advances in technology and the likelihood that carbon will soon have a market price – are sure to create future markets for cleaner power. By meeting this growing demand, BP believes it can benefit both society and its shareholders. It aims to grow Alternative Energy five to tenfold over the next decade, helping to reduce future greenhouse gas emissions by as much as 24 million tonnes each year.

Within its first year, the new division has announced relationships with GE. Furthermore, over the next three years, it plans to treble sales of solar products, begin construction on two of the world's first industrial-scale hydrogen power plants (in the UK and the US), build a new gas-fired power co-generation capacity and develop a significant wind power business.

Product

At the heart of BP's approach is the so-called 'energy paradox': people and businesses want the benefits of heat, light and mobility, but they don't want to think about the consequences. BP has long been aware that the only way to resolve this paradox is to provide customers with

1909	1940s	1954	1965
The Anglo-Persian Oil Company (as BP was first known) is formed.	After World War II, BP's sales, profits, capital expenditure and employment all rise to record levels as Europe is restructured.	The company name becomes The British Petroleum Company Limited.	BP finds the West Sole gas field – the first offshore hydrocarbons to be found in British waters.

alternatives that give them the benefits they want, with less environmental impact. The company continues to develop its portfolio of products based on this principle, with the simple aim of providing customers with a better quality of life.

Launched in 2003, BP Ultimate is a prime example of BP's approach. An advanced performance fuel, available in unleaded and diesel, BP Ultimate burns more smoothly and completely than traditional fuel and has outstanding engine cleaning power. In short, it gives drivers more performance with less pollution.

BP has a global strategic relationship with Ford that has extended the company's commitment to cleaner, higher-performing fuel from the forecourt to the manufacturers. The two companies have also collaborated on hydrogen vehicle trials in the US and on a Europe/US fuel filler cap initiative – reflecting its commitment to improve efficiency, performance and emissions.

BP continues to invest heavily in natural gas, transforming itself from a mid-size gas marketer into a gas marketing leader. Today, natural gas makes up more than half of BP's energy production, making it the largest producer and supplier in the US.

BP's Aromatics & Acetyls business uses leading edge technology to manufacture essential raw materials, which become a part of everyday life for millions of people everywhere around the world. For example, one tonne of purified terephthalic acid makes 50,000 0.5L cola bottles.

Recent Developments

A notable element of BP's communication in 2005/06 has been an effort to help educate people about their own household emissions. BP's carbon footprint calculator, for example, helps estimate the scale of a household's emissions and suggests ways these might be reduced.

BP is equally committed to minimising the environmental impact of road transport, as demonstrated by the UK launch of targetneutral. This not-for-profit initiative gives drivers a practical, affordable way to help neutralise CO_2 emissions from their cars.

At www.targetneutral.com, drivers can calculate how much CO_2 their car emits, find out how to reduce these emissions and learn more about global projects to minimise CO_2. They can also make cash contributions, usually about £20 per year, to help neutralise their car emissions. BP also makes a cash contribution for every litre of BP fuel purchased by targetneutral members using their Nectar cards.

Biofuels will play a major role in meeting the growing world demand for transportation fuels, and BP is investing in various biofuel-related activities. The aim is to make biofuels more widely available, and so bring them into the mainstream. Innovation begins with research, and BP plans to invest US$500 million over the next 10 years to establish the world's first research laboratory dedicated to biosciences energy: the Energy Biosciences Institute.

Since 2003, the company has also been working with DuPont to explore new approaches to biofuels development. The first product of this collaboration, an advanced biofuel called biobutanol, is well on its way to production.

Promotion

BP's brands, each with its own unique heritage and history, are recognised and respected around the world. Together, they make BP the force it is today, and BP is continually building its brands through investment and an innovative approach to brand management and positioning.

The Aral name remains one of the leading German retail brands, a byword for outstanding products and customer service on forecourts across the country.

BP's investment in consumer and B2B advertising and sponsorships for Castrol demonstrates the brand's continuing performance, especially in motor sport racing and sponsorship.

ARCO is the largest volume supplier of retail gasoline on the US West Coast. Alongside ARCO fuels stands BP's franchised forecourt retail brand, ampm, which has been a household name in the US for more than 20 years.

Brand Values

In all it says and does, BP aims to be performance driven, innovative, progressive and green.

Performance driven means setting global standards of performance in every area; from safety and the environment to increasing growth and delivering greater satisfaction for customers and employees.

Being innovative means using the creative know-how of BP's people, combined with cutting-edge technology, to develop breakthrough solutions to business challenges and the needs of BP's customers.

Progressive means BP is always looking for new and better ways to do things. In touch with the needs of its employees, customers and local communities, BP aims always to be accessible, open and transparent.

Lastly, green means demonstrating environmental leadership. It also means overcoming the trade-off between providing access to heat, light and mobility and protecting the environment.

In summary, all BP employees aim to bring to life these brand values in their day-to-day work.

www.bp.com

Things you didn't know about BP

BP's aviation business, Air BP, was launched in 1926, and now supplies aviation fuels at more than 1,200 locations across the world.

BP LPG business unit has more than 10 million bottles in circulation in Europe alone.

BP's international marine business delivers marine fuels and lubricants in over 800 ports worldwide.

BP Biofuels
a growing alternative

It is now possible to drive in neutral.

Road transport generates about 22% of the UK's CO_2 emissions. As well as driving more efficiently, you can now neutralise the impact of your car's CO_2 emissions at targetneutral.com. Initiated by BP, targetneutral is a not-for-profit scheme; drivers make a small annual payment towards funding alternative and renewable energy projects which, in turn, offset the equivalent to their car's emissions. Through this scheme all our fuel tankers delivering to UK petrol stations are now CO_2 neutral.

Find out more at targetneutral.com

bp

beyond petroleum

bp.com

1975
BP pumps ashore the first oil from the North Sea's UK sector when it brings the Forties field on stream.

1997
BP becomes the first in its industry to state publicly the need for precautionary action on climate change.

1998–2001
BP's main mergers and acquisitions take place – merging with US giant Amoco, and acquiring ARCO, Burmah Castrol and Veba Oil – turning it into one of the world's largest energy companies.

2005
BP Alternative Energy is launched, dedicated to the development and wholesale marketing and trading of low-carbon power.

BSI Group is a leading independent professional services business, delivering assurance to organisations worldwide. It does this through: independent certification of management systems and products; product testing; development of private, national and international standards; performance management software solutions; management systems and standards training; and delivery of information on standards and international trade.

Market

The Group has over 2,100 employees and has clients in over 100 countries. Some of the world's best known companies rely on BSI's authority in establishing reliable and respected benchmarks. In 2005, its turnover was £234.8 million.

BSI works for clients operating in a myriad of sectors, including communications, banking, engineering, electronics, food and drink, agriculture and consumer goods. Its clients include 25 per cent of companies listed on the FTSE 100 index and one sixth of Fortune 500 businesses. In order to compete and inspire their customers' trust, BSI's clients increasingly rely on industry benchmarking and quality assurance, including the Kitemark®,

widely seen as one of the most trustworthy marks available in the UK market. BSI remains one of the leading providers of standardisation documents, covering every aspect of the modern economy.

Achievements

Since its inception in 1901 as the Engineering Standards Committee, BSI Group has grown into an independent commercial business providing standards-based solutions which inspire confidence and deliver assurance to customers worldwide. The Group today operates globally through its four business units: BSI British Standards, BSI Management Systems, BSI Product Services and BSI Entropy International.

BSI British Standards was the world's first national standards body, which provided the model for other countries to follow, and instigated the formation of the International Organization for Standardization (ISO) in 1946. Today BSI produces an average of 1,700 new standards annually.

It has remained at the forefront of the international standards industry ever since, with a proud tradition of innovation. For example BSI also leads the international standards committee on nanotechnology and pioneered new guidelines on information security, risk management and sustainability. Furthermore, it developed the world's first standard in relationship management and assisted in the development of the only internationally recognised food safety management standard.

BSI British Standards is also increasingly building bi-lateral relations with other countries and their National Standards Bodies to advance the interests of British businesses internationally, including signing co-operation agreements with the National Standards Bodies of China and Japan. British Standards is also a major provider of technical assistance to countries around the world and has undertaken projects in countries including Russia,

Turkey and Albania, assisting in developing and improving their emerging standardisation infrastructures.

In addition, BSI Management Systems is one of the world's largest independent certification bodies, with over 60,000 certified locations and clients in over 100 countries. Indeed, the internationally accepted concept of management systems standards was pioneered by BSI. The ISO 9000 quality series, which has been adopted by over 750,000 organisations in 161 countries, was developed from British Standard BS 5750, first published in 1979. Furthermore the most widely accepted environmental management systems standard, ISO 14001, was derived from BS 7750 and has been implemented in 138 countries.

Product

BSI's four businesses provide a wide range of services. BSI British Standards is the National Standards Body of the UK and develops standards and standardisation solutions to meet the needs of business and society. It works with Government, businesses and consumers to represent UK interests and facilitate the production of British, European and international standards. British

1901	1903	1929	1953	1979	1992
BSI Group is founded as the Engineering Standards Committee (ESC). One of the first standards to be published is to reduce the number of sizes of tramway rails.	The British Standard Mark, now known as the Kitemark®, is registered as a trademark.	The Engineering Standards Committee is awarded a Royal Charter and in 1931, the name British Standards Institution is adopted.	In the post-war era, more demand for consumer standardisation work leads to the introduction of the Kitemark® for domestic products.	BS 5750, now known as ISO 9001, is introduced to help companies build quality and safety into the way they work. The Registered Firm mark is also introduced.	BSI publishes the world's first environmental management standard, BS 7750, now known as ISO 14001.

Standards' products and services help organisations to successfully implement best practice, manage business critical decisions and achieve excellence.

BSI Management Systems provides independent assessment, certification and training of management systems, including ISO 9001 and ISO 14001 (Quality and Environmental Management respectively), Greenhouse Gas Emissions Verification as well as ISO/IEC 27001 (Information Security Management) and ISO/IEC 20000 (IT Service Management) where it is a global market leader. BSI also holds this position in the Aerospace and Automotive management systems certification market.

BSI Product Services is best known for the Kitemark®, the UK's best known product quality mark which was first registered in 1903. It also provides CE marking under 17 European Directives for companies wishing to trade in the European market. BSI Product Services helps industry develop new and better products and to make sure they meet current and future laws and regulations, from commercial construction to motorcycle helmets, from mobile phones to fire extinguishers, from car headlights to healthcare.

Finally, BSI Entropy International, which joined BSI Group in 2006, is a software solutions company. It enables organisations worldwide to improve environmental, social and economic performance. The Entropy System™ is a market-leading, web-based application for enterprise-level risk and compliance management that helps businesses improve internal control and corporate governance.

Recent Developments

BSI Group continues to innovate and recently developed the world's first integrated management specification – PAS 99. In 2005 BSI achieved two new accreditations for SA 8000, the new Social Accountability standard, and in the following year gained accreditation for OHSAS 18001 which covers Occupational Health and Safety. Also in 2006, BSI

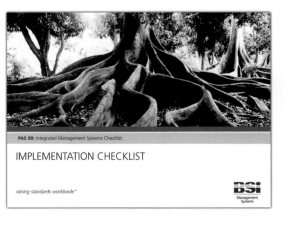

PAS 99: Integrated Management Systems Checklist

IMPLEMENTATION CHECKLIST

raising standards worldwide™

was one of the first organisations to be accredited to ISO 22000, the new food safety management system standard and has been instrumental in developing BS 25999, a new standard for business continuity management.

BSI has also developed a new range of Kitemark® schemes for the service industry. These include the Automotive Services Kitemark® scheme, which ensures the quality of vehicle repair, and the Kitemark® Crash Repair Scheme.

The Group has also continued its strategy of expansion through acquisition, most recently acquiring the major German certification business NIS ZERT. It also bought the UK and Canadian-based Entropy International Ltd, and in Australia it acquired Benchmark Certification Pty Ltd, Australia's second largest certification body.

Promotion

BSI has been investing heavily in marketing over recent years. In July 2002 it created a single BSI brand and now enjoys a consistent and clear visual identity across the Group's global operations. In addition, all BSI staff across the Group's divisions understand the importance and power of the brand and aim to deliver it consistently.

BSI's marketing focuses on achieving the long term goal of a coherent global brand identity. It uses a full range of communication tools, interacting with external and internal stakeholders. Public relations plays a strong role, as does its business magazine, Business Standards

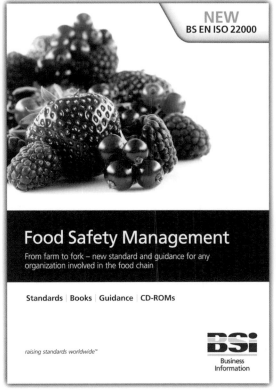

(www.businessstandards.com). It also uses sponsorship, lending its name to the BSI Sustainability Design Awards scheme, run in conjunction with London's Royal College of Art. This aligns BSI Group with the best in contemporary design and positions BSI as a leading player in sustainability issues.

To reinforce the brand internally, BSI's brand identity website is a crucial tool, making the corporate guidelines and brand elements easily accessible to staff and key suppliers worldwide.

Although the Group follows a carefully defined brand strategy, the business units tailor their marketing campaigns to meet the specific requirements of their individual customers across varying regions. Subsequently, the majority of BSI communications are now regionally focused, instead of being UK-centric.

Brand Values

BSI Group's brand values are integrity, innovation and independence. They are the foundation of the BSI brand, supporting the organisation as it strives towards its vision of inspiring confidence and delivering assurance to customers through standards-based solutions.

BSI continually strives to deliver its brand values, with the aim of building a powerful, globally recognised brand, ultimately satisfying the needs of clients, staff, Members and other key stakeholders.

www.bsi-global.com

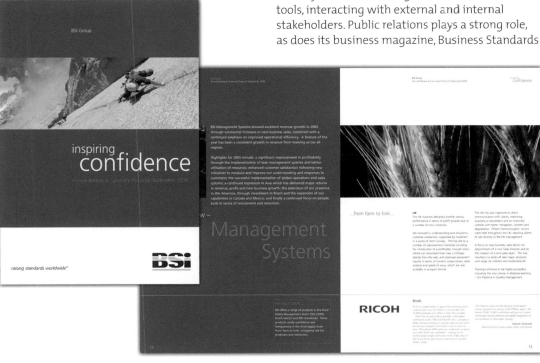

1999	2002	2004	2006
BSI acquires Mertcontrol, a leading certification company in Hungary, and ISC, a Singapore-based certification organisation.	KPMG's ISO registration business in North America is acquired, making BSI Group the largest certification body in the world.	The Group acquires KPMG Certification B.V. to provide an enhanced range of services to businesses across the Benelux region and continental Europe.	BSI acquires German certification company NIS ZERT, UK and Canadian-based software solutions company Entropy International Ltd, and Australia's second largest certification company Benchmark Certification Pty Ltd.

BT is one of the UK's best-known companies, providing communications services to more than 20 million business and residential customers around the globe. Its transformation from an 'old-fashioned telco' to a modern communications services provider is accelerating as the convergence of IT, communications and networking technologies continues.

Market

BT operates in a thriving, multi-trillion pound industry that spans the whole world. In recent years the global communications market has been focused on convergence, where the boundaries between telcos, IT companies, software businesses, hardware manufacturers and broadcasters have merged to create a new communications industry. Driven by the relentless evolution of technology and insatiable customer demand for innovative communications solutions, BT is at the forefront of providing world class networked IT services.

Billions of pounds continue to be invested in new networks and technology making BT well positioned to become the UK's first truly converged provider of information, communications and networking services and a major force in the digital networked economy.

Achievements

More than 80 per cent of the FTSE 100 and 60 per cent of the largest Fortune 500 companies rely on BT for networking, applications and system integration. Organisations including the National Health Service, the Ministry of Defence, Fiat, Microsoft®, Philips, Reuters, Unilever and the Bavarian Government are working with BT to exploit the power of networked IT and communications services.

BT is also the driving force behind the success of 'Broadband Britain' investing millions in a nation-wide network providing blanket coverage across the UK.

Industry recognition includes BT being named as the 'Best Global Carrier' at the World Communication Awards and highly commended as 'Best Brand' for its global scale and capability. BT Infonet was named Communications Business Service Company of the Year by Frost & Sullivan in 2005, while Technology Marketing Corporation singled out BT Fusion – the world's first seamless fixed-mobile phone service – as the winner of the Communications Solutions Product of the Year Award for 2005.

For the sixth year running, BT has been recognised as the world's top telecommunications company in the Dow Jones Sustainability Index (DJSI). DJSI assesses companies worldwide on their performance in areas such as corporate governance, environmental management, community investment, human rights, supply chain and risk management.

Product

BT provides a wide range of communication services for all sectors of the business market. It offers networked IT services focused on messaging and conferencing, CRM (customer relationship management), convergence, outsourcing and security as well as consultancy services to help businesses gain advantage in the digital networked economy.

Specifically, BT is pioneering the take-up of public wireless broadband in the UK that enables business customers on the move to surf the web, check emails and download documents at more than 8,500 BT Openzone 'hotspots' in the UK, and now over 30,000 sites across the globe. BT is also pioneering a new large scale city wireless scheme providing extensive coverage in 12 city areas including Westminster, Cardiff, Birmingham and Glasgow.

The award-winning BT Fusion offers businesses significant savings on the cost of making calls both on the move and in the office. When out and about, BT Fusion works just like a normal mobile phone, while calls made in the office are routed over a broadband connection.

BT's support for SMEs continues to grow with broadband increasingly critical to the success of small firms. This is backed by a portfolio of value-added services tailor-made for SMEs including

1984	1991
British Telecom is privatised making it the only state-owned telecommunications company to be privatised in Europe.	British Telecom is restructured and re-launched as BT.

BT Business Broadband Voice, its first 'flat top' internet telephone or VoIP call package for broadband customers. Many SMEs have opted for BT's Total Broadband package which gives users the opportunity to experience the full potential of broadband using BT's stylish and revolutionary BT Home Hub.

BT's vision is to provide customers with access to all their applications and information, wherever they are, on their choice of device, whilst utilising the best network available.

Recent Developments
The last year has seen BT at the forefront of technological innovation with the launch of new higher speed wholesale broadband services across the UK. The upgraded BT ADSL Max and BT ADSL Max Premium services mean that more than 99.6 per cent of UK homes and businesses are now able to benefit from broadband speeds of up to 8Mbit/s.

BT is also investing more than £10 billion to create a '21st century network' (21CN) – one of the most advanced in the world delivering converged services to both residential and business customers.

A new part of BT, Openreach has also been created to deliver installation and maintenance services for the UK's telephone and internet service providers. Containing almost all of BT's field force of engineers, Openreach has been created as part of a groundbreaking regulatory deal with Ofcom.

Promotion
In bringing its view of the digital networked economy to life, BT has created new and innovative communications channels to reach that illusive audience – senior business people.

Advertising provides strong air cover to establish the digital networked economy and build BT's credibility. The use of below-the-line media helps support BT's capability messages.

Brand Values
BT's corporate identity defines the kind of company it is today – and the one it needs to be in the future. Central to that identity is a commitment to create ways to help customers thrive in a changing world. To do this BT focuses on 'living' its brand values, which are as follows: Trustworthy – doing what it say it will; Helpful – working as one team; Inspiring – creating new possibilities; Straightforward – making things clear; Heart – believing in what it does.

The BT strapline – Bringing it all together – conveys leadership in the way BT enables global business customers to profit from convergence.

www.bt.com

2003
BT unveils its current corporate identity and brand values reflecting the aspirations of a technologically innovative future.

2005
Following the Telecommunications Strategic Review (TSR), BT signs legally-binding Undertakings with Ofcom to help create a better regulatory framework.

2006
Openreach opens for business and is responsible for managing the UK access network on behalf of the communications industry.

Also in 2006 BT is recognised as the world's top telecommunications company by the Dow Jones Sustainability Index for the sixth year running.

Things you didn't know about BT

BT processes 320 million transactions per day with sub one second response speeds.

BT, through its Global Services division, employs 27,500 professionals in 53 countries, serving customers in 170 countries worldwide.

More than nine million broadband users are connected to BT's network in the UK.

At the end of the 2006 financial year, BT had 453,000 BT Business Broadband customers.

BT provides remote support for 24,000 PCs for SME customers.

CIMA, the Chartered Institute of Management Accountants is a leading membership body that offers an internationally recognised professional qualification in management accountancy, which focuses on accounting for business. Headquartered in London and with 12 offices outside the UK, CIMA supports over 158,000 members and students in 161 countries.

Market

CIMA's members work in all sectors of industry, commerce, not-for-profit and public sector organisations and small and medium sized enterprises (SMEs). No other UK accountancy body has such a high proportion of members – 98 per cent – in business or the public sector.

In today's business environment, it has never been more important for accountants to demonstrate integrity and ethical standards. CIMA plays an essential role in this, protecting the public interest by regulating its members and contributing to the ongoing development of the profession through technical research and development.

With its emphasis on strategic business skills, CIMA's qualifications framework helps individuals and employers both within and outside financial management. Four out of 10 of its members work in areas such as operations management, project management and IT.

Demand for CIMA qualifications comes from all over the world, with 270 of the world's top organisations working with CIMA to support their students through the CIMA qualification. Australia, China, India, Ireland, Hong Kong, Malaysia, South Africa and Sri Lanka are among its international markets. Overall, 698 of CIMA members are employed within the top management of the FTSE 350 and 42 members of CIMA operate at group board level in the FTSE 350.

Achievements

CIMA provides more management, management accounting, project management and strategy than any other UK accounting qualification.

It supports some of the world's leading employers and course providers around the world and prides itself on the commercial relevance of its syllabus which is regularly updated to reflect the latest business developments and employer needs. It is also committed to upholding the highest ethical and professional standards and to maintaining public confidence in management accountancy.

CIMA's membership has grown by 23 per cent over the last five years. With 60 per cent of its working members in the UK employed by organisations with annual turnovers of £50 million or more (Source: CIMA Member Survey 2006), and seven per cent of its working members being chief executive officers, managing directors or other directors, it is not surprising that CIMA is seen as an increasingly influential body.

In 2006, CIMA's own research revealed high levels of satisfaction with its services showing that 90 per cent of its members rate satisfaction with CIMA as good, very good, or excellent compared to 79 per cent in 2004. In total, 93 per cent said that they would recommend CIMA to others and 95 per cent agreed that a CIMA qualification enhanced their career prospects.

Product

CIMA's training is dedicated to providing more than basic accounting skills. It aims to give business professionals a strategic view of the future. Due to this, and backed by the views of CIMA members, the CIMA Professional Qualification is regarded as the most relevant and internationally recognised financial qualification for business today.

With offices around the world CIMA's approach is used by individuals and employers all over the world – providing more management and strategy insights. Its syllabus tests for business awareness and cognitive skills of analysis, synthesis and evaluation.

There are other unique elements of the syllabus, designed to help members develop their careers including access to an extensive range of learning resources to assist students in their ongoing careers. CIMA also provides guidance on professional standards, networking facilities and access to exclusive work opportunities with reputable third parties.

CIMA supports its qualification framework with a range of complementary products and services. Management accounting books, guides and CDs are provided by CIMA Publishing, while CIMA Mastercourses offer an extensive programme of financial and business management seminars held throughout the UK.

Recent Developments

As a Chartered Institute, CIMA has a duty to protect the public interest. As part of this commitment, CIMA's new Code of Ethics was launched in January 2006 and distributed on CD to all members and students. All new students receive the CD when they register with CIMA. The Code is principles-based, rather than rules-based, making it more widely applicable and in the public interest. To support this CIMA delivered a series of 16 free 'ethics road shows' for members and students in the UK, Sri Lanka, Singapore, Malaysia and South Africa between May and November

1919	1975
The 'Institute of Cost and Works Accountants' is founded, its objective being to provide the range of information needed to plan and manage modern business.	The Institute is granted the Royal Charter.

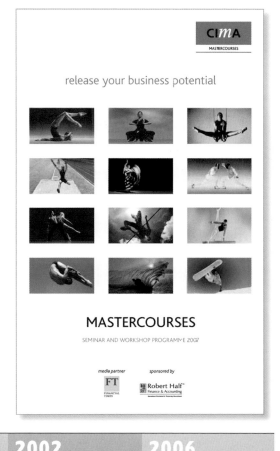

2006. At these events, delegates learnt how CIMA's Code of Ethics can support them, using discussion groups and real-life case studies. Over 600 members and students attended.

CIMA is constantly refreshing its syllabus. For example, in 2006, it updated the CIMA Certificate in Business Accounting, which is the entry level Certificate to CIMA's professional examinations, with more content relating to accounting ethics.

Launching in early 2007, CIMA has established a new Centre of Excellence, designed to support the long term development of members' professional development (CPD), and others working as accountants in business.

Other new developments include the introduction of over 50 new CIMA Mastercourses in 2006, including Management Accounting: Developments from the Cutting Edge, Effective Transfer Pricing and Information that Influences.

CIMA has been particularly active on the international scene, appointing a new Director of Development for Asia Pacific, and establishing a Shanghai Representative Office in 2006. In Hong Kong and New Zealand, CIMA signed agreements for closer collaboration with the respective national professional accounting bodies and in South Africa, CIMA saw a 42 per cent increase in registered CIMA Training partners and a 50 per cent increase in students on 'learnerships' – an initiative promoted by the South African Government.

Promotion

CIMA markets itself primarily to employers and students, using a range of tools to communicate its difference in the market.

For example, CIMA recently commissioned research through Bath University to contrast the differences between its syllabus and leading competitors in the UK and international markets. As a result, it published a white paper clearly stating key points of differentiation, such as its greater coverage of management and strategic issues, its focus on a broader base of management skills and the way in which the CIMA syllabus successfully develops leadership qualities.

Events are a valuable promotional tool, including national CIMA Training employer conferences, attended by employers and potential students, and the annual FD Forum. This is a key marketing

opportunity for CIMA, attended by 280 finance directors. In addition, CIMA sponsors the Accountancy Age Awards and the Guardian Public Services Awards, and various similar awards around the globe.

Financial Management, CIMA's monthly magazine, is circulated to all CIMA members and students, as well as other subscribers. CIMA's views regularly feature in other key media, with 'press hits' in 2006 generating an advertising equivalent value of over £2.5 million.

CIMA invests in printed marketing literature to promote specific courses, seminars and events and also publishes a newsletter, Insight, which has a circulation of 102,000. The CIMA website is another powerful communications platform, with over three million people visiting the site in 2006.

Brand Values

CIMA is positioned as 'The qualification for business'.

Everything CIMA does reflects five core values that drive its relationships with students and members, ensuring a consistent internal company culture and one that is understood, supported and lived by all CIMA employees. These values are: customer focused; professional; open; accountable; and innovative.

CIMA also identifies a purpose, vision and mission to pinpoint its sense of direction. Its 'purpose' is to achieve ever greater employability for CIMA members, its 'vision' for its members is to be driving the world's successful organisations and its 'mission' is to be the first choice for the qualification and development of professional accountants in business.

www.cimaglobal.com

Things you didn't know about CIMA

CIMA members are ranked among the UK's most powerful business leaders, with eight ranked as the key movers and shakers in The Times Power 100 list 2006.

CIMA member Helen Weir, Group FD, Lloyds TSB is currently the only FTSE 100 female FD.

CIMA is a £1 million investor in leading academic research into management accounting and related business issues.

CIMA is working with the Arcadia Retail Group to raise awareness of retail and finance careers among school pupils in the UK. Part of Arcadia's Foundation for Schools, the initiative offers the CIMA Certificate to 16-18 year-olds.

CIMA is the only body to focus on interpersonal skills as a requirement of the new professional qualification.

CIMA co-sponsors the extreme accounting website which documents some of the more bizarre habits of accountants – www.extreme-accounting.com.

1986	1995	2002	2006
The Institute changes its name to 'The Chartered Institute of Management Accountants' recognising the importance and commercial relevance of management accountants.	CIMA's members are given the right to use the title 'Chartered Management Accountant'.	Due to the growth of the institute, it relocates to its new global head quarters.	CIMA opens an office in Shanghai.

COMPASS
GROUP

Compass Group is the world's leading foodservice organisation with annual revenues of £11 billion and employing more than 400,000 people in over 90 countries. In the UK and Ireland, Compass Group has annual revenues of £2 billion, employing 90,000 people. As the largest foodservice organisation in the UK and Ireland, Compass Group provides high quality catering and support services at 8,500 locations and serves nearly three million meals a day.

Market

Compass Group has close to a 50 per cent market share of the contracted UK catering market. Services such as staff restaurants, student refectories, hospital patient meals, coffee shops, cafe bars, food courts, corporate hospitality and executive dining are provided to clients, ranging from blue chip company head offices to military bases, from universities to sports stadia and from schools to hospitals.

The UK & Ireland operating subsidiary companies of Compass Group are specialists in their markets, including Eurest, Scolarest, Medirest, Restaurant Associates, Leiths, Milburns, Letheby & Christopher and Eurest Support Services Worldwide. Each Compass Group company enjoys the benefits of Compass' purchasing power, financial investment, leading-edge IT and commercial support as well as products and service innovation.

This varied portfolio of catering brands allows Compass Group to operate with expertise in all its target markets, including business and industry, education, healthcare, defence, offshore, sports, leisure, fine dining and support services.

Achievements

At the heart of Compass Group's vision is 'great people' and the company places high importance on nurturing and developing employees to reach their full potential. A key avenue for developing skills and raising the profile of its employees is through culinary competitions. Compass Group's culinary team has won an abundance of prestigious culinary accolades on a regional, national and international level including a string of gold medals at the Culinary World Cup and over 1,000 awards over the past seven years.

The company's teams and employees have also been recognised by a plethora of industry awards which in the past year have included three Craft Guild of Chefs awards, three Springboard awards, the Olive Barnett award, five Cost Sector Catering awards and three Acorn awards.

Compass Group has an active Corporate Responsibility programme, and has won many awards for work in this area. These include a raft of accolades for Compass' flagship initiative – the Juniors Chefs' Academy (JCA) – including The Lord Mayor's Dragon Award, a Big Tick from Business in the Community, two Springboard awards, and the Innovation award from the Charities Aid Foundation.

The JCA has become an integral part of Compass UK's training and development programme, providing many young people with an introduction to the hospitality industry at the very earliest point. The 15-week course takes place on Saturday mornings at Further Education colleges around the country and provides students, aged 12-16 years, with a basic grounding in food preparation and cooking, with over 60 per cent signing up for NVQs.

1941	**1968**	**1987**	**1988**	**1993**	**1994**
The Contract Catering industry in UK is 'founded' with Factory Canteens Ltd.	Factory Canteens Ltd is acquired by Grand Metropolitan.	A management buyout of Compass from Grand Metropolitan takes place.	Compass is floated on the UK stock market.	Compass acquires SSP.	Compass acquires Canteen Corporation.

Product

There are four distinct operating divisions within Compass Group UK & Ireland, each with its own portfolio of operating companies. The divisions provide food services across all key market sectors targeted by Compass Group: Business and Industry (including offshore); Sports, Leisure and Hospitality; Healthcare, Education, Defence and Government; and Fine Dining.

Compass Group also offers facilities management (FM) solutions to clients across all four operating divisions, including the provision of the full spectrum of soft and hard FM services – from technical support, building maintenance and supply logistics to hotel services, transport, pest control and communications.

Recent Developments

In 2006, Compass divested its travel concessions business, Select Service Partner including Moto, in order to fully focus on its core contract foodservice market and growing business in the support services sector. Accordingly, Compass Group also sold the last hotel on its books, the Strand Palace Hotel in London, and announced its intention to sell its vending business, Selecta.

With a renewed focus on foodservices and FM, Compass is able to provide the full spectrum of soft and hard support services, from cleaning to portering and building maintenance across multiple sites and countries. This capability proved key in gaining a new contract with Shell in 2006, worth upward of £250 million total turnover based on over £50 million per annum over five years with an option to extend.

Innovation is at the heart of Compass' business strategy, and one foodservice solution that has seen strong demand in 2006 and has enormous potential for future application is Dream Steam. This revolutionary food concept utilises microwave technology to generate steam, resulting in fresh, high quality meals in minutes. The system's differential cooking method, using a unique valve to control pressure within special packaging, means an array of food items can be cooked together for the optimum amount of time. The system is utilised by Compass in the healthcare, education, business and industry sectors, with the potential for widespread application in other market sectors, particularly those facing space limitations such as the prison service.

Compass' healthcare business, Medirest, has been using the technology under the brand name Steamplicity to great success. The concept's benefits include increased flexibility of meal times, higher nutritional value, and reduced wastage. A Bournemouth University study showed the introduction of Steamplicity increased patient intake by 36 per cent and reduced food waste by a third. Compass Group is currently supplying over 10,000 Steamplicity meals a day across 30 hospitals.

Another key focus at Compass Group is around the issue of healthy and lifestyle food choices. Rather than dictate to customers, the company looks to provide a full range of food options to clients and customers, providing the tools for them to make an informed choice. The company's Balanced Choices programme, launched in 2005, uses an icon system to identify healthier, more environmentally friendly or lifestyle food choices, such as 'low fat', 'vegetarian', 'dairy free' or 'sustainable fish stocks'. Designed by a task force of dieticians and nutritionists, Balanced Choices incorporates nutritionally analysed recipes, information leaflets and other promotional material for customers and training in basic nutrition for chefs and catering managers.

Promotion

The Compass Group brand, as well as the company's individual operating company brands, is promoted via targeted press releases, PR campaigns and press calls. The company also sponsors key industry events, such the Hotelympia and Hospitality culinary competitions and Springboard's FutureChef culinary competition for aspiring young chefs.

To help promote its brands and foodservice concepts, Compass Group has created an 'innovation centre' based in Chertsey. Clients and prospective clients can visit the centre to see the company's brands at first hand, as well as touch and taste the products. Visitors can tour a convenience store, sit down for a latte in a coffee bar and eat lunch at a deli. A transition zone is transformed during the visit, from a standard staff restaurant, to a Compass branded area, bringing the company's brands to life.

Brand Values

Compass Group's mission is to be the most admired catering and support services provider in the UK & Ireland, and its vision is 'great people, great service, great results'. It aims to deliver outstanding service with a commitment to quality that customers and clients have come to expect. Its brand values are simply stated as 'win through teamwork, embrace diversity, share success, a passion for quality and a can do attitude'. To live up to these values, Compass Group focuses on attracting, training, developing and retaining the best people, offering the best possible services to its customers and understanding what they need.

www.compass-group.co.uk

Things you didn't know about Compass Group

Nearly three million meals are served by Compass Group per day in the UK and Ireland.

Compass caters at some unusual locations, from Bristol Zoo and Twickenham Rugby Stadium to Belmarsh prison and oil platforms in the North Sea.

Over 25,000 hospitality covers were served by Compass Group over four days at the 2006 Ryder Cup held in Ireland.

1995	1998	2000	2001
Compass acquires Eurest International.	Compass plc joins the FTSE 100.	The Granada Compass merger takes place.	Demerger and hotels disposal takes place.

conqueror

the art of communication

Conqueror is an internationally recognised symbol of quality in external business communications. Leveraging a century-strong heritage and awareness levels of over 80 per cent in the UK, Conqueror has long been recognised as setting the gold standard for business stationery. It has more recently been successfully extended into applications such as brochures, reports, advertising and promotional materials, packaging and labelling by image conscious companies in 120 countries around the world.

Market

The art of communicating in a world of message overload is now more important than ever before. Conqueror communications campaigns cut through busy business environments, convey differentiation and can stand alone or integrate effectively with other, electronic messaging mediums.

The Conqueror range is regularly updated to reflect trends in fashion and contemporary styling, as well as environmental and technological trends. Tangible and distinctive, its visual impact and tactile qualities can convey everything from style and creativity to professionalism and a bold corporate image.

Achievements

Conqueror is one of the few paper brands requested by name and although it remains most synonymous with quality business stationery, a wide variety of modern day usages continue to prove that Conqueror has the solution, whatever the application.

Throughout its 118-year history, Conqueror has pre-empted the demands of the market, embraced change, and in doing so has moved successfully from the era of pen and ink, through the advent of typewriters to the sophisticated world of multiple print technologies and digital communications.

Best-in-category performance in recent years has confirmed Conqueror's status as one of the best

known and most favoured brands of paper. This is frequently proven and substantiated through blind and branded tests, in which the brand is consistently chosen as the best quality and overall preferred sheet available.

Product

All Conqueror ranges are driven by trends and developments in technology, the environment and fashion. Whether it's the ground breaking, multi-functional products with guaranteed performance for the very latest of print processes, environmentally friendly ranges, or the hugely popular fashion-influenced ranges, Conqueror products achieve standout.

1888	**1920**	**1945**	**1960s**	**1990**	**1993**
Conqueror paper first rolls off the paper machine at Wiggins Teape.	Due to an increase in demand, a new dedicated paper machine is introduced at the mill.	Changes in the production of Conqueror are developed, as well as quality control and specialised colour matching.	Conqueror continues to develop and grow its export business.	Arjo Wiggins Appleton group is formed from the merger of Wiggins Teape with the French paper manufacturer Arjomari and the US manufacturer, Appleton Papers.	The brand logo is changed to a horseman representing William the Conqueror alongside the Conqueror name.

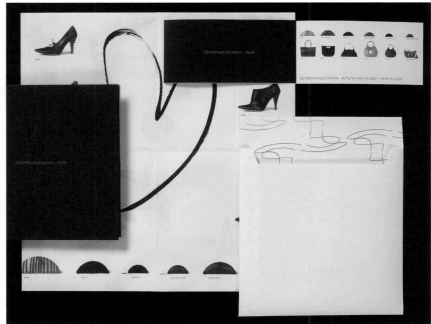

The extensive range of Conqueror products is grouped into five sub brands: Conqueror Smooth/Satin is fresh and contemporary; Conqueror Concept/Effects, futuristic and trend setting; Conqueror Digital is high performance and developed for digital printing technology; Conqueror Connoisseur, luxurious and classic; and Conqueror Texture is traditional and tactile.

Through its innovative and contemporary selection of colours, finishes, textures and watermarks, available in a complete range of co-ordinated papers, boards and envelopes, Conqueror guarantees to deliver the look and feel of effortless style and professionalism and ultimate interest and impact, whatever the application.

Recent Developments

In the last five years, Conqueror has worked hard to continually develop and evolve its positioning, range and product offering in order to ensure maximum relevance within an ever-changing market place.

May 2001 saw a global relaunch for the brand following a thorough strategic review that identified a need to bring the Conqueror brand to new audiences for a broader variety of applications, but without alienating its existing customer base or damaging its long established reputation.

In 2003 Conqueror launched a specific collection of products into the Office and Retail channel, focusing on the home-based as well as small and medium sized businesses.

Most recently, the brand has updated its range with new, patented Multi Technology products that work, uniquely, across both traditional and digital print processes. Three new iridescent shades were added to the Concept/Effects range, that achieved 30 per cent year on year growth versus 2004, and a collection of environmentally friendly FSC Certified and Recycled papers in a number of different finishes to meet the most stringent CSR (corporate and social responsibility) requirements.

Promotion

Conqueror has successfully developed a sustained 'push-pull' marketing strategy that focuses on distribution partners, printers, designers and end-users. Applications driven and with a strong emphasis on brand awareness and brand building, global communications deliver a consistent image and clear, targeted messages that are tailored to these key audiences.

Recent and future activity includes a multi-million pound television and press campaign

targeting the 'e-generation' of 25-35 year-old business users, which was launched in 2004.

The following year, a number of specially tailored promotions to both the print and design communities announcing the various launch activities throughout the year were undertaken. Following this, 2006/07 sees an integrated end-user communications campaign.

Brand Values

Conqueror provides a high quality range of distinctive papers, which can be specified with confidence globally, for both professional and creative communications needs. The value of the Conqueror brand lies in its quality, versatility, wide choice and availability as well as its reliable technical performance. Conqueror delivers ultimate attention, interest and impact for image conscious businesses with a need to make their customers feel extremely valued.

Development and testing ensures that Conqueror continues to meet the performance demands of both traditional printing processes and the latest digital technologies, while inspiring creativity through contemporary and versatile products.

www.conqueror.com

2001
A new, contemporary, stylised logo and identity based on the Conqueror name is launched. In addition, iridescent papers are also launched into the Conqueror Concept range.

2004
Conqueror Digital Multi Technology is introduced as the only fine paper that is printable on offset and digital presses.

2005
Arjowiggins offers the ultimate environmentally friendly proposition through the launch of a Conqueror FSC Recycled range.

2006
Arjowiggins continues to be the world's leading manufacturer of technical and creative papers.

Things you didn't know about Conqueror

If all Conqueror made within one week were in the format of 100g A4 sheets, laid end to end these would stretch twice around the world.

Today, there are some 600 different line items available within Conqueror. Users range from Royalty and huge corporates to one-man businesses the world over.

Concern for the environment is one of Conqueror's priorities and its production processes are therefore as environmentally friendly as possible. For example, its mills are accredited with the international Environment Management Standard ISO 14001. In addition, Conqueror invests heavily in CHP (Combined Heat and Power) generation to significantly reduce greenhouse gases and acidifying emissions. It also invests in reducing its use of water and effluent volume processes. All effluent plant residue is put to product re-use, thus eliminating the need for landfill disposal.

corus

Corus is an international steel company which stands for 'Value in steel'. Its aim is to outperform the competition using world-class processes to create a comprehensive and differentiated product range backed up by an unrivalled service package, as well as pursuing a strategy of selective growth. This approach – 'The Corus Way'– is summed up as 'creating value for all stakeholders in a safe and sustainable environment'.

Market

Corus has an annual turnover of over £10 billon, and employs more than 41,000 people in over 40 countries. It has major facilities in the UK, the Netherlands, Germany, France, Norway and Belgium as well as a global network of sales offices and service centres. While Corus is focused on value, not volume, it produced 18 million tonnes of crude steel in 2005.

Corus is one of the leading suppliers to some of the most demanding markets – automotive, aerospace, packaging, rail and engineering, as well

as building and construction. Through its process capabilities, technical excellence and market understanding, it helps its customers to achieve results. Corus aims to provide the right solution, on time, supported by the right advice.

Achievements

Launched in June 2003, the Restoring Success programme was designed to deliver a £635 million improvement in earnings before interest, tax and amortisation by the end of 2006. This set the scene for 'The Corus Way'.

A group-wide continuous improvement programme, based on the principles of lean thinking, was launched during 2005 in support of The Corus Way. The aim was to attract and retain the best employees through development in people, harnessing talent to become an employer of choice with the end result being motivated employees, committed to their work such that they feel fulfilled and able to contribute passionately to delivering business goals.

Product

Corus manufactures, processes and distributes many steel products for a range of demanding applications. For example, a wide range of

construction products and services are available for the world's most impressive buildings. This includes structural sections, plates, floor decking and cladding products used in building structures, as well as a range of products used in building interiors, such as ceiling systems and partitions. Strip steel is widely used in automotive applications and its special sections product range is used extensively in earthmoving equipment. Tube products are available for the manufacture of hot finished and cold formed welded steel tubular products; rail products and services are made available to rail networks; packaging steels for food, drinks and aerosols, as well as for promotional and speciality packaging; bar and billet is produced for engineering industries; and electrical steels for the generation, transmission and distribution of electrical power.

Recent Developments

The launch of The Corus Way in 2005 saw the creation of a platform on which Corus differentiates itself from its competitors. The aim was to become the 'best supplier to best customers' with 'world-class processes', achieved through 'passionate people' operating in a safe and sustainable environment with a focus on 'selective growth'.

'Best supplier to best customers' means that Corus provides a responsive service and offers differentiated, value-added products. Its enhanced production capabilities and improved routes to market mean that it delivers its products to its customers reliably and consistently. Corus positions its products so that it benefits from brand recognition and association.

'World-class processes' means achieving best-in-class, effective processes not just in manufacturing, but also in the supporting functional and office environments. Corus reduces stock levels while increasing productivity. Its aim is to run the most efficient processes in its industry.

'Selective growth' means that Corus will not increase in size just for the sake of it. It is not the biggest or the lowest cost steel company – but aims to offer the best value. The strategy of selective growth through investment places it in a position of strength. Corus is now looking to improve its competitive position further by ensuring that it has access to low-cost steelmaking and high growth markets.

Its approach to continuous improvement, based on lean thinking principles, aims to ensure that The Corus Way can become a reality. Continuous improvement gives its people the opportunity to become passionate about what they do and to contribute fully to enhancing business performance.

Promotion

The name Corus was initially chosen because it was distinctive, fresh, modern and easily recognisable. It conveys the idea that all the operations within Corus have different strengths but are more powerful when their voices join together.

The strongest relationships are built on trust

corus

Safety
Our health and safety standards apply equally to contractors and Corus employees. A safe workplace: not without you.

The Corus Way
Value in steel

Following the initial brand launch advertising campaign in 2000 to promote 'the future in metal' in international newspapers, Corus has concentrated its promotional activity on media relations as the main vehicle for its corporate messages. The company has also invested significant effort in ensuring that its internal communications are fully aligned to Company strategy and that all Corus employees are engaged in The Corus Way and Continuous Improvement. The communications effectiveness is routinely measured to ensure that employees understand the corporate messages.

Brand values have been communicated through poster campaigns such as 'we're not just making metal, we're making a difference' designed to inspire pride and motivation in the company's products and applications. The key proposition was to change the way the world looks at metal. The Corus Way poster campaign, together with the associated 'Not without you' mood film, aimed to engage employees around The Corus Way and Continuous Improvement. Meanwhile, the health and safety poster campaign was created to communicate the importance of the Company's health and safety policy.

At the same time, market promotional activity has been targeted at the key market sectors, namely construction, automotive, packaging, rail and the energy sectors. Corus exhibits all over the world at targeted exhibitions. In addition, Corus sponsors young designers, through, for example, the Coventry University automotive design awards, the student packaging design awards and Young Architect of the Year awards, to demonstrate its commitment to inspiring young designers.

In 2006, Corus announced its sponsorship of British Triathlon for an initial two-year period. The sponsorship embraces Corus' commitment to world-class performance and underlines its

ambition to outperform the competition. The sponsorship will support grassroots activity and elite triathletes as well as a number of community-based initiatives including a nationwide development programme for school children – known as 'Corus Kids of Steel' – and initiatives to support athletes with a disability.

Brand Values

The essence of the Corus brand is about creating value for customers, shareholders and employees. Corus has behavioural values to support its strategic business objectives and the goal is to be best in class. They include safety, strong leadership, reliability, trust, openness, respect and integrity.

The Corus brand offering is about being perceived as an innovative and inspiring partner who helps its customers to realise their projects, ideas and dreams. It looks at its business from its customers' perspective to ensure that innovation and development are driven by what its customers actually need. This translates to a differentiated and specialised product mix, better lead times, and unrivalled quality and efficiency.

www.corusgroup.com

Things you didn't know about Corus

Steel is 100 per cent recyclable and maintains its strength and durability no matter how many times it is recycled. Every tonne of recycled steel packaging makes the following environmental saving: reduction of air emission by 86 per cent and reduction of water pollution by 76 per cent.

Corus produces carbon steel by the basic oxygen steelmaking method at four integrated steelworks – Port Talbot, Scunthorpe and Teesside in the UK and IJmuiden in the Netherlands. Engineering steels are produced in Rotherham in the UK using the electric arc furnace method.

Corus has reduced its direct emissions of CO_2 by over four million tonnes since 1999. Over the last 30 years, the energy used to make one tonne of steel has reduced by around 40 per cent.

1999	2005	2006	
Corus is created through the merger of two very strong brands in the steel industry, British Steel and Koninklijke Hoogovens in the Netherlands.	'The Corus Way' is launched to establish a way of thinking and working. It is about unity and making connections with people and processes.	The Corus look and feel evolves to reflect the brand's new positioning of 'Value in steel'. The aim is for a more sophisticated, assured and refined look and feel.	In July, Corus announces an initial two-year sponsorship of British Triathlon.

Costain is one of the UK's best-known construction and engineering companies, undertaking some of the world's largest and most challenging construction projects. It works in a wide range of sectors, including water, roads, health, education, nuclear, rail, retail, marine, oil and gas.

Market

The construction industry is one of the largest and most important in the UK. Providing housing, infrastructure, employment and being a key indicator of economic health, the UK construction industry was worth £107.01 billion in 2005, a rise of 4.5 per cent on 2004 (Source: KeyNote).

Low interest rates and good employment levels have kept the industry growing in the UK, rising for 10 consecutive years (Source: MBD).

The construction sector is extremely wide, but principally consists of five areas: housebuilding, infrastructure, industrial construction, commercial construction and building materials. By value, the most significant sector is commercial work, followed by housebuilding, and together these account for approximately 45 per cent of total construction output (Source: KeyNote).

The market is extremely fragmented, comprising some 167,178 companies (Source: MBD), of which 32 per cent are engaged in specialist trades. It is an industry spanning very small and very large players, with 71 per cent of companies earning less than £250,000 in 2004. According to MBD, only one per cent of companies earn more than £5 million.

With a turnover of £773 million in 2005, and employing nearly 12,000 people worldwide, Costain falls into this category of international construction groups, competing against other major players such as Carillion, McAlpine and Bovis.

Costain aims to build market-leading positions in key commercial sectors. It is already the number one contractor in the water market, and holds the number two position in the road-building sector.

Achievements

For 140 years Costain has been at the forefront of UK and international construction. For example, in the mid 1920s, Costain built thousands of houses throughout south east England and in 1935, built 11 miles of the Trans-Iranian Railway, seven tunnels and two viaducts in isolated mountainous terrain.

More recently, the company's portfolio has included prestigious engineering projects, such as The Thames Barrier, the new headquarters for the Met Office and the Tsing Ma Suspension bridge in Hong Kong – the world's longest combined road and rail bridge.

It is also responsible for developing St Pancras and the Stratford tunnels for the Channel Tunnel

Rail Link as well as redeveloping Kings Cross Underground Station for London Underground.

Another significant contract is a £22.5 million project to upgrade the Grade 1 listed St Martin in the Fields Church, in London's Trafalgar Square.

The company had a record order book for 2005, totalling £1.9 billion, compared to £1.1 billion in 2004. This included a large percentage of repeat business, reflecting the high degree of customer satisfaction amongst Costain's clients.

Costain has built its success on a reputation for technical capability and exceptional customer service. The company also prides itself on its commitment to safety and, in 2005, was awarded 34 Royal Society for the Prevention of Accidents Occupational Health and Safety Awards.

The company has a peerless reputation in the water sector, recently delivering over £600 million of capital work to the UK water companies, comprising 700 separate projects. It is also involved in a £750 million contract for Southern Water.

In the roads sector, Costain has won a major contract to improve the M1 motorway – the company's largest road contract to date – and qualified for a Private Finance Initiative (PFI)

project to extend the M25, valued at £1.5 billion. This is the largest single PFI road scheme in the UK.

The company has also made great strides in its building division, growing revenue 36 per cent in 2005 and winning Building magazine's 2005 Major Contractor of the Year Award and the 2006 UK Major Contractor of the Year Award from New Civil Engineer magazine.

Product
Costain's primary markets include water, health, roads, rail and education.

The Building Division undertakes complex projects throughout the UK, from its five regional offices: London, Southern, Eastern, Midlands and Northern. Costain takes pride in the relationships it has developed within the construction community and seeks to deliver value and quality through innovation and technical excellence.

Costain has established itself as a leader in the Asset Management market. This work involves clients who want long-term, expert, building and maintenance care for their valuable assets. Costain has won most of this business in the water sector, winning long-term contracts with Thames Water, Yorkshire Water, Wessex Water, Dwr Cymru Welsh Water, Bristol Water, United Utilities and Southern Water.

Costain Oil, Gas & Process is an international process engineering contractor, delivering safe, cost-effective solutions for investments in the worldwide energy and process sectors.

Recent Developments
In September 2005, Costain appointed a new chief executive, Andrew Wyllie. Formerly managing director of Taylor Woodrow Construction, Wyllie initiated a strategic review of the business. Entitled 'Being Number One', the strategy sets out clear objectives, focused on developing market-leading positions in targeted market sectors of water, roads, rail, health, education, retail, nuclear, marine, oil and gas. The strategy aims to instil a common culture whereby people share best practice and work together towards the goal of making Costain the market leader in everything that it does.

To do this, the company plans to adopt a greater focus in fewer areas of operation, enabling it to commit more resources to these areas where it believes it can build a real competitive advantage and market leadership.

Promotion
To reach its target audience of construction clients in the public and private sectors, Costain promotes itself in a variety of ways, using national and international trade fairs and events, as well as advertising in key technical titles, and key business-facing newspapers such as the FT.

Costain also uses its news magazine, Blueprint, as a means of raising awareness of current projects and new developments. Blueprint was named the UK construction industry's 'Company Magazine of the Year' in 2004 and since then, has received two more national awards in subsequent years.

Another of Costain's promotional channels, Building Awareness, performs an important social role, raising young people's awareness of the construction industry through direct involvement and partnership with schools.

Costain and its partners are committed to providing resources and funding to support initiatives giving students and teachers the opportunity to find out more about what the company does and boost young people's perception of construction as a career.

Brand Values
While the new 'Being Number One' mission statement drives Costain forward, based on striving for leadership through focus and excellence, the company also maintains a clear set of brand values.

The key element underpinning Costain's brand is a desire to be 'Relationship Driven'. In pursuit of this, Costain's vision is to be the leader in the delivery of sustainable engineering and construction solutions.

Its mission is to embark on a path of Business Excellence involving innovation, initiative, teamwork and high levels of technical and managerial skills.

The Costain brand itself can be dissected into seven key values: Customer Focused; Open and Honest; Safe and Environmentally Aware; Team Players; Accountable; Improving Continuously – with the aim of making Costain the 'Natural Choice'.

www.costain.com

Being Number One

1865	1933	1939–45	1971
Richard Costain, a 26 year-old jobbing builder from the Isle of Man founds a construction business in Liverpool.	Costain floats as a public company, with a share capital of £600,000.	The company plays an active role in the war effort, with wartime work including 26 aerodromes, part of the Mulberry Harbours, munitions factories and 15,000 post-war prefabricated Airey houses.	Costain becomes the first UK contractor to win the Queen's Award for Export Achievement – and has since won nine further Queen's Awards.

Things you didn't know about Costain

Costain created the largest and deepest hole ever made in London clay during construction of the Aldersgate office complex.

The Kariba township in Zimbabwe was built by Costain in 15 months to house 10,000 people.

Costain completed Hong Kong's first cross-harbour tunnel in 1972 – a 1,850m steel immersed tube tunnel.

More than 10,500 drawings were needed to design the £232 million Dubai Dry Dock.

Specialist pre-cast concrete sleepers were produced by Costain for the rail track through the Channel Tunnel and for rail networks both in the UK and overseas.

›DATAMONITOR

Datamonitor is a market leader in the business information industry, providing online data, analytic and forecasting platforms for key industry sectors. It helps 5,000 of the world's largest companies profit from better, more timely decisions. Datamonitor's research covers six major industry sectors: automotive and logistics; consumer and retail; energy and utilities; financial services; healthcare; and technology.

Market

The market for business information continues to show good growth. Demand has been spurred by consolidation and globalisation across industries and the blurring of traditional business boundaries. Strong market and competitor intelligence play a fundamental role in helping businesses make winning decisions.

Datamonitor prides itself on having moulded its offering to meet the needs of the changing business world. While many business information providers maintain a narrow focus, specialising in data or analysis for one particular industry, Datamonitor is unique in offering a 'total' solution for clients with both data and analysis from an industry-specific and cross-industry perspective. No other provider equals Datamonitor's breadth of industry coverage and depth of analytical insight.

Achievements

The Datamonitor brand has achieved outstanding growth over its 18-year history. Starting as a five-man operation, the company has developed quickly into today's global organisation of 1,000 employees with sales of US$200 million and double digit rates of growth.

This growth has been accelerated by the acquisition of a number of businesses that

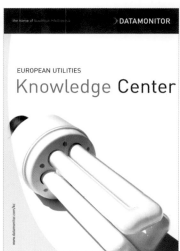

complement Datamonitor's core offering, for example Butler Group, Verdict Research, Life Science Analytics and, at the time of press, Datamonitor has announced the proposed acquisition of Ovum. Such acquisitions, in addition to impressive organic growth, have fuelled the company's international expansion. Today, Datamonitor operates globally including offices in London, Frankfurt, New York, San Francisco, Tokyo, Sydney and Hyderabad.

The Datamonitor brand has also achieved global recognition through extensive press coverage.

During 2006, the Datamonitor Group appeared in the press on average 730 times per month, with frequent mentions in the Financial Times, Wall Street Journal, The Economist, Washington Post, Investors Business Daily, Sydney Morning Herald, and the South China Morning Post. Appearing with such regularity and also across prestigious broadcast channels, such as CNN, BBC and Sky, means that the brand has high visibility and has built a reputation for publishing leading research and opinion amongst the business and journalist communities.

Product

Datamonitor's research is available to subscribers through Knowledge Centers – a new delivery platform with in-built innovative functionality. Each Knowledge Center consolidates all Datamonitor information for a particular industry into a single customised online interface. In total that includes millions of data points, thousands of pages of analysis and daily news and comment articles. Content is easily searched and navigated with the help of advanced functionality which also enables users to download information straight to their desktop.

1989	1993	1995	1997	1999	2000
Datamonitor is founded by Mike Danson.	The first online delivery platform for Datamonitor products is launched.	Datamonitor opens its New York office. Datamonitor's primary website www.datamonitor.com is launched.	Datamonitor's first service-orientated offering is launched. A rebranding exercise is undertaken with the help of branding consultancy Interbrand, resulting in a new visual identity and new core values.	Datamonitor opens offices in Frankfurt and Hong Kong.	Datamonitor floats on the London Stock Exchange. Branding consultancy Hicklin Slade & Partners develops the distinctive Datamonitor orange arrow.

Non-subscription clients can purchase individual research products in the form of reports, briefs and databases from the Research Store – Datamonitor's online shop. It contains the full historical library of over 10,000 Datamonitor reports, traditionally the company's most popular product. Each report presents a detailed analysis of a particular market, issue or trend, from the EU emissions trading scheme to prepaid cards in Australia.

For clients with specific research needs, Datamonitor conducts custom consulting projects. These typically take the form of market entry analysis, product evaluations, end-user research, market forecasting or scenario planning projects.

Datamonitor also has a growing events business which organises regular management conferences and briefings. These provide clients with a forum to debate hot topics and hear from the industry's movers and shakers.

Datamonitor's diverse product and service offering is united by common research methodologies. Research is carried out by teams of in-house researchers who, at each step of the process, employ rigorous quality checking. All Datamonitor research is independently audited by a top four global audit firm which means the company can ensure a high level of accuracy and reliability in its data and forecasts, and quality of insight in its analysis.

Recent Developments

Datamonitor has continued to invest in its technology platforms, introducing new functionality to the Knowledge Centers to further enhance the user experience. Advanced searching and navigation makes information easy to find, at which point it is immediately available to use: it can be bookmarked for future reference, downloaded to the user's desktop in seconds or easily built into custom reports. Clients can post questions directly to Datamonitor analysts via the site and also sign up to receive email alerts relating to their areas of interest.

The Datamonitor brand is synonymous with cutting-edge research and over the last year the company has conducted pioneering work in brand new areas. Recent projects include a ground-breaking study of epidemiology in China where

clients were invited to submit questions for inclusion in large-scale surveys; and a compilation of 7,000 independent software vendor profiles, providing the most detailed and complete view of this market.

Promotion

Datamonitor employs a strict house style when it comes to representation of the brand in promotional campaigns. The company's in-house marketing team ensures the brand's visual identity, based around the corporate orange and blue, together with its brand values, are consistently communicated.

Datamonitor's promotional strategy spans a variety of different media. Marketing microsites and flash presentations demonstrate the company's newly developed online services. More traditional promotional brochures and the quarterly 'INSIGHT' magazine for Knowledge Center subscribers highlight the latest research. These materials are distributed to existing and potential clients via one-to-one sales meetings and highly targeted direct marketing campaigns.

Whilst email has proved to be a particularly successful medium for its promotions, Datamonitor still places emphasis on a fully integrated approach, running concurrent campaigns across direct mail and advertising channels. Advertisements and inserts are typically placed in trade magazines whose readerships match Datamonitor's target audiences. The brand also appears in these same trade publications via news articles, with the company's PR team helping it achieve widespread coverage in industry-focused trade publications, such as Marketing, Computer Weekly and Post Magazine, and also across broader business publications, such as The Economist, Forbes, Time and Business Week.

Brand Values

Datamonitor is committed to three core brand values: quality data, expert analysis and innovative delivery.

Quality data is guaranteed by the standard research process that's strictly adhered to by Datamonitor's dedicated research teams. This process is audited by one of the world's largest auditing firms to give clients the assurance of

reliability and accuracy. Furthermore, Datamonitor places a strong emphasis on primary research having established the Datamonitor Panel – a knowledge network of over 600,000 opinion leaders, experts, industry personnel, consumers and end users. This robust source of quality data forms the foundation of all Datamonitor's analytical work.

Expert analysis is provided by a skill base made up of over 1,000 multilingual, professional people from a wide diversity of backgrounds, including corporate finance, management consultancy, and graduates from the world's leading business schools. Datamonitor also recruits people from the industry sectors themselves, bringing practical experience of the realities of the marketplace. This mix results in an in-house global analysis team with the deepest possible insight into markets.

Innovative delivery is the brand value associated with Datamonitor's cutting-edge online delivery platform: the Knowledge Center. This platform has been developed with the latest search, browse and download technology that helps users increase the efficiency of their research processes. The Knowledge Center represents a brand new concept in business information provision and places Datamonitor at the very forefront of its industry.

www.datamonitor.com

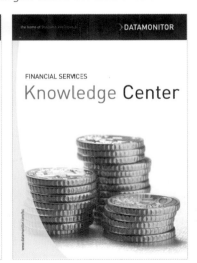

2002	2004	2005	2006
ComputerWire is acquired. In addition, offices open in Tokyo and San Francisco.	Datamonitor acquires Productscan Online and eBenchmarkers.	Butler Group and Verdict Research are both acquired.	Datamonitor launches Knowledge Centers, a new delivery platform for subscribers. Life Science Analytics (MedTRACK) is acquired and an office in Hyderabad is opened.

A Passion to Perform.

Deutsche Bank

Deutsche Bank has established itself as a leading global investment bank with a strong and profitable private clients franchise and provides a full range of financial services to corporate, institutional, high net worth and retail clients in all of the world's major markets.

Market

Deutsche Bank has built an outstanding franchise in sales and trading (both equity and fixed income) and commands a strong reputation for innovation and intellectual leadership in derivatives and other high-value product areas. The bank has also developed a leading global corporate finance platform, together with highly successful cash management, trade finance and other corporate banking services.

Deutsche Bank has also become one of the world's leading asset managers. It has significant positions in both institutional and retail asset management and is a leading mutual fund provider both in the US and Europe. The bank has a substantial global Private Wealth Management business, and is the leading retail bank in Germany with a strong retail presence in Italy and Spain.

To get all the attention, you have to be a star. Or a client of Deutsche Bank.

A Passion to Perform.   Deutsche Bank

In the past two years the bank's franchise has been expanded significantly through a series of acquisitions in the US, Germany, the UK, Russia, China, Mexico and Turkey.

Achievements

Also in 2005, Deutsche Bank's transformation into a leading global investment bank, operating at benchmark return levels was widely recognised. Deutsche Bank has a world-class platform with global resources, far-reaching industry insights and excellent know-how.

In 2005, International Financing Review (IFR) named Deutsche Bank as its 'Bank of the Year' for the second time in three years. In the same year it was also named 'Bank of the Year' by IFR Asia.

Over the past year, Deutsche Bank has also been named 'Derivatives House of the Year' by IFR, Risk, AsiaRisk and Derivatives Week and was ranked the number one provider of FX services in Euromoney's FX Poll. It also won a plethora of awards in Euromoney's annual Awards for Excellence including Best Investment-Grade Debt House, Best Emerging Market Debt House and Best Risk Management House. Deutsche Bank was also named House of the Year in Risk Advisory, Prime Brokerage, Leveraged Finance and High Yield Bonds by The Banker magazine.

Deutsche Bank is the 'National Champion' for the German banking market, has a leading position in Europe and is part of the so-called 'global bulge-bracket' of investment banks.

Product

Deutsche Bank believes that satisfied clients are the key to sustained corporate success, so it offers its clients a broad range of banking products and services.

The Private Clients and Asset Management Division comprises three areas: Private and Business Clients, Private Wealth Management and Asset Management. Private and Business Clients provides private clients with an all-round service extending from daily banking offers to holistic

Bank of the Year.

A Passion to Perform.   Deutsche Bank

investment advisory and tailored financial solutions. Private Wealth Management caters to the specific needs of high net worth clients, their families and select institutions worldwide. Asset Management combines asset management for institutional clients and private investors. As a global provider, it offers customised products in equities, bonds and real estate.

The Corporate and Investment Bank (CIB) comprises two areas: Global Markets and Global Banking.

Global Markets handles all origination, trading, sales and research in cash equities, derivatives,

1870	**1870s**	**1873**	**1917**
Deutsche Bank is founded in Berlin to support the internationalisation of business and to promote and facilitate trade relations between Germany, other European countries, and overseas markets.	The first branches are established in Bremen and Hamburg, followed by Frankfurt am Main, Munich, Leipzig and Dresden.	The first foreign branch is opened in London.	Deutsche Bank M&A transactions begin.

foreign exchange, bonds, structured products and securitisations and thereby occupies a leading position in international foreign exchange, fixed-income and equities trading as well as in derivatives.

Global Banking comprises the Global Cash Management, Global Trade Finance and Trust & Securities Services business divisions and handles all aspects of corporate finance, advises corporations on M&A and divestments, and provides support with IPOs and capital market transactions. Global Banking also covers global corporations, financial institutions and the German 'Mittelstand' (mid-caps) through strong relationship management teams.

Recent Developments

Deutsche Bank competes to be the leading provider of financial solutions. To turn this mission into reality, Deutsche Bank has undergone significant organisational developments over recent years. Between 2002 and 2003, it placed focus on its core businesses – selling marginal activities, making divestments and concentrating on revenues – to achieve a reduction of its operating cost base. Deutsche Bank also aimed to optimise the capital base/balance sheet through its share repurchase programme, as well as optimise the Private Clients and Asset Management (PCAM) business by streamlining its structure and increasing efficiency and profitability.

In late 2006 Deutsche Bank introduced the next phase of its management agenda which focused on leveraging its global platform for accelerated growth. The key elements of this phase are: maintaining its cost, risk, capital and regulatory discipline; continuing to invest in organic growth and 'bolt-on' acquisitions; further growing its 'stable' businesses in PCAM and GTB and building

on its competitive edge in the Corporate and Investment Bank (CIB).

Its current restructuring process focuses on increasing efficiency in the CIB by integrating its sales and trading activities, improving client coverage, streamlining the Asset Management Business and strengthening the regional Management within the organisation.

Promotion

Deutsche Bank's communication initiatives leverage its strong and globally renowned brand icon, the global symbol for 'growth in a stable environment' that was designed by the graphic artist Anton Stankowski and was first introduced in 1974.

The Deutsche Bank global brand communications concept stages the brand icon as the carrier of the corporate messages. Introduced in March 2005, the 'Winning with the Logo' concept gives the logo physical attributes thus giving Deutsche Bank a tangible face for effective and globally aligned communication of its 'winning' corporate story. The campaign visuals convey Deutsche Bank's enhanced brand image, depicting leadership, global performance and client-orientated delivery. Each execution reflects a different interpretation of the Deutsche Bank logo to a very specific market.

The communication is targeted at people with a modern mindset, a can-do, achievement-oriented attitude. To ensure impact and brand alignment of its communications initiatives, Deutsche Bank regularly monitors progress of brand-related key performance indicators.

Deutsche Bank is highly aware of its role as a corporate citizen and aims to go far beyond the provision of financial resources alone. For many decades Deutsche Bank has been a dedicated patron of the arts and music, and has supported community development projects and educational programmes. With the bank's commitment in these areas, the goal is always to enable individuals to push their limits, to discover their talents and to realise their full potential.

The bank's foundations and charitable institutions play a key role, firmly anchoring its Corporate Social Responsibility (CSR) activities around the world. With a global CSR budget of 90 million euros, 4.4 million euros is dedicated to the UK. Projects have included numerous volunteer programmes in disadvantaged areas of London, working closely with over 65 non-profit

partner organisations. In addition, the bank owns the world's largest corporate contemporary art collection and uses its knowledge of business and the arts to support new creative businesses, encourage art appreciation and mobilise art and culture to contribute to sustainable and healthy communities. The Deutsche Bank Microcredit Development Fund is an exemplary combination of social commitment and professional expertise. Since 1997, the fund has provided loans of over US$4 million to 40 microfinance institutions in 24 countries.

Brand Values

Deutsche Bank has streamlined its brand platform to emphasise its core positioning as a European global powerhouse dedicated to excellence, constantly challenging the status quo to deliver superior solutions to its demanding clients and good value to its shareholders and people.

The brand is supported by four key 'pillars' that have a different emphasis in different markets where Deutsche Bank is active. These are: pursuing excellence; leveraging unique insights as a multi-cultural bank; delivering innovative solutions; and building long term relationships.

This all goes to show that 'A Passion to Perform' applies not only to the Bank's relationships with its clients, but to every aspect of life at Deutsche Bank – it is the way Deutsche Bank does business.

www.db.com

Things you didn't know about Deutsche Bank

Deutsche Bank provides substantial funding and additional support for community and cultural projects across the globe.

Eight notable graphic artists were commissioned to create a new logo for Deutsche Bank. In 1974, the bank introduced a symbol created by the painter and graphic artist, Anton Stankowski.

Deutsche Bank employees 6,300 people in London and is one of the largest employers and occupiers of space in the Square Mile.

1926	1970s	2001	2006
Major deals in the UK include a number of advisory roles for a leading UK based oil company BP. Deutsche Bank advises on and finances the £2.6 billion London Underground Financing.	Deutsche Bank pushes ahead with the globalisation of its business, when today's Deutsche Bank Luxembourg S.A. was founded and additional offices were opened in Moscow, Tokyo, Paris and New York.	On 3rd October Deutsche Bank lists its shares on the NYSE.	Today, the bank offers financial services in 73 countries throughout the world with roughly 1.1 billion euros in assets and more than 67,500 employees.

For many years DHL has been synonymous with fast, reliable services around the world, and today DHL is the number one logistics provider worldwide – offering a wide range of cutting-edge solutions through the whole logistical supply chain that free customers to concentrate on their core competencies.

Market

Driven by globalisation and liberalisation, the express and logistics sector is one of the world's largest growth markets. According to Global Insight, world trade will increase by 9.5 per cent in 2007, compared to 7.2 per cent in 2006. The volume of road and rail freight worldwide will also grow – according to the forecast for 2007 – by four per cent, ocean freight by 4.2 per cent and air freight by 8.9 per cent. It is expected that in 2007, 28 million 20ft containers will be shipped from Chinese harbours alone – mostly with destinations in the US and Europe, and that number is increasing. In all segments of the express and logistics market, DHL is in a strong position to strengthen its sales and revenue.

Achievements

Thanks to its competence in air, road/rail and ocean transport, DHL is the world's leading brand for express and logistics services. DHL has 285,000 employees around the world, more than 76,000 vehicles and more than 420 airplanes. Each year around 1.5 billion DHL consignments arrive at almost 120,000 shipping destinations in more than 220 countries and territories.

DHL's unique market position is the result of consistent alignment as a one-stop-shop for companies of every size. In the courier express parcel sector, DHL is the market leader in core European, Asian and emerging markets. Both in air and ocean freight, as in contract logistics, DHL is number one in each of these markets – often a clear distance ahead of its competitors.

DHL Exel Supply Chain demonstrates exemplary customer focus and professionalism: the customer list for contract logistics comprises more than 2,000 large and prominent companies in 40 countries, including three quarters of Europe's Top 500 companies.

Product

The DHL brand consists of five strong service fields: DHL Express, DHL Global Forwarding, DHL Exel Supply Chain, DHL Freight and DHL Global Mail.

DHL Express is globally present with same-day, overnight and classic parcel services. Its network includes fully automated trans-shipment centres, a high performance IT infrastructure, 4,000 subsidiaries and links to 120,000 destinations worldwide.

As market leader for air and ocean freight, DHL Global Forwarding offers many useful value-added services, such as a house-to-house service, group shipments and customs clearance. This DHL service field is also heavily represented with regards to project shipping and heavy cargo, with transport

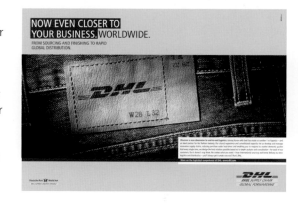

for industries such as oil, gas, petrochemicals, electricity and mining.

DHL Exel Supply Chain takes over all complex, global logistical tasks using custom-built solutions along the entire supply chain. With regards to procurement logistics, storage and sales logistics, the range of products available also includes upstream and downstream services such as packaging, co-packing, price marking, billing and order processing.

DHL Freight specialises in international and domestic road and rail transportation for full or partial loads within Europe. Qualified specialists integrate innovative IT applications to develop custom-built transport solutions for industry and retail.

Finally, DHL Global Mail is one of the world's leaders in the international mail business, with offices and production facilities on four continents and direct links with more than 200 countries. As well as its cross-border mail business, in many countries DHL Global Mail is increasingly focusing on domestic services, expanding upon its mail related value-added services.

Recent Developments

One of the central tasks in 2006 was to integrate the contract logistics provider, Exel, into the DHL brand. Under the management of former Exel CEO John Allen, all worldwide logistics activities at DHL were restructured and bundled into a

1969	1971
DHL is founded by Adrian Dalsey, Larry Hillblom and Robert Lynn in San Francisco.	DHL expands its network rapidly and becomes a trusted partner of many companies.
	Expansion into the Far East and Pacific Rim takes place.

separate executive division. The first quarter of 2006 saw the start of Exel rebranding. By the end of the year the switch to yellow and red was almost complete.

Building on DHL's uniform visual presence, the company is intensifying its content direction to turn the brand into a global brand. The new DHL brand positioning pulls together the common values of a globally active provider integrating around 285,000 people from different cultures, with different traditions, languages and religions. DHL's employees are at the hub of the organisation as active ambassadors of the brand.

At the start of the 2006 season, DHL strengthened its logistics partnership with Formula One racing. The amalgamation with Exel meant that DHL was able to offer an enhanced portfolio for teams, management and sponsors. This included ocean transport of the racing cars, engines, tyres, replacement parts and TV equipment for the most popular racing series in the world. Furthermore, DHL transported more than one million litres of petrol for the 18 races which took place on four continents.

Traditionally, DHL has used its logistics knowledge to support aid campaigns after natural disasters, such as the South Asia tsunami or Hurricane Katrina. Based on these valuable experiences, in 2006 the company set up two DHL Disaster Response Teams (DRTs) in Singapore and Florida. They are available to the UN Office for the Co-ordination of Humanitarian Affairs (OCHA) and support this international community with relief efforts. As volunteers, members of DRT bring their experience in transportation and logistics to co-ordinate aid deliveries at airports and near areas affected by a natural disaster.

Promotion

The three core elements of the DHL brand positioning – personal commitment, proactive solutions and local strength worldwide – are also fundamental to the present DHL global branding campaign. For this reason, DHL employees are seen as the heroes of the campaign.

DHL presented itself as logistics partner for the film Mission: Impossible III during its launch in March 2006. The introductory motif showed dedicated employee, Dirk Ravensteiner, with a roll of film tucked under his arm, appearing to deliver the film to every cinema in the world.

The TV ad mixed film sequences – including some with Tom Cruise – with images of the agile DHL deliveryman, underlain with original music from the film.

'DHL is now even closer to your business' is the core message of a specialist campaign run in logistics and retail magazines. It promotes DHL's new strengths to logistics decision-makers in 23 countries after the integration of Exel into the areas of contract logistics and freight forwarding. Jeans, tablets, chocolate and computer chips all stamped with DHL's brand logo show how close the DHL logistics division is to key industries such

as Fashion, Healthcare, Consumer, Technology, Automotive and Retail.

Brand Values

By integrating a whole range of express and logistics companies, the global brand DHL has developed rapidly within only a few years. Uniform company clothing, vehicle decoration and advertising creates a strong visual presence. The aim of DHL's consistent brand management is to be front of mind for its target audiences around the world. Moving forward, DHL aims to increase the proportion of customers who say they prefer DHL to a level higher than its actual market share. An important means to this end is the clear global brand positioning of DHL, which consists of three core elements.

Firstly, 'personal commitment' which means each individual in the company takes on responsibility, from the executive board to the front line, that interact with customers. The second element is 'proactive solutions' – instead of merely reacting to problems, possible issues will be anticipated in advance in order to develop appropriate resolutions. The third element is 'local strength worldwide'. If DHL is able to successfully combine local expertise with global resources, quality and continuity, then customers will truly receive the best of both worlds.

www.dhl.co.uk

Things you didn't know about DHL

DHL UK & Ireland was chosen for the second year running as International Express Operator of the Year in 2006.

Two live manatees became the most unusual item of DHL freight of recent times when they were transported from the zoo in Cincinnati, Ohio to SeaWorld in Orlando, Florida.

According to a 'following the sun' principle, the three DHL computer centres in Scottsdale (USA), Prague (Czech Republic) and Kuala Lumpur (Malaysia) each take on the primary role in DHL IT worldwide for eight hours per day.

1974	2002	2003	2005
The first UK office is opened in London. Globally, DHL now has 3,052 customers and 314 staff.	Deutsche Post World Net becomes the major shareholder in DHL from 1st January. A 100 per cent shareholding is completed by the end of the year.	DHL's corporate colours become yellow and red. In April, the worldwide visual transformation of all vehicles, packing materials and buildings begins.	Deutsche Post World Net acquires Exel, the British logistics corporation. Around 111,000 employees will be put under the umbrella of DHL.

Eddie Stobart

Eddie Stobart is the UK's largest independent logistics company with a turnover of £170 million, a fleet of over 850 trucks, 1,500 trailers, 27 depots, 3.5 million sq ft of warehousing and 2,000 employees. During its 37-year existence, Eddie Stobart has steadily increased its market share and developed internationally.

Market

Within the UK haulage industry, 80 per cent of companies have less than 20 vehicles so there are a relatively small number of large operators. The current trend in the industry is towards consolidation and rationalisation. Other fierce market challenges include the introduction of the working time directive, rising fuel costs, competition from overseas and a national shortage of skilled drivers.

The intense competition, low margin and high level of investment required in both equipment and systems are typical characteristics of the haulage industry. Delivery lead times, especially to the national retailers, have reduced to 12 hours which has forced a high level of specialist equipment and systems. Eddie Stobart has a unique brand offering symbolised by its commitment to provide a one stop solution to clients' distribution needs.

Achievements

From a small village in Cumbria, Eddie Stobart has become the largest independent contract distribution company in Europe and has built a reputation for running clean trucks, with smart, uniformed drivers who arrive on time at their destination.

All lorries are named by their drivers or lucky fans who can wait years for their chance to christen a truck. Eddie Stobart's response to public enquiries became the foundation of the present Stobart Members Club with its extensive range of merchandise and members who come from all over the world.

Eddie Stobart's other achievements have been recognised through a number of high-profile awards including the 'Supplier of Excellence Award' by the Institute of Transport Management and the PricewaterhouseCoopers 'Middle Market Award', but perhaps its most prestigious to date is 'Haulier of the Year' in the National Motor Transport Awards. In addition, Eddie Stobart Chairman, Andrew Tinkler, was recognised as the

North West Director of the Year by the Institute of Directors in 2006.

Product

Collection and delivery is the core function of Eddie Stobart. The company operates 365 days a year throughout the UK and Europe, transporting a diverse range of products from manufacturing to consumer goods. Eddie Stobart has vast experience in handling every type of consignment and load combination, offering a single or multi-drop option to and from any location. The service is supported by efficient vehicle planning and modern communication systems to ensure accurate tracking of vehicles and to maintain time-sensitive delivery schedules.

This is of particular importance in the refrigerated transport service which offers next day delivery into Europe using state-of-the-art temperature controlled facilities.

The International division has significantly grown over the past decade, with vehicles

operating cross channel and throughout Europe. This diverse work is carried out by seasoned professionals with years of continental driving experience.

Storage and distribution is a fast moving, highly skilled discipline within the logistics industry. Eddie Stobart operates over 3.5 million sq ft of warehousing, strategically located throughout the UK and Europe, with a wide variety of storage options. 'Paperless' warehouses use a range of sophisticated bar-coding and tracking systems that can locate batches or individual pallets quickly.

Process management is an added-value service, which enables manufacturers to 'contract-out' all logistics related activities, allowing them to release resources to concentrate on their core business.

Recent Developments

Eddie Stobart is investing heavily in mobile technology which has the benefit of satellite navigation for better routing of vehicles. On-board

1950s	**1970s**	**1980**	**1988**	**1992**	**1998**
Eddie Stobart establishes an agricultural contracting business in the Cumberland fellside village of Hesket Newmarket.	The business becomes incorporated as Eddie Stobart Ltd to develop its transport and distribution interests.	Re-location to a new depot in Carlisle takes place. The fleet of eight vehicles largely consists of tippers, but soon evolves into more versatile articulated vehicles with both flat bed and curtainside trailers.	Eddie Stobart opens its second depot in Burton on Trent with 50 vehicles and 450,000 sq ft of warehousing space.	Eddie Stobart is voted 'Haulier of the Year' for the first time by the Motor Transport Industry.	Eddie Stobart's International business is established in Belgium with a fleet of 750 vehicles and nearly three million sq ft of warehousing, creating an annual turnover of £98 million.

computers use Global Positioning Systems (GPS) and Radio Data Systems (RDS) to provide drivers with vital operating data. Route, fuel and engine diagnostics are also combined within the technology.

Investment in large plasma planning screens allows the real time monitoring of accurate vehicle utilisation and efficiency, keeping empty vehicles and miles to a minimum thus enabling better planning through peaks and troughs.

In 2006 new purpose built premises near the M6, Warrington, opened to form a central control for Eddie Stobart's general haulage fleet.

Following Eddie Stobart's 2004 takeover by WA Developments International, a substantial investment programme has been put in place which will see 250 new vehicles and 360 new trailers added to the fleet each year under a three year replacement programme. Focus has also been placed on a dedicated Driver Training and Recruitment department, to ensure a constant supply of highly skilled personnel is readily available to the company.

In September 2006 Eddie Stobart expanded from road to rail with the launch of its first rail freight service, which will replace over 13,000 lorry journeys each year, generating substantial environmental benefits.

In addition to Stobart Rail, Stobart Air has been formed, following the multi-million pound acquisition of Carlisle Airport. Plans to develop it into an international airport, for both freight and passengers, is underway.

Promotion

The Eddie Stobart brand name enjoys 95 per cent brand recognition throughout the UK and acts as a magnet for clients looking to contract out their distribution needs, however tough competition means that the company can not afford to rest on its laurels.

The principle marketing channel used to promote Eddie Stobart is the trucks themselves, as they carry the distinctive green livery and company contact details. An obvious approach to maximum exposure and to keeping advertising costs low.

Much of Eddie Stobart's promotional activity is to build brand awareness through trade publications, press releases, brand merchandising and sponsorship. Great publicity has come from Eddie Stobart's venture into motorsport. It has its own rally team competing nationally and internationally with the likes of British star Matthew Wilson being the only British driver contesting the 2006 World Rally Championship and for the last two years Stobart Motorsport has

won the British Rally Championship. The Stobart Honda Superbike team also competes on the British Superbike circuit. Eddie Stobart continues to be a major sponsor of Carlisle United Football Club, an association of more than 12 years.

Eddie Stobart produces a quarterly magazine to keep existing and prospective clients and employees informed, as well as its website, which has been designed to be of use to both customers and fans of the company.

Eddie Stobart has won several high profile marketing awards over the years; these include the SWOT Marketing Excellence and Marketeer of the Year awards.

Brand Values

Eddie Stobart places great importance on keeping the brand fresh and exciting. In June 2004, the company revealed a new corporate identity, heralding a bright new era. The livery graphics utilise the latest sign making technology to present a powerful image. This rebranding has further enhanced Eddie Stobart's identity and captures its core values of honesty, respect for people and the environment, and commitment to what it says it will deliver.

www.eddiestobart.co.uk

2001	2004	2005	2006
Eddie Stobart has a fleet of 900 vehicles operating from 27 depots with a turnover of £130 million, 2,000 staff and warehousing space of in excess of three million sq ft.	Eddie Stobart is acquired by WA Developments International. A major rebrand takes place involving changes to the distinctive truck livery, new uniforms and upgraded premises.	Eddie Stobart Ltd won its first Tesco Distribution Centre contract.	Eddie Stobart's parent company acquires Carlisle Airport and Stobart Air is formed. Stobart Rail is launched to offer a rail freight service. New central control at Warrington is built.

Things you didn't know about Eddie Stobart

Eddie Stobart trucks do some 85 million miles per year, which is the equivalent to 3,662 laps of the earth.

Each week Eddie Stobart delivers over 11 million cans of Coca-Cola products.

Stobart's vast Daventry warehouse complex covers 60 acres – equivalent to 20 Wembley stadiums.

The fuel saving made by the Stobart train is equivalent to taking the entire Eddie Stobart fleet of vehicles off the road for three weeks every year.

ExCeL LONDON

Since opening in November 2000, ExCeL London has staged over 2,000 events. More than five million people from 193 countries have visited, experiencing everything from music industry award ceremonies, religious festivals and medical congresses to high octane sporting events and exhibitions. ExCeL London is home to eight of London's top 10 trade shows, and two out of three of the UK's largest consumer shows, plus dozens of blue chip corporate client events and international conferences.

Market

ExCeL London is the UK's premier venue for exhibitions, events and conferences, a market currently worth £20 billion.

The venue operates across the sector, and markets itself as being able to handle almost any event imaginable. Two large halls, totalling 65,000 sq m – which can be sub-divided or used in their entirety – plus an additional 25,000 sq m of meeting space within a 100-acre campus, offer event organisers unrivalled space and a blank canvas where they can create truly unique event experiences. When combined with over 30 bars, restaurants and cafes, six on-site hotels and a host of additional services, ExCeL London boasts an impressive package for event organisers, both in the UK, and across Europe.

ExCeL London works with the biggest names in the exhibition business, including Reed Exhibition Companies, CMPi, Haymarket, Emap, Clarion Events, IMIE and National Boat Shows.

The Conference & Events Division, set up in 2004, has already built an enviable client list, including Philips, Tesco, Barclays, Rolls-Royce, the NHS, HSBC, Oracle and Royal Mail.

Achievements

ExCeL London has been rewarded with an impressive range of industry awards. It won the accolade for Business Venue of the Year (gold) at the Visit London Awards 2006 and was voted Best Live Events Venue (gold) and Best Exhibition Venue (silver) by the Event Awards 2006, following its win of Best Exhibition Venue (gold) at the 2005 Event Awards.

Further to which ExCeL London was awarded Best Website (silver) at the MIMA Awards 2006, as well as Best Purpose-built Venue in the Conference & Incentive Travel 2005 reader poll and Venue Customer Service Award at the 2005 aeo Awards.

The venue has the additional accolade of being at the forefront of London's eastside regeneration,

and will play host to six events during the 2012 Olympic Games.

Product

ExCeL London is a £300 million international venue located on a 100-acre, waterside campus alongside Royal Victoria Dock. It is the largest and most versatile venue in London, boasting 90,000 sq m of available multi-purpose space, compared to the 65,000 sq m offered by its nearest competitor.

The Platinum Conference Suite can stage conferences and dinners for between 400-1,100 delegates, whilst an additional 45 meeting rooms – many with dockside views – can cater for between 20-200 delegates. There are six on-site hotels, providing 1,500 bedrooms, ranging from budget to four star, 4,000 car parking spaces and three on-site DLR stations – linking to the Jubilee line. London City Airport, which is five minutes away from ExCeL London, offers

1855	1950s	Mid 1960s	1981
The Royal Victoria Docks site, on which ExCeL London now sits, is opened by Prince Albert as a working dock. It becomes the first dock to take iron steam ships and to use hydraulic cranes, handling shipments of tobacco, beef and produce from New Zealand.	Traffic through the Royal Docks reaches its peak.	Containerisation and other technological changes, together with a switch in Britain's trade following EEC membership, leads to a rapid decline.	The dock is finally closed.

over 200 flights each day, from more than 30 European destinations.

Recent Developments

ExCeL London is involved in a constant process of improvement and enhancement to ensure the visitor and event planner experience is of a high standard. Recent developments include the new undercroft car park, which opened in June 2006. This £5.5 million investment added 1,600 new car parking spaces directly beneath the venue.

In June, the venue completed its Wayfinding Project, which saw the installation of over 800 prominent, directional signs across the venue – crucial in a building and campus of this scale to ensure that visitors and delegates are easily able to find their way from A to B.

ExCeL London has also seen the installation of state-of-the-art fibre optic cabling with direct links to the BT Tower, enabling live outside broadcasting. Technology plays an important part in the events hosted at the venue so it is vital to stay cutting-edge.

In addition, new restaurants and retail outlets have opened across the campus in the last few months, including a Caribbean themed restaurant, a convenience store and dry cleaners. More are scheduled to open during 2007.

Future plans include a possible Phase 2 development, which would add an additional 36,000 sq m of event space to the existing venue (taking the total to 100,000 sq m), plus more bars, restaurants and potentially a new casino.

Promotion

The marketing team targets two distinct audiences – the exhibitions industry and the conference and events market.

UK exhibition organisers are targeted via a variety of communication channels including email broadcasts, sales literature, PR and the ExCeL London website. The venue also undertakes as much face-to-face marketing as possible, through organiser forums, corporate hospitality at key events and Strategy Days with key organisers.

Unique to the exhibitions campaign is an award-winning marketing and PR support package, tailored for trade and consumer show organisers. This involves working with each organiser to support them with their visitor and exhibitor marketing in order to drive up attendance levels. The support packages are made up of a variety of elements, such as inclusion on event listing materials, local PR, support with exhibitor days and familiarisation trips and contra-deals with local organisations (including the DLR, Canary Wharf and London City Airport) and media partners. The support package was recently valued in excess of £100,000.

The conference and events marketing campaign targets both UK and international event planners and is very much focused on promoting the venue in the context of London, a key city in Europe. To this end, much of the international activity is executed in conjunction with Visit London where the destination and the venue are jointly promoted.

As with the exhibition organiser's campaign, a great deal of face-to-face marketing is employed where the sales and marketing team make direct contact with potential clients in order to be able to tailor the product to their particular needs. This entails exhibiting at international shows, involvement with key industry bodies, hospitality events, speaking at industry seminar programmes and organising UK, European and US road shows, as well as press and client familiarisation trips.

Brand Values

ExCeL London is more than a simple exhibition and conference venue. It's an organisation that promises its clients and staff 'space to perform'. This promise is underpinned by a commitment amongst staff to deliver the ultimate environment in which events can flourish; a blank canvas providing creative inspiration and flexibility; a meticulous approach to every aspect of a project; a caring attitude to the environment and to its neighbourhood.

www.excel-london.co.uk

Things you didn't know about ExCeL London

ExCeL London is a 2012 Olympic Games venue and will be hosting: boxing, wrestling, judo, Tae-kwon-do, weight lifting and table tennis, as well as five Paralympic sports.

Will Young started his road to stardom at the Pop Idol auditions held at ExCeL London in 2002.

The test drive scene for the Batmobile in Batman Begins was filmed at ExCeL London.

As 007, Pierce Brosnan filmed the boat chase scene in the Royal Docks alongside ExCeL London for the film, The World Is Not Enough.

1988
Architect, Ray Moxley, is approached by the Association of Exhibition Organisers (aeo) to locate and design a new exhibition and conference centre within the M25.

1990
A turning point is reached when the 100-acre Royal Victoria Dock site is found.

1994
The London Docklands Development Corporation launches an international competition to appoint a preferred developer, which is won by ExCeL London. Today ExCeL London is one of Europe's largest regeneration projects.

2000
ExCeL London opens in November.

FedEx ® Express

FedEx Express is the world's largest express transportation company, providing fast and reliable delivery to more than 220 countries and territories. FedEx Express can deliver all kinds of time-sensitive shipments, from urgent medical supplies, last minute gifts and fragile scientific equipment, to bulky freight and dangerous goods.

Market

The global economy and rise of the multinational corporation means that today's businesses rely on being able to send and receive shipments all over the world. The opening up and rapid growth of markets such as China and India are further fuelling growth in international courier services.

According to McKinsey, 20 per cent of manufactured items are sold across borders, but, by 2020 some 80 per cent of all production will be distributed globally. E-commerce, in particular, is changing the way the world does business.

FedEx Express has a fleet of over 670 aircraft and 40,000 local delivery trucks. But it faces intense

competition, with rival global operators such as DHL and UPS, as well as a host of smaller and local operators, competing to meet clients' ever-increasing expectations for speed, security and cost-efficiency.

Achievements

There are few companies that can claim to have invented an entire industry, but FedEx did exactly that. The idea that Frederick Smith came up with while at university has grown into a global organisation, generating revenues of US$32.3 billion and net profits of US$1.8 billion in 2006.

FedEx has scored numerous industry 'firsts'. It invented overnight delivery in the early 1970s, and the 'hub and spoke' system, where shipments from 'spokes' all over the world are flown to a central hub to be sorted, loaded onto planes and despatched to their final destinations. This has since been adopted by the entire airline industry.

It was the first to offer money-back guarantees and to offer real-time package tracking over the

phone. It developed barcode technology in the 1980s to track packages on every step of their journey and introduced a dedicated computer network for use in its customers' offices when PCs were rarely sighted.

A pioneer of e-commerce when the internet was unknown to most, FedEx has constantly sought to anticipate the technology its customers will need tomorrow and introduce it today.

FedEx now operates 26 weekly flights in and out of China – more than any other international express carrier – and 400 weekly flights within Asia. Thanks to its two direct, around-the-world flights between Europe and Asia, it connects these locations in just two days.

FedEx is consistently recognised as one of the world's most admired and respected companies. In 2006, it ranked fourth in Fortune's list of the 'World's Most Admired Companies'. Furthermore, it ranked second in the 2006 list of 'America's Most Admired Companies' and has been among the '100 Best Companies to Work for in America' every year since the list's inception in 1998.

1973	**1980**	**1985**	**1992**
Federal Express creates an express delivery service with 389 employees serving a fleet of 14 Falcon jets that carries 186 packages to 25 US cities.	DADS™ (Digitally Assisted Dispatch System) is introduced, making Federal Express the first air express carrier with computers in vans.	Federal Express begins regularly scheduled flights to Europe.	The introduction of Tracking Software enables customers to track and trace their packages from their own workplace.

Product

FedEx offers time-definite, door-to-door, customs-cleared delivery to over 220 countries and territories worldwide. Its service is backed up by the most extensive flight and vehicle network in express delivery.

FedEx offers global transportation, logistics, e-commerce and supply chain management solutions. FedEx simplifies and speeds the shipping process by providing online ordering and processing facilities, free packaging, straightforward shipping documentation and bespoke e-business facilities.

FedEx divides the territories it serves into six regions: the US; Asia Pacific; Canada; Europe, Middle East and Africa; Latin America; and the Caribbean. For most of these territories, FedEx can offer delivery on the next business day. To keep customers up-to-date with the progress of their delivery, each shipment is scanned 17 times on average, allowing its precise location to be tracked by email, on the internet or by telephone, 24 hours a day.

Recent Developments

In January 2006 FedEx announced a strategic investment in the long term growth of China by agreeing to acquire the domestic express network of DTW Group along with its 50 per cent share in the FedEx-DTW International Priority express joint venture.

In the 2006 financial year, FedEx also expanded its service in India. FedEx was the first express company to serve this important market with direct international air routes. This expansion connects more of India – 4,348 cities and towns – to more of the world, faster. FedEx inaugurated the first overnight express flight from India to China and doubled its capacity from Europe to Asia through an eastbound around-the-world flight, mirroring its westbound counterpart launched in the 2006 financial year.

Also in India, FedEx recently announced its intention to purchase the leading Indian transportation company, Prakash Air Freight (PAFEX). PAFEX is one of FedEx's established partners in India.

Promotion

FedEx has a long heritage of brand promotion. In 1975, it became the first cargo carrier to advertise on television and in the consumer press, announcing itself with the line: 'America, you've got a new airline'. Since its first campaigns, FedEx has set the industry standard with classic commercials such as the 'Absolutely, positively, overnight' series in 1979.

Nowadays, FedEx continues to use a wide range of marketing tools, including television, press, posters, radio, internet, sponsorship and direct marketing.

To help communicate its enhanced services to and from China, FedEx recently initiated an 'Asia Direct' campaign, targeting business customers with details of its 26 weekly flights in and out of China.

It has also invested in direct marketing to promote its services to the US and Canada, communicating its 'next business day by 10.30' service. In Europe, the company turned to the internet to run an online advertising campaign featuring four 15-second mini-films and banner ads. The ads communicate FedEx's

'Purple Promise' of excellent customer experience by showing two different scenarios of poor service contrasting with the 'FedEx customer experience'. The scenarios are linked by the line: "If only I were treated like a FedEx package."

FedEx's sponsorship agreements include a new deal to sponsor the European Rugby Cup (ERC). Previously, FedEx has successfully sponsored the 2005/06 Heineken Cup and European Challenge Cup. The relationship highlights ERC and FedEx's shared vision of speed, reliability and teamwork.

Brand Values

A cornerstone of the FedEx brand is the 'Purple Promise'. In essence, this is to 'Make Every FedEx Experience Outstanding'.

The Purple Promise is the basis for FedEx's long term strategy to develop loyal relationships with its customers and to delight them with outstanding experiences, every day, at every touch point and with every transaction.

'Innovation' is another key value, as FedEx constantly strives to invent new technologies that improve the way its customers work and live. 'Integrity' informs the way that the company honestly and efficiently manages its operations, finances and services and 'Responsibility' champions its approach to safety, health, the environment and local communities.

www.fedex.com

Things you didn't know about FedEx Express

FedEx was the first express delivery service to receive ISO 9001 certification for its entire worldwide operation.

FedEx was the first in the industry to give European customers a next-morning freight service to most of North America with ExpressFreighter® direct international flights.

FedEx shipped 17 classic Ferraris worth millions of dollars from Brussels to the US for a car show.

One of the largest items that FedEx has ever shipped is a windmill from Denmark.

1994	**1999**	**2003**	**2005**
Federal Express launches its website and changes its name to FedEx®. It also launches the slogan 'The World On Time'.	FedEx becomes the first major carrier to introduce a single tariff between certain countries in Europe. This initiative means that all package movements within the 'euro zone' are the same price.	FedEx celebrates 30 years since the first FedEx aeroplane took flight, and announces the addition of both Afghanistan and Iraq to its global network.	FedEx Express launches the express air cargo industry's first direct flight from mainland China to Europe. It also announces that it is doubling capacity from Europe to India and the rest of Asia.

First is Britain's biggest transport operator, carrying over two billion passengers a year, employing over 74,000 people across the UK and North America with an annual turnover of over £3 billion. First is a leader in safe, innovative, reliable sustainable transport services – global in scale and local in approach.

Market

First provides customers with high quality public transport across the UK and North America.

First is the UK's largest rail operator with four passenger rail franchises: First Great Western, First Capital Connect, First TransPennine Express and First ScotRail. It also operates Hull Trains, a non-franchised open access operator and provides freight services through GB Railfreight as well as operating the Croydon Tramlink network.

First is also the UK's largest bus operator with a fleet of some 9,000 buses carrying 2.9 million passengers every day in over 40 major towns and cities. It holds a market share of approximately 23 per cent nationally.

Other operations include First Student UK, which has an existing and essential operating base in more than 40 towns and cities across the country. As a result they have substantial economies of scale ranging from fleet purchase, through to operational flexibility and experience.

Achievements

First prides itself on innovation and investment, and aims to create a new standard of transport services across the UK. For example, on the First TransPennine Express network, it has introduced a modern, high-quality intercity fleet of 100mph

trains, with air conditioning, advanced passenger information systems and on-board CCTV.

The company has also led the way in modernising bus services. 'The Overground' system, which offers an underground-style bus network with colour-coded routes and interchange points, has now been introduced in over 30 towns and cities around the UK. In Glasgow a new system called 'streamline' has been developed to improve bus information and signalling systems, which has seen journey times reduced by almost 10 per cent.

In May 2006, the company launched a new premium urban travel concept, called ftr, in York. These high-tech vehicles look like trams but have the flexibility of a conventional bus, using normal roads.

Across the group, several awards have been won recently. First ScotRail received UK Public Transport Operator of the year 2006. First's bus operations in Aberdeen were short-listed for 'Public Transport Operator of the Year' at the National Transport Awards in July 2006. The ftr project won 'Innovation of the Year' at the 'routeone' Operator Excellence awards. In addition, First was the winner of a National Green Apple Award for environmental best practice in the transport and freight industry category 2006. Finally, Hull Trains won the Rolling Stock Excellence of the Year award 2006 and was runner up in the Rail Business of the Year award 2006.

Product

First is divided into three principal divisions: UK Bus; UK Rail; and its North American business. UK Bus generates over £1 billion per year in turnover, and runs a fleet of 9,000 buses. Recently, the group has acquired high quality, low-floor buses, comprising an investment of over £95 million in 2006 alone. This modern fleet means that all buses now comply with EU IV emission standards.

UK Rail, which generates a turnover of £1.164 billion per annum, is the market leader in the UK, running over 4,500 train services per day, and carrying over 250 million passengers per year. First has grown thanks to sustained investment and attention to customer service. One of its newest enlarged franchises, First Great Western, has, for example, increased passenger journeys by more than 50 per cent.

1995		1996	1997
First Bus is born out of a merger between Grampian Regional Transport and Badgerline Group. The two companies (both listed on the stock exchange) merged to form FirstBus plc.	Also in 1995, the company is listed on the London Stock Exchange and is registered in Scotland with operational offices in Aberdeen and London.	First acquires a 24.5 per cent holding in Great Western Holdings. The company that operates the Great Western Trains franchise.	The name is changed to FirstGroup plc to reflect the growing interests of the business in rail and international.

First's involvement has boosted the performance of many other franchises. For example, passenger numbers at First TransPennine Express increased by 11 per cent since the start of the franchise in February 2004. In Scotland, First ScotRail has reduced operator-attributed delay by 26 per cent since 2004. In Hull, six weekday services are now operated by Hull Trains and new 125mph trains have recently been introduced onto the network.

First also runs trams in Croydon, south of London, carrying 22 million passengers per year. Furthermore, in the rail freight business, GB Railfreight, is a leading player in the UK. GB Railfreight carries over one million letters per day between London and Scotland for Royal Mail. The flexible service can be tailored to meet changing levels of demand. First can provide more services to help move some of the 120 million pieces of mail to be delivered each day.

Recent Developments
First was awarded two important new enlarged rail franchises in 2005 – First Great Western and First Capital Connect, worth over £1 billion in revenue per year for up to 10 years. Operations for these two franchises began in 2006.

First Great Western operates services across the south and west of England, and South Wales. The Group will invest over £200 million on new and improved station facilities, trains and staff over the

first two years. The train fleet is being upgraded with some 30 per cent more seats being provided during the morning and evening peaks.

First Capital Connect operates services across London and the South East. The Group is also committed to improving service here, investing £52 million, the majority of which will be spent during the first three years of the franchise. This investment aims to help improve customers' comfort, safety and satisfaction.

The ftr scheme in York has been designed and manufactured in partnership with Wright Group to deliver a unique vehicle unlike any other passenger transport vehicle. The scheme has also started in Leeds and is being evaluated to be included in cities such as Sheffield, Swansea, Reading, Bath and Glasgow.

First's pioneering Workplace initiative in partnership with The Transport and General Workers Union, has been a great success. There are now 40 learning centres reaching approximately 60 per cent of UK employees.

Promotion
The Group has created a strong visual presence across all areas of the business. Its vehicles are the strongest representation of its brand, which has helped establish First as the leader in public transport provision in the UK. The brand has developed in recent years to allow for innovation and to encourage the profile of strongly branded products such as ftr and companies such as First ScotRail. First is also investing heavily in its website to help customers plan their journeys.

Brand Values
First has a clear vision: to transform travel by providing public transport services that are safe, reliable, high quality, personal and accessible.

It aims to be the 'best in class' in everything it does, delivering the highest levels of safety and service, and constantly building on its reputation for innovation, investment and improvement.

Safety is the number one priority for the Group, and it has created a culture of 'Safety First' throughout the business. It supports this with a simple message: 'if you cannot do it safely, don't do it'.

www.firstgroup.com

1999	2003	2004	2006
The Group makes a significant entry into the North American transport market with the acquisitions of Bruce Transportation and Ryder Public Transportation (RPTS).	First completes the acquisition of a 90 per cent stakeholding in Aircoach, Dublin.	First are successful in winning the ScotRail bid. This franchise is now known as First ScotRail. It also acquires a new franchise, which is now called First TransPennine Express.	First wins two new enlarged rail franchises, First Great Western and First Capital Connect. First now employs some 74,000 employees in the UK and North America.

first direct ◆◆
Member HSBC Group

first direct revolutionised the UK banking market in 1989 with the introduction of 24-hour telephone banking. Its high levels of service, delivered to 1.3 million UK customers, have made it the UK's most recommended bank for 13 consecutive years (Source: Research International December 2006).

Market

The retail banking market has undergone a transformation over the last decade. The domination of the 'high street bank' has disappeared as more and more banking services moved first onto the telephone and then onto the internet. According to Key Note, over 20 million people in the UK now bank online. Retail banking has also attracted a host of new entrants, ranging from supermarkets such as Tesco and Sainsbury's to off-shoots of established banking names such as The Co-Operative Bank's smile.co.uk, Abbey National's Cahoot and HSBC's first direct.

Many of these, including first direct, are targeting a more distinct group of customers than their mass-market parents. Enhanced service, a personalised approach, customer loyalty and word of mouth recommendations are the watchwords, with first direct and its immediate competitor brands going after quality, not necessarily quantity of customers. For example, first direct has 1.3 million customers, giving it a two per cent share of the UK current account market. However, first direct's competitors are not confined to the financial sector alone. As it cements its reputation for superior service, it finds itself being considered alongside the emerging breed of online 'service brands', such as Amazon and eBay.

Achievements

When it launched in 1989, first direct invented a new way of 'direct' banking. At the time, the idea of banking outside of high street branches was unheard of. Its model of 24-hour telephone banking, seven days a week and 365 days a year, was a radical departure, but it proved that 'remote' banking didn't have to mean an impersonal or detached service. In fact, it proved the very opposite, delivering high levels of service that raised the bar for the banking industry as a whole. It proved that it could build a trusting relationship with its customers, without them needing to stand in a queue or travel to a branch. Allowing people to take control of how they wanted to bank, and treating them like individuals, was an immediate hit with a discerning part of the UK public.

Soon, a host of other banks followed first direct's lead and 24-hour telephone and, subsequently, internet banking, became a standard part of the retail banking mix. But it was first direct's innovation that changed the shape of the UK banking industry.

Indeed, research shows that it has had the most satisfied customers and been the UK's most recommended bank for the last 13 years consecutively (Sources: MORI, NOP & RI). It has won a host of awards, including being voted Best Current Account Provider at the 2005 Guardian

Consumer Finance Awards, for the fourth consecutive year. It also recently won a coveted place in The Sunday Times '100 Best Companies to Work For' 2006 list. It was named Best Online Bank or Building Society at the 2005 Online Finance Awards and scooped Gold in the recent Direct Marketing Association Awards in the Financial Services and Consumer Direct Marketing categories.

In July 2006, first direct received a major accolade when it was named Direct Brand of the Decade by Precision Marketing magazine, beating off stiff competition from Tesco, Cancer Research UK, Gordon's Gin, Honda (UK) and Nectar.

Product

first direct has 1.3 million UK customers, 840,000 of whom use its internet banking service, while 460,000 use SMS text message banking. This makes first direct the largest text messaging bank in the UK and, to serve those customers, it sends its SMS customers around 3.5 million text messages every month.

Whether they are holders of first direct's award-winning current account, hold an e-savings account, a loan, mortgage, credit card, or use the bank for its share dealing service, first direct serves its customers in any way that suits them. It employs 3,400 people, 2,800 of whom work in its

1989	1991	1995	1997
first direct opens for business on Sunday 1st October. Over 1,000 phone calls are taken in the first 24 hours.	By May, 100,000 customers have joined the bank.	The 500,000th customer joins first direct.	first direct introduces PC Banking.

two call centres, one in Leeds and the other in Hamilton near Glasgow. They handle over 235,000 telephone calls a week, and 13,000 per day outside of working hours.

The bank prides itself on its ability to convert its strong customer relationships into customers taking more than one of its products, with nearly half of its customers having more than one account with first direct. This 'share of wallet' is one of the highest in the market.

Recent Developments

first direct recently built on its reputation for ground-breaking innovation in the banking market with the announcement that it is to trial 'video call' mobile banking. Teaming up with the 3G mobile phone operator, 3, the trial will allow first direct staff to take video calls from customers who have a video-enabled mobile phone. The pilot is designed to test what customers want from mobile phone banking, and with so many of its customers choosing to interact with the bank via SMS, first direct wants to see how the latest mobile phone technology can further enhance their experience.

In another development that sees first direct tapping into how consumers integrate new technology into their daily lives, the bank is launching a community 'chat and blogging' site for its customers. first direct Interactive responds to the social networking trend popularised by websites such as MySpace and Bebo, but also recognises how many of its customers already see first direct as a 'club'. first direct Interactive is not a banking platform, but provides a forum for customers to discuss common interests, recommend books and restaurants, or just chat.

In a further initiative to improve its service, first direct has also launched 'Internet Banking Plus', giving customers a single, transparent view

of their finances, however many accounts they hold. In addition, it recently launched a podcast, with contributors including the bank's chief executive, Chris Pilling, discussing issues such as online security and the secrets of good customer service.

Promotion

first direct has a strong pedigree in above and below-the-line marketing, collecting accolades for its direct mail, television, internet and mobile communications from a host of high-profile awards.

Unlike some mass-market banks, first direct uses marketing to target a niche audience, building a dialogue with its existing customers and carefully targeting prospective new customers. This means that targeted communications such as direct mail have always played an important role. Some of its financial services and consumer mailing

campaigns helped it win Gold in the recent 2005/06 Direct Marketing Association Awards.

Above-the-line, first direct spends the bulk of its marketing budget on advertising on the internet – proving to be a particularly effective tool for customer acquisition. It spends less on television campaigns than some of the high street banks, but it has invested in some award-winning work, such as the 'Customer Testimonials' campaign, in which real first direct customers spoke on-camera about why they liked the bank. Hundreds of customers expressed an interest in being featured, before 15 were chosen to make the ads.

Corporate Social Responsibility is extremely important to the bank and it undertakes a wide range of promotions in support of community and charity. For example, first direct recently announced that for every life insurance policy it sells, it will give £10 to Marie Curie Cancer Care while every home insurance policy it sells will generate a £10 donation to the homeless charity, Shelter.

Brand Values

Being personal and having a human touch with its customers lies at the core of the first direct brand. It is not trying to be its customers' closest friend, but maintains a professional relationship and dialogue. Its aim is to ensure that its customers have control, allowing them to interact with the bank whenever they want, by phone, text, internet or mobile. But, however they choose to deal with the bank, it aims to ensure that the dialogue always has the same recognisable 'first directness' about it. Other key values of the first direct brand are its transparency, openness and a desire to give something back to its customers and to the community.

www.firstdirect.com

1998
first direct launches its website and a year later introduces text message banking.

2000
A new current account, savings account and credit card are launched on firstdirect.com.

2001
The first direct Offset Mortgage is launched.

2004
Internet Banking Plus is launched.

flybe.com

Flybe was formed in Jersey in 1979 and has grown to become the number one UK regional airline with more domestic bases and flights across the UK than any other airline. Flybe operates 37 aircraft to 47 airports in 10 countries, carrying six million passengers and employing 1,700 people.

Market

The boom in budget airlines over the last decade means that short haul air travel has never been more popular. According to Key Note Research, the number of passengers carried by UK airlines in 2005 increased by eight per cent to 124.3 million and the number of seat kilometres used was up by 8.8 per cent to 290.48 billion. Meanwhile, the revenue generated by UK airlines in 2005 is estimated to have reached £15 billion, a 1.9 per cent increase.

The explosion in budget air travel means that the market is highly competitive, with tight margins. Increases in the price of oil, rising taxation on air travel, higher airport charges, and pressure from environmental groups on airlines to reduce carbon emissions, are all factors likely to have a profound effect on airlines' business over the next decade.

Achievements

Flybe has chalked up 27 years of continuous operations, evolving from its roots as Jersey European into a successful, innovative market leader within the low cost airline industry.

It has marked out a clear territory in the crowded airline marketplace. With a key focus on 'low cost travel on your doorstep' by flying from the UK regions, and offering business travellers the country's only true low cost business service, Flybe has skillfully positioned itself in the industry. Business travellers can enjoy executive lounges, pre-assigned seating and the UK's most generous frequent flyer programme.

The airline has also been highly successful in driving ancillary revenue – a key aim for any low cost operator. It was also the first airline in the world to charge for hold baggage, an initiative which has been followed by the industry, and reward hand baggage only passengers. In addition, Flybe has become the market leader in in-flight sales, taking a higher spend per passenger than any other short haul scheduled airline.

Flybe is also spearheading efforts to reduce the environmental impact of air travel and promote sustainable growth. Taking steps to minimise emissions from its flights, it has invested heavily in aircraft. Its orders for Bombardier Q400 and Embraer 195 aircraft will give Flybe one of the youngest and most environmentally friendly fleets in the world.

Flybe strives to connect with the community it serves and has a strong track record of investing in local environmental and community projects. Over the last three years the airline has invested over £4 million in a range of local initiatives. As well as ploughing investment back into the community, the airline is also thriving commercially. Flybe recently announced its strongest ever summer trading period, resulting in an un-audited operating profit of £20.5 million for the six months to 30th September 2006, a 65 per cent increase on the same period in 2005.

Product

Currently, Flybe operates 37 aircraft serving 47 airports and 10 countries. Its route network is unique in the industry, being split into 80 per cent UK domestic, 10 per cent sun and ski, and 10 per cent regional France. The average length of these routes is 300 miles, and the average size of its aircraft is 90 seats. Flybe has opted to provide a simplified aircraft type, designed to suit the diversity of the network. The aircraft also provide suitable capacity to offer high frequency services within the UK and Europe.

1979	**1983**	**1991**	**1993**	**1993/94**	**2000**
Jersey-based entrepreneur and successful businessman Jack Walker founds Jersey European.	The airline is taken over by the Walkersteel Group.	Jersey European gains its first London route from Guernsey to London Gatwick.	The Business Class Service is launched, making Jersey European the first domestic airline to offer two classes of service.	Jersey European wins the 'Best UK Regional Airline' award at the Northern Ireland Travel and Tourism awards.	Jersey European changes its name to British European.

Low cost... but not at any cost.

The South West's low fare, low emissions airline.

For the business market, a key part of the airline's product offering is Flybe Economy Plus. As well as free executive lounge access across the UK and Europe, this offers a range of other features such as: lower minimum check-in times; fully changeable tickets; dedicated check-in; and generous baggage allowance. The ongoing enhancement of Flybe Economy Plus now means that customers have access to many more executive lounges across the UK and Europe. More of these lounges are being equipped with wireless internet access.

Another important part of Flybe's offer is the UK's most generous frequent flyer programme, Passport to Freedom, offering more points per flight than any other UK airline. Customers flying Flybe Economy Plus can collect Freedom Points which can be redeemed against a selection of rewards.

In addition to the airline, Flybe is a major player in Aviation Services, offering aircraft engineering for not only the Flybe fleet, but also third party maintenance including British Airways. The business, which has won several industry accolades, employs over 500 staff at its Exeter site plus further line engineering teams across the UK and has recently invested £14 million in brand new hanger facilities in the South West.

Recent Developments

In 2006 Flybe became the first airline to take delivery of the new EMBRAER 195 aircraft. Its high environmental performance features include greater fuel efficiency and a reduction in noise levels, whilst also offering superior cabin service and passenger comfort. The 26 aircraft order will create one of the youngest fleets in the world.

For summer 2007, Flybe has 15 new European routes planned providing travellers with further

door to door links to the UK and abroad without having to travel via London – a cause championed by Flybe as it continues to bring convenient, low-cost travel to the regions.

Promotion

Since relaunching as Flybe in 2002, the airline has focused on developing a highly visible retail brand.

This has been achieved through a high frequency and aggressive marketing programme, using multimedia channels on a national and regional level.

Customer Relationship Marketing is at the heart of Flybe's long term marketing strategy to increase

the life time value of its customer base. Flybe's strategy is at the forefront of the industry with a highly segmented database and a communications strategy that is fast, bespoke and personalised.

Sponsorship is another important tool for Flybe, with the airline recently signing a deal to sponsor three football clubs, Norwich, Birmingham and Southampton Football Club. The airline attracted media attention when it announced it would forgo its right to add its name to the Southampton stadium, St Mary's, saying that its decision to keep the original name reflects its support of football in the local community.

Brand Values

Flybe's brand is built on a vision to be modern, different, environmentally and socially responsible, transparent and customer-driven. Its investments in the local community, advocacy for regional 'on your doorstep' services, and strong regional heritage all feed into the identity of the brand. Innovation and offering its customers a different choice of services, is another key value.

www.flybe.com

Things you didn't know about Flybe

Flybe's aircraft fly a total of 44.4 million kilometres per year.

The fleet uses 1,800 aircraft tyres per year.

Flybe is the first airline in the world to take delivery of the new Embrear 195 aircraft.

If all the tubs of Pringles sold on board in one year were placed on top of each other they would be 12 times higher than the tallest building in the world, Taipei Tower, Taiwan.

All of the bottles of mineral water Flybe sells in a year could fill up an Olympic sized swimming pool, 15 times.

2002	**2003**	**2005**	**2006**
British European becomes Flybe.	Flybe is voted the 'Most Recommended UK Low Fares Airline' by Holiday Which?	Flybe is voted most popular UK Domestic and France-bound airline in Holiday Which?	Flybe becomes the first airline to offer online check-in to passengers carrying hand and hold baggage. In addition, a self-service check-in facility is launched.

GATWICK 'EXPRESS

Gatwick Express, established in 1984, is the longest running dedicated airport service in the world and carries approximately 14,000 passengers between Gatwick Airport and London's Victoria station throughout the day, with a non-stop journey time of 30 minutes and with trains departing every 15 minutes.

Market

Gatwick Express is owned by National Express Group. They acquired the franchise in 1996, and hold more than 70 per cent of the rail market between Gatwick Airport and central London.

Achievements

Gatwick Express has the highest customer satisfaction levels of any train operating company in the UK. In the 2006 spring National Passenger Survey, Gatwick Express scored 94 per cent, an industry record and the sixth consecutive time over a three-year period that Gatwick Express has held the number one position.

Delivering excellent customer service is a constant challenge and the demands of customers are constantly evolving. Gatwick Express is always looking for innovative ways to improve the way staff interact with customers. To meet the needs of an increasingly sophisticated and customer service focused market, Gatwick Express shifted its focus to providing flexible, positive and personal customer service. As a result, the innovative and award winning 'Leading Lights' training programme was developed.

Designed as a training programme that proactively engages its workforce by using drama and theatrical elements to spark interest and maintain attention in trainees, Leading Lights helps frontline staff identify different types of customers so they can deliver customer service that meets the passenger's individual needs. Its emphasis is on achieving targeted, long term change in day-to-day behaviour and performance.

Gatwick Express has the highest levels of employee satisfaction (as tracked in the National Express Group employee survey) across all Group companies, and in March 2006 Gatwick Express

saw their satisfaction ratings increase from 78 per cent in 2005 to a record 85 per cent in 2006.

Product

Gatwick Express is a dedicated, non stop, high speed rail-air link operating between Gatwick Airport and central London.

The purpose built modern Juniper Class 460 trains, run from 3.30am-12.30am from London Victoria and from 4.35am-1.35am from Gatwick Airport.

Gatwick Express has its own dedicated platforms in Victoria station to allow passengers quick access on and off the trains. Similarly, the railway station at Gatwick Airport is at the heart of the South Terminal.

Gatwick Express welcome hosts are situated at the front of the platform to help customers with

queries about the service and onward travel into London. In addition, Gatwick Express has installed flight departure boards on the platforms at Victoria to allow passengers to check the status of their departing flight.

Whether travelling for business or pleasure the emphasis is on comfort. Gatwick Express' First Class interiors provide a calming and spacious, air-conditioned environment for customers to make the most of their time whilst travelling to or from the airport. These customers have access to the departures Fast Track security channel at Gatwick Airport. The service includes a quick route through airport security control, access to a priority till in Duty Free and a dedicated foreign exchange desk.

Express Class includes modern, comfortable seating, air-conditioned surroundings and

1936	1939	1955	Late 1950s
Gatwick Airport opens with one terminal which is known as 'The Beehive' due to its distinctive cone shape. The airport station is situated one mile south of the current station, and is used to service Gatwick Racecourse.	World War II sees the airport used as a military base.	The airport is sold by Airports Limited to the state and a period of major development begins.	A new airport terminal is built and the Gatwick Racecourse station is developed into a dedicated airport station. The train link to Gatwick is limited, using dedicated carriages from part of another service.

attentive staff, a full refreshment trolley service and room for luggage.

Recent Developments

Gatwick Express was the first train operating company in the UK to utilise an e-ticketing solution, allowing customers to book their ticket online. To support e-ticketing, Gatwick Express recently upgraded its website to simplify and speed up the booking process. Customers' personal details and favourite tickets can be securely retained and those holding accounts can be notified of planned or unplanned disruptions on their date of travel.

In keeping with its commitment to excellent customer service, a major enhancement programme of the first class train carriages, which will be operational in spring 2007, is underway.

Promotion

In order to reach its customer base, from both the UK and internationally, Gatwick Express uses press, outdoor and online communications to execute its promotional strategy.

In summer 2006, Gatwick Express launched a new advertising campaign specifically targeted at the time sensitive air traveller. A new strapline 'Anything else is a risk', was introduced, replacing the previous 'Timing is everything' line. The new strapline – still underpinned by the essence of 'certainty' in the Gatwick Express brand – takes a more competitive approach by referring indirectly to competitors between central London and the airport.

The main messages in the advertising is to create reassurance and highlight the speed, the non-stop nature of the service, the frequency and its strong customer service record.

Gatwick Express advertises in the inner London press to target the UK business and leisure audience, a strategy supported by online advertising at key times of the year on popular travel and business websites.

The majority of outdoor poster activity is concentrated at Gatwick Airport, Gatwick Airport Station and Victoria Station, aiming to reassure

customers that they are making the right decision and to convert undecided travellers.

The focus for below-the-line activity is working and developing relationships with airlines at Gatwick Airport, such as Gatwick Express' partnership with Virgin Atlantic's Flying Club programme. Silver and Gold members receive an allocation of First Class upgrades to use on Gatwick Express. This has proved to be extremely successful since its launch in 2003, supporting the premium nature of both brands and adding value to the customer's travelling experience.

Foreign travellers are targeted through airline partners; Gatwick Express has developed solid relationships with growth airlines, such as easyJet and Monarch, as a mechanism for reaching potential customers during the booking process or during their flight. Jointly branded microsites, reciprocal weblinks, in-flight announcements and advertising in in-flight magazines have all been effective ways for generating sales.

The focus for Gatwick Express in 2007 will be on customer relationship marketing, with the objective of ensuring consistent and frequent communication with the customer base, providing news about promotions, new products and service enhancements.

Gatwick Express also realises the potential of the ski and snowboard market and is targeting this market through sponsorship of the Time Out Ski & Snowboard Europe guide. With a large number of flights departing from Gatwick Airport, the luggage space and a 'four for two' promotional

offer, this market has seen great growth potential. This sponsorship is supported by concourse promotions at London Victoria and online advertising on high profile ski websites.

Brand Values

Regardless of the passenger type there is a common belief that 'some journeys are simply more important than others'. It is acknowledged that there is heightened tension on a trip to the airport; for most air travellers, the consequences of a delay can be significant. Gatwick Express therefore, bases its brand promise on the certainty that passengers will arrive in a timely fashion.

This promise is broken down into the emotional and rational benefits of using the service. Rational benefits include the speed and frequency of the service, as well as its punctuality and reliability.

Emotional benefits include the dedicated service, trust and reassurance, premium feel and the belief that the Gatwick Express is the 'official' way to travel to and from the airport.

It is the combination of these rational and emotional values that enables Gatwick Express to have such a dominant share of the rail market to and from the airport.

The Gatwick Express 'voice' that delivers these brand values in the advertising has been developed to represent that of an airline captain with wit and charm – someone who is confident, comfortable and unflappable.

www.gatwickexpress.co.uk

Things you didn't know about Gatwick Express

Every year 1.6 million miles are travelled by Gatwick Express, the equivalent to over six times the distance to the moon.

Gatwick Express actively recruits multi-national and multi-lingual customer service staff to reflect an increasingly non-English speaking customer base. As a result, more than 35 languages are now spoken across the team. All employees who speak a foreign language are given name badges with flags to depict which languages they speak.

Each day, 14,000 passengers travel on Gatwick Express trains.

1980s	1984	1990s	2005
The current station building is erected and business at Gatwick Airport expands rapidly.	The first dedicated Gatwick Express service is formed to provide a rail-air link to the airport.	Gatwick Airport continues to expand.	Gatwick Airport has 32 million passengers passing through it. This is expected to grow to 40 million by 2008.

GENERAL DYNAMICS
United Kingdom Limited

General Dynamics United Kingdom Limited is a leading prime contractor and complex system of systems integrator working in partnership with the UK's Ministry of Defence and other allies. With more than 1,700 highly skilled employees and over 40 years experience delivering complex systems, General Dynamics UK has the technical leadership, manufacturing expertise and prime contract management skills to deliver future network-enabled battlespace capabilities. Its annual turnover is in excess of £500 million.

Market

General Dynamics UK works primarily in the UK defence industrial sector, with additional work in the Homeland Security sector. Its principal UK customer is the MoD, with overseas success in the export markets including the Netherlands, Romania, and others in the near future.

Today, General Dynamics UK is the fourth largest UK defence company and the third largest defence prime contractor in the UK. It is part of the General Dynamics Corporation, one of the top six defence companies in the world with more than 81,000 employees and revenue of US$24.1 billion in 2006.

As a prime system of systems integrator it takes leading products and technologies and performs the complex integration work required to enable their effective use at the system of systems level. This means that General Dynamics UK's market share is underpinned by a diverse supply chain, including a major contribution from SMEs.

Achievements

General Dynamics UK has achieved massive growth on the back of major project successes since 2000 and has invested more than £14 million in facilities. Its workforce has more than tripled in size with over £900,000 being invested in employee training in 2005 alone. Since 2002, more than 1,000 jobs have been created in Wales, adding over £30 million to the UK economy. In fact, every job created contributes on average £55,000 to the local economy.

General Dynamics UK takes its corporate responsibilities seriously and is very aware of the local communities in which it works and over the past few years has given more than £250,000 in charitable contributions and sponsorships. General Dynamics UK also actively supports several charities and benevolent funds associated with the military, including SSAFA (Soldiers, Sailors, Airmen and Families Association), the Army Benevolent Fund, the RAF Benevolent Fund, and Combat Stress.

Product

General Dynamics UK is structured around four core business units: C⁴I (UK), Mission Systems, Network Solutions and Ground Systems.

C⁴I stands for Command, Control, Communications, Computing and Information. It is the integration of technology and networks that give commanders the vital information they need, when they need it.

General Dynamics UK's C⁴I business is successfully delivering Bowman – a tactical communications system – to the UK forces, giving them a decisive advantage by integrating digital voice and data technology to provide secure radio, telephone, intercom and tactical internet services. The programme includes the conversion of over 18,000 platforms, including vehicles, helicopters, naval vessels, landing craft and fixed HQ buildings.

As the leading provider of ISTAR (Intelligence, Surveillance, Target Acquisition and Reconnaissance) capabilities, the Mission Systems

1899	1952	1962	1979	1990	1997
The Electric Boat Corporation is established.	The Electric Boat Corporation becomes General Dynamics.	The Computing Devices Company (CDC) is established in London to support an avionics project for the Anglo-Canadian Nimrod Mk1 maritime patrol aircraft.	The first major contract is won – a leading role in Tornado Missile Management System.	RAF use Computing Devices' Real-Time Tactical Reconnaissance System in the Gulf War – the first world use of this technology.	General Dynamics Corporation acquires Computing Devices International.

team delivers a family of capabilities. Products range from operational flight programmes with integrated digital mapping and recording for the Future Lynx helicopter, to safety critical design for 'ground to air' and 'air to air' data networks.

The Network Solutions team provides C⁴I solutions, like Bowman, for the export market, together with UK-based Chemical, Biological, Radiological and Nuclear (CBRN) Protection capabilities. In addition, General Dynamics UK is a key partner in the Atlas DII consortium through the Network Solutions business.

As a technology-independent Prime System of Systems Integrator, General Dynamics UK is able to draw from the global marketplace, bringing together the best solutions for the UK Armed Forces. The extensive experience of its parent company – General Dynamics Corporation – aids in offering the right solutions to customers, at the appropriate technology and system readiness levels.

Ground Systems is a recently formed business unit, established to build on a UK-based capability for armoured fighting vehicles and related sub-systems. The core activity within this business unit is associated with the development of solutions for the UK Future Rapid Effects System (FRES) programme.

Recent Developments
General Dynamics UK has successfully demonstrated the latest stage of the Bowman CIP tactical communications and data system to its key customers from the UK Armed Forces. The system is constantly evolving to respond to changes in experience on operations, evolving doctrine, updated requirements and advances in technology. The latest update provides the Armed Forces with a more robust tactical internet which allows soldiers to pass data and key information around the battlefield.

In addition, General Dynamics UK has won a second contract to develop the Defence Technology Centre in Data and Information Fusion (DIF DTC) for a further three years. This is a research consortium, led by General Dynamics UK in partnership with the Ministry of Defence. It recently featured in The Daily Telegraph, providing an insight into the technology of the future.

General Dynamics UK has developed a leading position in the British Army's Future Armoured Fighting Vehicle programme, FRES (Future Rapid Effects System). FRES is the key element of a new medium force capability for the British Army. It is the largest ever Army programme with an acquisition value of around £16 billion, and through-life costs of £60 billion. It will also transform the industrial landscape in the armed fighting vehicle sector. It represents another major opportunity for General Dynamics UK to help transform the way the British Army operates.

This builds on the Company's experience and facilities in the UK – digitising thousands of military vehicles for Bowman – as well as the track record of General Dynamics Corporation as the world's leading supplier of armoured vehicles.

Promotion
General Dynamics UK works hard on reputation management using a variety of channels, including a comprehensive corporate responsibility programme.

As an integral part of General Dynamics UK, the Research Foundation exists to foster understanding of the evolving nature of technology and warfare, with particular emphasis on command and battlespace management.

The Research Foundation sponsors periodic conferences under the Whither Warfare banner to promote debate of topical issues. These conferences attract defence chiefs, defence policy makers and industry, and acknowledged experts from academia to present their views and to participate in discussion with an audience drawn from across the defence community.

With a customer centric culture, the majority of promotional activities are centred around face-to-face communication using advertising and promotion selectively. Long-standing relationships based on trust, and a firm belief that General Dynamics UK will deliver its promises on time, every time, is key.

Due to its rapid growth, promotion has been focused on the recruitment of staff. General Dynamics UK has launched a vigorous campaign to recruit and develop the best graduate engineers for its current and future business. Targeted branding and materials have supported an active presence at recruitment events and key media outlets.

Brand Values
Being dynamic – characterised by energy and effective action – is at the heart of General Dynamics UK. This manifests itself through five main aims.

Firstly, to keep customers satisfied through maintaining close contact and understanding their needs; maintaining integrity throughout the Company; taking the right action at the right time, encouraging its people to take calculated risks and being prepared to accept and learn from mistakes; working in partnership with other groups for the success of mutual goals and delivery of the best results; valuing the contribution of others – recognising and appreciating different viewpoints.

www.generaldynamics.uk.com

Things you didn't know about General Dynamics UK

In Tactical Reconnaissance Systems, General Dynamics UK pioneered the move from celluloid film to digital video-based technology – allowing imagery to be interpreted in real/near real time in the cockpit. The RAF had this system operational during the Gulf War in 1990 – the first world use of this technology.

The General Dynamics UK facilities in South Wales have been developed on the site of former coal mines and have been described by the First Minister of Wales as the 'jewel in the crown' of the regional economy.

2000	2001	2005	2006
CDC becomes General Dynamics UK, formed to support the UK MoD.	General Dynamics UK wins the Bowman contract from UK MoD worth £1.9 billion, followed in 2002 by the CIP information and data contract, bringing the total value of Bowman to £2.4 billion.	General Dynamics UK reports turnover of more than £500 million.	General Dynamics UK creates its Ground Systems division to focus on delivering the next generation of armoured fighting vehicles to the British Army.

Group 4 Securicor

Created in July 2004 through the merger of Securicor and the security businesses of Group 4 Falck, G4S is the world's largest security company, with a market value of over £2 billion, 430,000 employees and operations in over 100 countries.

Market

Worth £48 billion per year, the global market for security services is highly fragmented, with the five leading players accounting for less than a third of revenues. However, the market is consolidating as companies seek to provide a co-ordinated multi-territory service for multinational clients. This drift towards globalisation, combined with the increased threat of terrorism following 9/11, has prompted companies to invest more in security and seek a consistent service. This trend was one of the factors behind the merger of two of the industry's best-known names, Securicor of the UK and Group 4 Falck of Denmark. The resulting company, G4S is now the world's largest security company, and is leading the market in most of the territories in which it operates.

The industry is seeing strong growth outside the main markets of the US and Europe. These emerging markets now make up 20 per cent of G4S' revenue and demand is growing fast, fuelled by rising crime, expanding economies, and the privatisation of former state-owned industries. China and Russia are two key countries with strong potential for future growth in security spending.

Achievements

One of the key achievements of G4S in recent years has been to merge two of the world's largest security businesses so quickly and successfully. The ambitious marriage of the two firms, creating an entity with 430,000 employees in over 100 countries, was achieved in just 15 months, instead of the two years many expected. The resulting synergies will save the combined group £30 million per year.

Ensuring a new corporate culture was communicated and bedded down swiftly was a priority for the newly merged firm. As well as launching a new brand identity, G4S, the group has also invested in its people, including an award-winning global leadership development programme. This was designed to help high-level employees develop their leadership skills and progress to senior management positions. The programme won 'Best Executive Development Programme' at the Human Resources Excellence Awards 2006.

The group has also achieved a great deal in its community support programmes, comprising a wide range of company-supported events around the world which raise money and awareness for charities and other good causes. In 2006, the company ran events raising awareness of HIV and AIDS in Zambia, holding a Christmas party for a children's village in South Africa and a bicycle donation project in the US as well as

1906	1935	1951	1960
Sophus Falck establishes the guarding company Redningskorpset for København og Frederiksberg A/S.	In the UK, Edward Shortt creates 'Night Watch Services', a modest enterprise with four bicycle-riding guards dressed in ex-police uniforms.	'Night Guards' become known to the public as 'Security Corps'. Considered too military by the Home Office, the name is shortened to 'Securicor'.	Securicor becomes a wholly-owned subsidiary of Kensington Palace Hotel and develops into a nationwide operator in the UK with numerous branches and a radio communications network.

agreeing a major long-term strategic sponsorship arrangement with Skandia Team GBR, the Olympic gold medal winning sailing team, for the next three years.

Product

G4S is a familiar face in daily life; providing the guards we are accustomed to seeing in banks and shops, airports and events as well as transporting and delivering cash. G4S also supports the police and prison services, providing officers and electronic equipment, such as tags, to track and remotely monitor offenders.

These various lines of activity see G4S organise its business into three divisions: security services, cash services and justice services.

Recent Developments

In its first full year of trading G4S delivered impressive results, reporting an eight per cent growth in turnover and 16 per cent leap in profits to £254 million (before interest, taxation, amortisation and exceptional items). This underlines the success with which the new organisation has been brought together, while

continuing to drive growth and build a platform from which the company can move forward.

Having steered successfully through the merger, Nick Buckles, the chief executive of G4S, has ambitious plans for the group. With low debt levels, G4S is keen to expand through acquisition and recently grew its portfolio with the addition of HISEC, a Danish security alarm company, and One-Service, a diamond-shipping firm, based in the US. More acquisitions are on the horizon, which G4S hopes will fill the remaining geographical gaps and help it achieve its aim of being market leader within each sector in which it competes.

Promotion

In May 2005, G4S introduced its striking new brand identity across its global business following a major brand and culture research project involving customers and senior managers. This new brand identity was implemented across all territories by December 2006. This was a huge task for the business to undertake; consulting with customers on the new uniform style and rolling out the new uniform to its employees, rebranding the vehicle fleet and upgrading building signage. Alongside

this activity of physically rebranding the business, a Group-led project has begun to ensure that the values which support the new brand identity are lived by its people and become an everyday part of the business. With over 430,000 employees in more than 100 countries, the challenge ahead will be to ensure that the values are meaningful to all people at every level within the organisation.

Brand Values

G4S has defined its values around six pillars. In Customer Focus, it aims to understand its customers, their markets, and deliver the highest standards of service. In Expertise, it stakes its claim as the world's leading experts in security services. In Performance, it focuses on service performance for its customers, and financial performance for the organisation and its shareholders. It also aims to attract, keep and develop the Best People in the security business, and operate with an Integrity that is shared by everyone in the group. Equally, Teamwork and Collaboration is the glue that binds the organisation together.

www.g4s.com/uk

Things you didn't know about Group 4 Securicor

G4S provides Fire Protection and Emergency Response Services at Kennedy Space Centre.

Event security at major sporting events such as the Wimbledon tennis championships, PGA golf tournaments and in 2004, the Athens Olympics, is provided by G4S.

It also provides protection to 32 commercial nuclear plants in the US (46 per cent of all plants in the US).

With a market value of £2.2 billion, G4S is just outside the FTSE 100 index of the UK's most valuable companies.

Every year, in the UK alone, the group transports more than £300 billion in cash, and processes cash worth more than £25 billion.

G4S is the global leader in offender monitoring services, and is developing a new electronic tag based on satellite tracking technology.

1974	1991	2000	2004
The third generation of the Philip-Sørensen family take over the Group 4 business.	Group 4 wins the contract to manage the first privatised prison in the UK, at Wolds in Humberside.	Group 4 and Falck merge and the business is rebranded Group 4 Falck.	Group 4 Falck's security business merges with Securicor to create G4S, now the world's largest security provider.

Heathrow express   ⊗

Serving the world's busiest international airport, Heathrow Express is one of the most successful high-speed rail-air links in the world. The service carries over 15,000 passengers a day on the 15 minute journey between Heathrow Airport and central London.

Market

Every year, some 63 million passengers pass through Heathrow Airport. Compared to many other international airports, Heathrow has historically been one of the hardest to get to, with passengers travelling to and from London facing the choice of a long journey by tube, or risking traffic congestion by car or taxi.

Heathrow Express has tapped into a growing trend among world airports to offer a premium, dedicated and high-speed train service, giving passengers an easy, reliable and fast option for travelling between city centre and airport. It reaches the airport in just 15 minutes, compared to 40 minutes by London Underground, or 40-140 minutes by taxi.

The Gatwick Express, linking Victoria Station in London with Gatwick Airport, is a similar example, and, internationally, there are airport express services in Oslo, Vienna, Stockholm, Rome and Moscow. In most cases, these services compete with the city's public transport services for passengers, but they also play an important role in easing road congestion. Carrying over five million passengers per year, Heathrow Express is one of the leading airport rail links in the world.

Achievements

Since its launch in June 1998, Heathrow Express has gained market share over both the London Underground and taxi travel to the airport from central London, firmly establishing itself as a favoured route for both business and leisure passengers. The service removes approximately 3,000 journeys from the regional roads every day, and has made savings to the UK economy in terms of time, compared to the use of tube, taxi or bus, of over £444 million.

St Paul's Cathedral. London. 11.33pm July 22.

Steal the last kiss on top of the Eiffel Tower. 11.59pm. July 3.

Heathrow Express has also eased congestion on London's roads with its Taxi Share scheme, introduced in 1998. Operated in conjunction with the Licensed Taxi Drivers Association, this enables passengers to share a taxi on their onward journey from Paddington Station. The lower fares and shorter waiting times generated by the scheme allow 40-75 per cent more people to leave Paddington by taxi during peak hours. Over 505,000 travellers have shared a taxi so far, saving about 975,000 taxi miles and easing the pressure on London's rush hour.

Heathrow Express has won a host of awards, and been recognised internationally as one of the most successful airport rail services. Its marketing has

attracted accolades, with its corporate identity and branding, developed by Wolff Olins, among the most comprehensive branding and design projects ever undertaken in transportation. This was recognised when the project became the 2000 Grand Prix Winner of the Design Business Awards.

More recently, in September 2006, Heathrow Express was judged to be the Customer Service Team of the Year at the National Customer Service Awards – the UK's most prestigious award for customer service.

Its reputation for performance, reliability and punctuality within the travel trade industry helped it win the best UK airport link in the 2006 Selling Long Haul and Short Breaks and Holidays awards.

Product

Heathrow Express is a dedicated, non-stop, high-speed rail-air link operating between Heathrow Airport and central London, with a journey time of 15 minutes. There are two dedicated stations at Heathrow: Heathrow Central (serving Terminals 1, 2 and 3) and Terminal 4, which is a further 6-8 minutes away. The Inter-Terminal Transfer service also provides an additional option for passenger movement around the airport, offering free travel between the two stations.

The design of the Heathrow stations ensures that they offer customers swift, convenient access to the train service. The purpose-built trains, capable of travelling at 100mph, run between

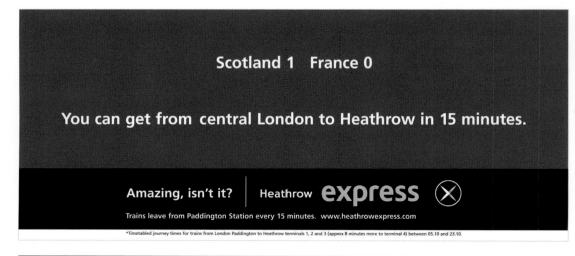

Scotland 1   France 0

You can get from central London to Heathrow in 15 minutes.

Amazing, isn't it? | Heathrow express ⊗

Trains leave from Paddington Station every 15 minutes. www.heathrowexpress.com

*Timetabled journey times for trains from London Paddington to Heathrow terminals 1, 2 and 3 (approx 8 minutes more to terminal 4) between 05.10 and 23.10.

5.10am and 11.30pm from Paddington Station 365 days a year (the only exception being on Christmas Day when the service usually runs every 30 minutes). The carriages are air-conditioned and have ergonomically designed seating, generous luggage areas and on-board TVs. There are also Quiet Zones on the trains where the use of mobile phones is prohibited and Express TV is not in use.

Heathrow Express is a member of Airport Express, a joint alliance between BAA plc and National Express Group which promotes and markets the Heathrow, Gatwick and Stanstead Express rail services. The alliance brings together the sales and marketing activities of all three operations to create a single point of contact for airlines, travel trade agents and tour operators.

Recent Developments

Heathrow Express has worked hard to translate its customer service ethos into action and, in October 2006, introduced a new team of Customer Service Station Managers. These are deployed at both Paddington Station and Heathrow Airport to ensure that customers receive an even higher level of support and service.

Heathrow Express is also working to maximise the experience of travellers on board its trains, and recently teamed up with T-Mobile to provide on-train WiFi internet access. The HotSpot service is currently being rolled out and will be fully operational in early 2007.

Heathrow Express has also recently enhanced its ground-breaking on-board TV service, Express TV. It was the first rail service in the UK to introduce on-board televisions at its launch in 1998. Created specifically to cater for the Heathrow Express passenger, it delivers a personalised bulletin covering domestic, international and business news. Express TV has been enhanced with entertainment clips, from the BBC show Top Gear and also the Comedy Channel.

Local authorities deny that speed cameras are there to make money.

You can get from central London to Heathrow in 15 minutes.

Amazing, isn't it? | Heathrow **express** ⊗

Trains leave from London Paddington Station every 15 minutes. www.heathrowexpress.com

*Timetabled journey times for trains from London Paddington to Heathrow terminals 1, 2 and 3 (approx 8 minutes more to terminal 4) between 05.10 and 23.10.

Promotion

Heathrow Express primarily uses press, outdoor and online to promote its service. For 2006/07 it has developed an advertising campaign called 'Amazing isn't it?' which highlights the convenience and speed of the Heathrow Express service. The campaign is directed at the business market, particularly within the UK, and aims to communicate the key benefits of the service. The objective is to encourage trial among prospective business passengers by focusing on the core business messages – speed, frequency, and convenience.

The campaign is based around amazing facts and includes news stories which feature in the current news agenda.

The company also uses below-the-line media to target its audience, investing in customer relationship marketing to boost frequency of use amongst its most loyal customers, and also developing marketing relationships with airlines at Heathrow Airport. Frequent travellers are the focus of joint initiatives run in conjunction with key airlines. For example, Heathrow Express is a partner within the Virgin Atlantic Flying Club programme, whereby Silver and Gold members receive an allocation of First Class upgrades to use on Heathrow Express. This has proved extremely

successful since its launch in July 2003, adding value to both brands. The partnership is communicated within membership packs, statements and email newsletters.

It also has sales agreements with various airlines, such as bmi, which sells Heathrow Express tickets in-flight.

Targeting the leisure market, Heathrow Express uses 'two for one' style promotions communicated through a number of channels including Time Out magazine, Visit Britain and airline frequent flyer programmes.

The four terminals at Heathrow Airport provide another valuable marketing platform, with strategically placed communications conveying Heathrow Express' key benefits and steering customers in the direction of the Heathrow Express platforms.

Promotions also play an important part, as with a new product called 'Carnet'. This offers loyal travellers 12 single tickets for the price of 11, in a pocket-sized wallet. It runs other promotions in its advertising and in partner airlines' in-flight promotions.

Brand Values

Heathrow Express' key brand values are speed, frequency and certainty. Recent research has shown that these are the benefits of the service that are most recalled by customers.

For both business and leisure customers, Heathrow Express aims to provide the high levels of comfort and customer service that air travellers have come to expect.

However, different aspects of the brand's personality are highlighted for the business and consumer markets. For the business traveller, the brand is portrayed as fast, frequent, reliable and convenient. When speaking to the leisure market, the brand is reflected as not being overly formal or austere while being fast, reliable, convenient, approachable, and family friendly.

www.heathrowexpress.co.uk

Heathrow **express** ⊗

Don't miss a minute

Downhillt to Davos. 2.47pm, Dec 21.

Heathrow Express is your fastest way to and from Heathrow Airport, and you'll find plenty of luggage space for your snow gear. Trains leave London Paddington Station every 15 minutes and reach Heathrow 15 minutes* later. So if you want to travel in comfort and arrive in plenty of time, take the Express.

Booking is quick and easy too. Just visit www.heathrowexpress.com

*Timetabled journey times. 8 minutes more to Terminal 4. First and last trains subject to different timings. See website for full timetable.

Timing is everything

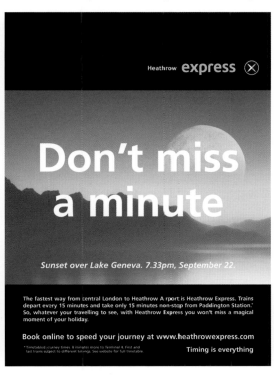

Heathrow **express** ⊗

Don't miss a minute

Sunset over Lake Geneva. 7.33pm, September 22.

The fastest way from central London to Heathrow Airport is Heathrow Express. Trains depart every 15 minutes and take only 15 minutes non-stop from Paddington Station. So, whatever your travelling to see, with Heathrow Express you won't miss a magical moment of your holiday.

Book online to speed your journey at www.heathrowexpress.com

*Timetabled journey times. 8 minutes more to Terminal 4. First and last trains subject to different timings. See website for full timetable.

Timing is everything

Things you didn't know about Heathrow Express

Every year, almost one million miles are travelled by Heathrow Express, the equivalent to almost four times the distance to the moon or 37 times around the world.

Since the service was launched in June 1998, it has carried almost 30 million people.

There is a special Meeter/Greeter fare for those travelling to the airport to see friends and family off, or to meet them on arrival.

1987	1991	1998	2001
The UK Government commissions the Heathrow Access Surface Study, concluding that a main line rail link from Paddington would provide the best option for increasing public transport to Heathrow.	The Heathrow Express Railways Act gives BAA the power to construct the Heathrow Express.	Heathrow Express is officially launched by the Prime Minister, Tony Blair.	Heathrow Express places an order for five new carriages, costing a total of £6.5 million.

IBM has a fundamental belief in progress, science and the improvability of the human condition through innovation. With its unique capabilities, IBM sees it as its responsibility to create opportunity and prosperity for businesses, industries, society and the world.

Market

Gone are the days when cost-cutting alone would deliver competitiveness. Today's business leaders must look for new ways to excel. For many, technology is the key to enhanced success, fuelling rapid growth in the global business IT market. Consulting firm IDC estimates that the market will be worth £720 billion by the end of 2009, with banking, manufacturing and Government the biggest technology spenders.

IBM has leveraged both its technology and business acumen to become a leading player in this IT services industry. In this high-end field of technology services and consultancy, it is about understanding businesses, how they work and delivering real value to the client's bottom line.

Achievements

During 2005, IBM again gained an impressive list of innovation credentials. These include receiving more US patents than any other company – an impressive 1,100 patents more. This is the eighth consecutive year that IBM was awarded more than 2,000 US patents. However, it is the results that IBM achieves for its customers that make it the world's third most valuable brand – and gaining in value each year (Source: Business Week, Interbrand 2005).

The company's innovations benefit more than its customers, however. With a fundamental belief in progress, science and the improvability of the human condition, IBM sees it as its responsibility to create opportunity and prosperity for businesses, industries, society and the world. Each year, IBM Corporate Community Relations invests

over US$140 million globally in a range of large scale, global programmes focusing primarily on innovative uses of technology in educational contexts to help raise standards of achievement.

For instance, IBM recently announced that two advocacy groups, The Human Rights Campaign and Gay Men's Health Crisis, are now part of its new research effort to help battle AIDS using the massive computational power of the World Community Grid.

Product

IBM's products span servers and systems, workstations, data storage, semiconductors, software and printing systems. It is also the world leader in business/technology consulting. IBM's broad suite of business solutions are designed to

what makes you ✳ **special?**

innovation for new business models **IBM**

1924	**1935**	**1952**	**1980**	**1981**	**1993**
The International Business Machines Corporation is established by Thomas Watson, providing companies with the latest in typewriters and calculating machines.	When the new Social Security Act requires the US Government to keep employment records, only IBM is able to meet the huge demand for punch card data-processors.	IBM develops a range of mainframes, compatible with multiple printers and drives as well as other peripherals, establishing IBM as an industry leader.	IBM Ireland sets up an international software development centre, one of only four in Europe.	The IBM Personal Computer is unveiled and becomes an overnight sensation.	IBM Global Services is launched.

Centre Court: 6-0 7-6 6-7 3-6 0-0 (30 - 15)

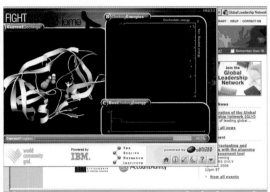

what makes you * special?

innovation for new ideas IBM.

integrate hardware, software, business consulting and IT services into answering the needs of clients worldwide.

Here are examples of what this innovation-focused approach has achieved:

Facing increasing pressure to raise productivity and cut drug development costs, pharmaceutical leader Bayer was determined to bring new drugs to market faster. Working with IBM Global Business Services, the company replaced its in-house Electronic Data Capture (EDC) application with Rave™, a global EDC system for collecting and managing trial data from Medidata Solutions Worldwide. This reduced the time spent gathering data from weeks to near real-time and made clinical trial information processing more efficient, so drugs were developed quicker.

The All England Lawn Tennis Club hosts one of the world's most important sporting events, The Championships at Wimbledon. For the past 17 years, IBM has worked with the Club to help it meet increasing business demands and to optimise revenue streams through e-commerce and increase the efficiency with which The Championships are organised and run. The result is that more courtside statistics, analysis and insights are available each year, and tennis fans around the world are brought closer to the action.

Recent Developments

During 2006, IBM announced plans to acquire three software companies: FileNet, MRO Software and Webify. As well as bolstering its sofware business, IBM has also been building its IT services portfolio with the recent addition of the online security firm, Internet Security Systems.

This investment strategy is designed to grow IBM's profits by creating a product portfolio that

1995	2006
IBM makes network computing – later to be called 'e-business' – the company's overarching strategy.	IBM celebrates its 50th anniversary in Ireland.

includes strong software and consulting revenues, as well as IBM's heritage of product.

Promotion

Between 1993 and 2005, IBM climbed from the 282nd position in Interbrand's league of the world's most valuable brands to third.

It achieved this by making huge strides in its marketing. In 1993, with the company using 70 different advertising agencies, IBM's brand identity had become severely eroded. To rectify this, IBM consolidated its communications into a single network, Ogilvy & Mather, which developed its first global advertising campaign.

'Solutions for a small planet' ran in 47 countries and 26 languages, helping reposition IBM as a market-focused, service-orientated solutions provider.

As IBM became aware of the enormous benefits the internet could provide to businesses, the company's solutions and communications had to reflect this, resulting in its second integrated global campaign, alerting and educating the market about the potential of 'e-business'.

In 2006, the 'what makes you special?' campaign was launched, establishing the need for businesses to start thinking differently about innovation, and weaving it into their thinking, their products, and their people.

Brand Values

A core value for IBM is that innovation matters. IBM has learned how and where to apply innovation to

help businesses get results. As companies realise that their continued success depends on re-thinking their approach to innovation, the real role of technology is to enable business transformation. An ability to identify and deliver this has driven IBM's own restructuring, with IBM Global Services aligned to meet specific customer requirements.

www.ibm.com/uk

Things you didn't know about IBM

In 1996, as IBM scientists experimented with ways to add ever more processing power to a microchip, they used the tip of a scanning tunnelling microscope (STM) to form the letters 'IBM' out of 35 individual atoms. The STM has since evolved into the IBM Atomic Force Microscope (AFM), an essential tool of the nanotech era.

The organisation's most high-flying intranet is 220 miles above our heads, in the International Space Station. IBM has been computing in space since Explorer I in 1958 – participating in the Mercury, Gemini and Apollo missions, as well as the Mars Rover exexpedition.

IBM recycles 96 per cent of its computer equipment worldwide.

INVESTORS IN PEOPLE

Investors in People delivers business improvement through people, by setting a benchmark for world-class practice in matching what people can do and are motivated to do, with what the organisation needs them to do. Designed to advance the performance of organisations through their people, Investors in People now offers two directly linked leading business improvement tools, the Investors in People Standard and Profile.

Market

Investors in People is committed to providing every UK employer with the opportunity to unlock the potential of their people across all sectors and sizes of company. Investors in People is used by over 60,000 organisations across the public and private sector, employing one third of the UK workforce (including 52 of The Sunday Times '100 Best Companies to Work For'), and has been exported successfully to 27 countries across the globe.

It competes in the marketplace of both standards and HR consultancy working to provide tailored business solutions, however in the current market there is no other tool that is a direct competitor.

Achievements

Investors in People has recently joined together with the Department of Health to examine the

emerging subject of health and wellbeing within the workplace and is currently piloting support for organisations. The Investors in People Standard already provides the foundation for emotional and psychological wellbeing at work within its current criteria. The current developments are therefore seen as a natural extension to the Investors in People Standard.

In the last five years the marketing of Investors in People has focused on readdressing the perception that Investors in People is just a training tool. The Standard has been repositioned as a business improvement tool that delivers real bottom line benefits and challenges organisations to evaluate exactly the benefit to them.

Investors in People sponsors The Sunday Times '100 Best Companies to Work For' as both celebrate the very best organisations in the UK. Currently 50 per cent of the list are already working with the Standard.

Product

Adopted widely throughout the UK and internationally, the Standard and Profile are flexible frameworks which organisations of any size or sector can work with. Investors in People helps businesses become more effective by developing and supporting best practice and ensuring they are getting the right return on investment as well as stimulating and challenging organisations to continually strive for improvement.

Investors in People's Profile builds on the breadth and depth of the Standard, but goes further to embrace a wider range of people management issues, exploring them in considerable depth. Through Profile, organisations can gain a deeper understanding of how they are performing against extensive criteria. It allows organisations to continuously improve through taking an in depth look at their strengths and weaknesses and also benchmarks an

1990		**1991**		**1993**	**1995**
The Employment Department is given the task to develop a national Standard which sets out a level of good practice for training and development to achieve business goals; Investors in People is created.	Investors in People is launched by Sir Brian Wolfson, David Gwyther and Sir Christopher Hogg on 18th October at the TEC Conference in Brighton.	Consultancies such as KPMG, Dent Lee Witte and Coopers & Lybrand become involved in testing the rigour of the Standard and its assessment processes in real company situations.	The first 28 'Investor in People' organisations – both large and small – are celebrated at the formal launch of Investors in People on 16th October 1991.	Investors in People UK is formed as a business-led non-departmental public body. The following year the first Investors in People week is launched.	The first review of the Standard is carried out. An operation is also established in Australia.

Delivering growth through people
Using Investors in People to improve performance

Taking your organisation further
An overview of the Profile framework

Unlock your organisation's potential
An overview of the Standard framework

organisation's performance against others. This enables organisations to prioritise their targets and raise the performance of the business.

Recent Developments

The business environment is continually changing and it is important that the Standard moves with the times and remains relevant to industry. To ensure this is achieved it is revised at least every five years. In 2004, following an 18 month long consultation and development process, a newly revised Standard was launched during Investors in People Week.

The revised Standard has been widely welcomed for the way in which it tests performance more fully, especially on issues of leadership and management. It is also seen as being more robust and a relevant and accessible business improvement tool. This version places an increased

emphasis on the involvement of employees within the organisation and on maximising their potential.

Profile was also redesigned and relaunched in November 2004 as a sophisticated business improvement tool. Profile is based directly on the structure and principles of the Standard, but its assessment process goes much deeper and probes more extensively into the way organisations operate, providing continued stretch and growth, benchmarking against world-class best practice.

Investors in People recognises the importance of Human Capital Management and has brought together a group of distinguished individuals to establish whether there is a generic set of human capital measures which would be relevant to most employers. It is hoped that over time these measures will form part of assessments against the Standard, encouraging organisations to continue to evaluate their practices.

Promotion

Investors in People's marketing strategy focuses on the promotion and positioning of the brand as a business improvement tool.

Investors in People carries out extensive direct mail and online campaigns that are targeted to different sectors, organisation size and business issues.

Investors in People thrives from word of mouth through trusted respected sources and has two programmes recognising the value of advocacy – The Champions Programme and The Ambassadors Programme.

Champions disseminate and share best practice with organisations of all sizes and within all sectors interested in Investors in People, engaging in other promotional activity to extend

understanding of the Standard and its benefits. A total of 33 organisations have now gained the prestigious status of Investors in People Champion.

Ambassadors promote and represent Investors in People through personal experiences and recommendations and strive to inspire other businesses and organisations. They take part in a series of high profile events and speaking platforms from a wide variety of sectors.

Investors in People carries out research which is focused on key topical business issues and is regarded as a credible voice in the media, enabling them to further develop and encourage organisations to take a business improvement through people approach.

Brand Values

Investors in People aims to ensure that its brand is inspiring and energising. It is distinctive in the marketplace but straightforward, with a proven framework for delivering business improvement through people, which is universally applicable.

www.investorsinpeople.co.uk

Things you didn't know about Investors in People

An assessment against the Standard requires no paperwork, as assessments are conducted through a series of interviews.

Reviews may take place anytime within a three year schedule and are always client focused and linked to key business priorities.

Investors in People operates in over 18 different languages, assessments have taken place in 70 countries and any organisation can be assessed worldwide.

Currently only one organisation has the prestigious result of achieving the top score of all level fours when assessed against the Profile framework, therefore demonstrating world-class practice in their people management.

1998	**2000**	**2004**	**2006**
Five international pilot projects get underway.	The Ambassador programme is launched.	The Champions programme is launched.	Investors in People celebrates 15 years of improving business and the first organisation achieves the top score of all level fours when assessed against Profile.
	Two years later the Profile framework is launched.	The revised Standard and Profile are launched.	

The Institute of Directors (IoD) is one of the UK's leading business membership organisations, and has branches throughout the world. The recent edition of hubs in Paris and Brussels has seen the IoD expand its physical presence internationally. The organisation has approximately 55,000 individual members from companies of all sizes, types and geographical locations.

Market

The IoD draws its membership from across the business spectrum – from media to manufacturing, e-business to the public and voluntary sectors. Its network reaches into every corner of business leadership, from the largest public companies to the smallest private firms.

The majority of members come from small and medium-sized enterprises (SMEs), which reflects the business demographic of the country as a whole. However, the organisation also has members on the boards of 92 per cent of firms listed on the FTSE 100.

Membership of the IoD is on an individual rather than corporate basis. Championing professionalism in the boardroom, the IoD offers a wide range of training and development services designed to ensure that individual directors are fully equipped to fulfil their role, and drive the success of their organisations. Overall, it is committed to ensuring that good practice is being observed by directors, no matter how large or small their organisation.

Achievements

The IoD has been running courses for directors since the early 1980s. The success and popularity of these professional development products increases year on year; in 2006 the IoD filled 3,110 course places and successfully developed 500 individuals to Chartered Directors through its specially developed programmes.

The IoD runs a full programme of business events, attracting high-profile speakers, including Jack Welch, Ronald Reagan, Sir Richard Branson, Bill Gates and Baroness Thatcher.

Its flagship event, the Annual Convention, has been held at the Royal Albert Hall since 1961 and is the biggest and one of the most important business events in the UK.

The IoD policy team is highly successful and influential in representing the views of its members to Government and in providing comment on significant events in business. It responds to more than 80 Government consultation documents a year, which help in shaping the business environment.

Product

The IoD has a wide range of products, including conferences, events, professional development, hospitality services, information and advisory services and also a policy unit which lobbies on behalf of the business community.

The IoD Policy Unit regularly meets with senior politicians and civil servants to discuss key issues facing IoD members in the current economic and political climate. The IoD's role is to represent the views of its members and to bring about change, not to support one particular political party.

The IoD takes its role as a centre for professional development very seriously, running an extensive range of courses, development programmes, and seminars. These equip directors with the all-round skills, knowledge and understanding needed to direct an organisation from a strategic perspective.

The IoD one-day business conferences and summits are designed to react swiftly to market trends and provide up to the minute information on key business issues. Expert speakers and case study presenters from a range of organisations are selected to share their knowledge and experience.

The organisation also runs breakfast seminars, offering a practical way to learn about more specific issues.

Altogether, the IoD holds over 1,000 events a year, including its Annual Convention and a variety of conferences, sporting dinners and local networking events.

1903	1921	1950	1976	1983	1999
The first group of senior directors meet to form the first 'Council of the IoD', responding to concerns about the creation of new company legislation in 1900-1901.	The forerunner to Director magazine, entitled Advance, is launched.	The IoD holds its first annual conference, moving to the Royal Albert Hall in 1961.	The IoD moves to its current headquarters, 116 Pall Mall.	Worldwide membership reaches 33,000 spread across 90 countries with 29 branches in the UK.	Approval is granted to establish a professional qualification for directors.

AFTERHOURS

cars | travel | wine | sports | antiques | interiors   winter 2004/5

CHRISTMAS GIFT SPECIAL MR & MRS SMITH IN
EUROPE MODERN DESIGN CLASSICS LUNCH WITH
CARLUCCIO WHERE TO SKI DAMON HILL 25 THINGS
THAT MAKE LIFE WORTH LIVING

Hospitality is also a very big part of the IoD's core product offering. The facilities available in its two Pall Mall premises in London include a restaurant, brasserie, wine bar, cocktail bar, rooms available for functions and meeting rooms. The IoD also has a nationwide network of premises where members have free access to meeting space with their guests.

Recent Developments

The IoD has introduced a development programme tailored specifically to the football industry. Developed in partnership with Soccerex, the Football Business Direction Programme aims to provide directors within the industry worldwide with specific knowledge and skills to succeed in this high growth and truly global market.

In order to better equip directors who are focusing on international market trends and business opportunities, the IoD recently launched its International Insight Series. Benefiting from the experience, practical knowledge and insights of high-level speakers, events to date have focused on China, India and Eastern Europe. Previous speakers include Lord Bilimoria, the founder and chief executive of Cobra Beer and HE Mr Kamalesh Sharma, High Commissioner of India.

To ensure the IoD is reflecting the up-to-date views of its members the Policy Panel was launched in April 2006. This is a group of IoD members who have expressed an interest in helping the organisation formulate policy and influence Government.

Promotion

The IoD promotes itself through a comprehensive portfolio of media, keeping members and non-members abreast of major developments in the Institute's product portfolio.

Publications are an important tool, with Director magazine having become a highly regarded and authoritative business journal for over 60 years. Circulated to all IoD members and to thousands of subscribers, it attracts high-profile contributions and comment from business leaders around the world.

Recently this has been joined by a sister title, After Hours. This is designed in recognition of directors' lives outside work, offering content that reflects members' attitudes, lifestyles and aspirations. Alongside features on travel, cars, watches and wine, it also runs editorial of more general interest, including profiles of unusual personalities.

The organisation also uses email to the full by building an email community on an opt-in basis and sending out the monthly 'e-News' bulletin.

Direct mail is an important marketing channel, with high-quality literature designed in-house and instantly recognisable under the IoD umbrella brand.

Perhaps one of the most significant promotional tools for the Institute is public relations. The IoD distributes regular press statements on a variety of business issues. This not only represents members' views on relevant issues, but also generates local and national coverage in all media on a daily basis, keeping the IoD's brand and identity in the forefront of the business arena.

Brand Values

Lord Avebury, the IoD's first president, defined the Institute's objective in 1904 as: "...to protect the interests of directors. It is much more important that it should enable directors to carry out the great responsibilities which they have undertaken; that it should be the centre from which they might obtain information upon various points of interest; that it should be the meeting ground on which they might consult together."

This ethos still holds true today, but to enhance the Institute's perceived relevance in the 21st century, the IoD now builds and promotes its brand on the following cornerstone values: professionalism, energetic, commercial and enterprising. This is especially relevant in the boardroom, where the IoD works to ensure that directors are aware of all their duties and responsibilities and are equipped to uphold them.

The brand's positioning is reflective of British business: incorporating past successes with innovation in an increasingly global context.

www.iod.com

Pierluigi Collina

Things you didn't know about IoD

During World War II the late King Haakon and senior officers of the Norwegian Forces used what is now the restaurant of 116 Pall Mall to hold their meetings whilst they were in exile. This is now commemorated with a plaque in the corner of the restaurant.

At the 1991 Annual Convention, Gerald Ratner famously said: "We even sell a pair of earrings for under £1, which some people say is cheaper than a prawn sandwich from Marks & Spencers, but the earrings probably won't last as long!"

The IoD premises were used as the setting for scenes in the 1982 film Gandhi, starring Ben Kingsley, as well as the well loved ITV series Foyles War.

| In March 1999 the IoD is granted approval from the Privy Council to establish a professional qualification for directors, called Chartered Director; it is endorsed by the Financial Reporting Council, Deutsche Bank and the Centre for Tomorrow's Company. | **2001** IoD 123, at 123 Pall Mall, is opened by Tony Blair. New regional premises open in Bristol. | **2004** IoD Paris is launched, followed two years later by a hub in Brussels. | **2007** The IoD launches a new qualification for directors in the football industry, the Football Business Direction Programme. |

JCB sells construction equipment to 150 countries around the world. It has 17 plants on four continents, employs over 6,300 people and sold more than 45,000 machines in 2005. It is now set for greater expansion, with the opening of its first factory in China.

Market

JCB is the fourth largest manufacturer of earth moving and construction equipment in the world.

It is the biggest privately-owned company in the market and the premier manufacturer of construction equipment in Europe. The company's iconic backhoe loader – the machine that JCB is most famous for – is the clear leader in the world market.

JCB sold more than 45,000 machines in 2005 – an increase of over 20 per cent on 2004. By 2010, the company hopes to double its sales to US$4.5 billion.

With a 9.6 per cent market share, JCB is close to its business objective of achieving 10 per cent of the world market for construction equipment. This is no small task, considering there are over 500 manufacturers in the industry.

Achievements

JCB is one of Britain's biggest industrial success stories. Over its 60-year history, JCB has won more than 50 major awards for engineering excellence, exports, design, marketing, management and for its care for the environment. Among them are 18 Queen's Awards for Technology and Export

Achievement, the latest being two Queen's Awards for Enterprise in the International Trade category in 2005 for JCB Earthmovers and JCB Heavy Products.

The company invented one of the most recognisable pieces of heavy machinery, the backhoe loader, also known as a 'digger'. This was first introduced by JCB in 1953. Since then it has become the brand leader virtually the world over and its yellow machines are a familiar part of the landscape and language. The JCB name ever appears in the Oxford English Dictionary and has become one of the most recognisable of all B2B brands.

Another major achievement was the introduction of the Loadall machine in 1977. This revolutionised aspects of the building industry, allowing bricks to be lifted in pallets instead of being carried in a hod by a labourer. JCB also developed the first and still the only road-legal high-speed tractor, the Fastrac, winning numerous awards, including the Prince of Wales Award for Innovation in 1995.

Another design classic is the Teletruk – the only forklift truck not to use cumbersome double masts at the front.

JCB's achievements in design have translated into business success, with 2005 being a record year. Pre-tax profits rose to £110 million as JCB's global market share climbed from 8.6 to 9.6 per cent. The company's sales turnover increased by 23 per cent to £1.42 billion, and machine production reached 45,000 units.

Product

JCB manufactures 257 different machines, exporting 75 per cent of its UK-made products to 150 countries.

Its wide range includes: backhoe loaders; loadall telescopic handlers; tracked and wheeled excavators; wheeled loading shovels; articulated dump trucks; rough terrain fork lifts; mini excavators; robot skid steers loaders; JCB Vibromax compaction equipment and groundcare equipment.

In addition, for agricultural markets, the company produces a range of telescopic handlers and the unique Fastrac tractor. JCB also manufactures the Teletruk forklift for the industrial sector.

JCB continues to increase the proportion of major parts manufactured in-house. In 2004, JCB's own off-highway diesel engine, the JCB

1945	1953	1964	1970	1979	1986
Joseph Cyril Bamford (Mr JCB) starts his business manufacturing a tipping trailer, made with a £1 welding set in a lock-up garage he rented in Uttoxeter, Staffordshire. He sold the product at the local market for £45.	The backhoe loader becomes the first product to carry the JCB logo. It is now universally known as a 'JCB'.	The JCB Dancing Diggers give their first performance.	The company sets up an American operation at White Marsh, near Baltimore, USA.	JCB commences production of backhoe loaders in India, at a plant in Ballabgarh, near Dehli.	'JCB' enters the Collins English Dictionary as an eponymous noun. The 100,000th backhoe loader rolls off the production line in Rocester.

DIESELMAX, went into production at a new plant in Derbyshire, following an investment of £80 million. The company already produces its own axles, transmissions, cabs, chassis, booms, hydraulic rams and excavator arms.

Recent Developments

2006 is an important year for JCB, marking the start of production of backhoe loaders and mini excavators at the company's newest manufacturing plant in Shanghai, China. Local production will ensure the company is well positioned to take advantage of the massive potential of the Chinese construction equipment market.

JCB is also expanding in India, where it is the clear market leader and has been manufacturing backhoe loaders at a plant in Ballabgarh, near Dehli, since 1979. The company recently invested US$50 million, opening a second factory in Pune, strategically located close to the port of Mumbai. The new factory has been built to produce excavators, while the original Pune plant has been expanded for the production of fabricated components.

In addition, JCB India is upgrading its Ballabgarh factory to include a new paint plant with the latest powder coat technology, conveyor production line system and new transmissions assembly.

Throughout its history, JCB has grown organically but, in 2005, it acquired the German compaction equipment producer, Vibromax.

The firm's compaction products are now being sold throughout the world under the JCB Vibromax name, and production at the Gatersleben plant, near Leipzig, has been boosted and new machines introduced. The JCB DIESELMAX engine now powers the VM115D/PD soil compactor machine.

JCB has a history of donating construction equipment to

grief stricken areas, and at the beginning of 2005, the company donated over £1 million worth of machines to help the relief effort in the wake of the Asian Tsunami disaster. JCB machines were employed in southern India, Sri Lanka and Indonesia. In the same year it also joined the global relief effort in India and Pakistan by donating over £500,000 worth of machines.

Promotion

JCB has a rich heritage of striking promotional activities, setting new standards in heavy equipment marketing.

As well as a tradition of award-winning advertising in the industry trade press, the company is also famous for its customer events featuring the 'JCB Dancing Diggers', in which backhoe loaders display their technical flexibility by 'performing' synchronised stunts to music.

Likewise, the company enjoyed huge PR success when 'The JCB Song' by Lizlopi rocketed to number one in the UK charts in December 2005.

But perhaps the most breathtaking example of JCB's dynamic approach to marketing was in August 2006, when it broke the world land speed record for diesel-powered cars with the JCB DIESELMAX car at a speed of 350.092mph. The car, developed in less than 12 months, was powered by two specially-modified versions of the JCB DIESELMAX engine. Breaking the record was the

ultimate demonstration of the engine's extreme performance and highlights JCB's commitment to world-class engineering.

Brand Values

The 'DNA' of JCB's brand is hard work, and the company's machines work hard to meet the demands put on them by customers.

JCB has also always been known for its attention to detail. A JCB machine is seen as world-class, innovative, high performance, strong and stylish. JCB carries out business with a sense of style and, being family-owned, JCB has a great sense of community and pays particular attention to helping those who are underprivileged.

It is also committed to protecting the environment. All JCB's factories aim to eliminate the releases of pollution, promote high standards of energy management and to prevent, recycle or safely dispose of waste.

Plus, every JCB machine is designed for maximum energy efficiency and minimum environmental impact.

www.jcb.co.uk

1996	2000	2004	2006
JCB becomes the 'World No.1' for backhoe loaders. A new HQ for JCB Sales Asia Pacific is established in Singapore. The 200,000th backhoe loader is driven off the production line by Sir Anthony Bamford.	The first machines to be manufactured in the US are produced in a new plant in Savannnah, Georgia. £1 million is raised by JCB employees for the NSPCC and matched by Sir Anthony.	Production of the JCB 'DIESELMAX' diesel engine begins at the Derbyshire plant. JCB donates £1 million worth of machines for relief work in devastated Asian Tsunami regions.	JCB opens its first plant in China. The 'JCB DIESELMAX car', powered by JCB's own diesel engine, breaks the world land-speed record for a diesel powered car – at 350.092mph.

JONES LANG
LASALLE®

Jones Lang LaSalle is a global leader in real estate services and money management. Its 22,000 employees provide comprehensive, integrated expertise across financial services, transactions, consulting, property and facilities management. The firm serves clients locally, regionally and globally covering over 450 markets worldwide. Its client roster includes many of the leading international real estate occupiers, investors and developers along with governments, public authorities and charitable organisations.

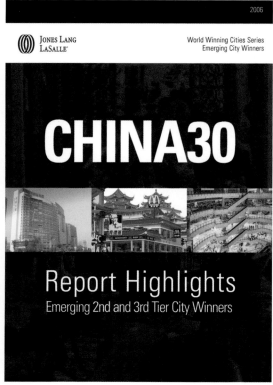

Market

The Real Estate Services sector has grown significantly in recent years, fuelled by a rise in demand from both owners and occupiers.

The increasingly global nature of big business has made occupiers' real estate choices more complex, with issues such as how to use real estate to improve your competitive position, if and where to offshore business operations, and whether to own or sell and leaseback real estate assets all having major P&L and balance sheet implications.

Forward-thinking companies are now looking to their real estate to deliver cost savings through more cost effective use of space, location and procurement and to deliver competitive advantage

in how their customers and staff experience their brand; as well as maximising value to shareholders.

In their search for maximum returns at acceptable risk levels, real estate investors are broadening their horizons and considering opportunities in new geographies and asset classes.

Large users of commercial real estate services continue to demonstrate a preference for working with single source providers able to provide seamless, integrated services and expert advice across local, regional and global markets.

To meet rising demand and increasingly complex client needs, the Real Estate Services sector has witnessed significant consolidation in

recent years, with a number of high-profile mergers and acquisitions of smaller players taking place.

Achievements

Jones Lang LaSalle prides itself on its integrated platform. The firm continues to grow both organically and through acquisitions, focusing on merger partners with a strong cultural fit who also place 'putting clients first' at the heart of their operations.

During 2005 the firm's global revenues totalled US$1.39 billion – up 19 per cent on the previous year and 55 per cent above 2001 levels. In the same year Jones Lang LaSalle completed capital markets sales and acquisitions, debt financings, and equity placements on assets and portfolios valued at US$43 billion. In addition, it completed agency leasing transactions of approximately 8.63 million sq m and had 54 million sq m of space under management.

Over 22,500 valuations, with an aggregate value of approximately US$286 billion, were performed in 2005. By the end of the year, the firm's money management business LaSalle Investment Management had approximately US$40 billion of assets under management.

In 2006 Jones Lang LaSalle gained a Top 50 Company listing in The Times 'Where Women Want to Work' Survey. In January 2007 Jones Lang LaSalle was named one of the Fortune '100 Best Companies to Work For' as well as one of the Forbes '400 Best Big Companies' – the only real estate services and money management company to earn either title.

Product

Jones Lang LaSalle takes pride in being the single source provider of solutions for its clients' full range of real estate needs in the UK and throughout the world. Its services include:

1783	1945	Late 1950s	1965	1968	1970/80s
Jones Lang Wootton (JLW) auctioneers is founded by Richard Winstanley.	With records destroyed and post-war confusion over boundaries and ownership, JLW locates the owners of small land parcels, securing licenses for development in the process.	The firm is established in Asia Pacific with an office in Australia; the operation expanded across the region including New Zealand, Singapore, Malaysia & Hong Kong.	The first office on the continent opens in Brussels, followed by other key European cities including Amsterdam, Paris and Frankfurt.	IDC Real Estate is founded in El Paso, Texas.	IDC changes its name to LaSalle Partners in 1977 and grows rapidly throughout this period. Jones Lang Wootton continues its expansion in North America, where it opens a New York office in 1975.

outsourcing; space acquisition and disposition for commercial, industrial and retail property; facilities and property management; project and development services; consulting; agency leasing; buying and selling properties; corporate finance; capital markets; hotel advisory; and valuations.

Jones Lang LaSalle is committed to building long term client relationships. The firm examines clients' needs and objectives before recommending solutions. This approach has built trust and forged enduring relationships with satisfied customers.

This focus on client satisfaction is backed by its 'best in class' research capabilities. Jones Lang LaSalle has a team of highly-qualified professionals who track and interpret market forces and economic trends that affect the real estate and money management businesses.

Recent Developments

Jones Lang LaSalle has seen significant but measured growth in recent times. For example, in the second half of 2006 the firm announced the creation of both an Indirect Investments team and a Derivatives team within Jones Lang LaSalle Corporate Finance. The team is focused on: providing both buy-side and sell-side advice on unlisted indirect investments to Jones Lang LaSalle's client base; executing the sale and purchase of units in the secondary markets; and raising funds from major UK and international investors in the primary markets for property investment vehicles.

In January 2006, the firm acquired Spaulding & Slye, a privately held US real estate services and investment company with offices in Boston and Washington. In May 2006, Rogers Chapman, a privately-held real estate services company with offices in west London and the Thames Valley, was acquired. Further to which, in September 2006 Jones Lang LaSalle acquired RSP Group, the leading Dubai-based real estate investment and advisory firm in the Middle East, adding immediate scale in the Middle East and North Africa region. Expansion continued in January 2007 when the firm opened its first Romanian office in Bucharest.

Promotion

Jones Lang LaSalle's primary marketing focus is on creating a positive client experience by delivering superior results and consistently high levels of customer service. A comprehensive client

relationship management programme is in place and a wide spectrum of marketing and communications initiatives are delivered to ensure that clients receive the dedicated attention and relevant information that benefits them the most.

The firm hosts client events annually throughout EMEA, centring around both strategic business content and industry networking. Playing an active part in moving the industry forward, Jones Lang LaSalle people invest time and energy into initiatives such as CORENET and the Urban Land Institute.

At both its own 'Leading Edge' seminars and external industry events such as The Financial Times Real Estate Conference and the Global Real Estate Institute Summit, Jones Lang LaSalle brings an array of specialists to the podium. The firm's intent is to keep clients and future clients ahead of the curve.

Jones Lang LaSalle co-sponsored the Gala Dinner Drinks Reception alongside the Mayor of London's Office, Transport for London and the London Development Agency. Pictured below are John Stephen with Ken Livingstone, Mayor of London and Richard Lambert, Director General of the CBI at the CBI Conference Gala Dinner 2006.

The firm's strong media relations capabilities help to deliver its brand message. The firm's views on local and international trends are regularly

sought, given the depth and breadth of its real estate business and the multitude of markets in which it operates. Its proactive approach and belief in sharing knowledge has resulted in powerful relationships with the local, regional and international media.

Jones Lang LaSalle's thought leadership profile has been built on years of delivering cutting-edge research and by providing timely and insightful opinion pieces enhances the contribution it makes to delivering news.

Brand Values

Jones Lang LaSalle's brand has always stood for the highest standards of knowledge and expertise. Its emphasis on training and development as well as industry-leading research capability has gained it a reputation as the 'teaching hospital' of the industry.

The firm has a rich heritage of providing advice to clients around the world. With its culture of teamwork and collaboration it leverages deep internal resources to help deliver client results. Its combined assets – talented people, extensive research resources, financial strength, technology platforms, reward and recognition programmes, ethics and its supporting organisational infrastructure – constitute the competitive advantage of Jones Lang LaSalle.

www.joneslanglasalle.co.uk

Photographer (far right image): James O'Jenkins

Things you didn't know about Jones Lang LaSalle

Jones Lang LaSalle created the first register of buildings in London following the blitz of World War II, identifying owners and paving the way for post-war redevelopment of the City.

The firm has been actively involved in advising on three out of the last four Olympics.

It was one of the first Real Estate firms to open a Research and Information function in 1979 and the first International Real Estate Services firm to open an office in Moscow.

Jones Lang LaSalle has established a global Energy & Sustainability board to provide leadership in energy use and sustainability in commercial buildings.

Late 1990s	1998	1999	2000s
Strategic acquisitions of Alex Brown Kleinwort Benson Realty Advisors Corporation; CIN Property Management Ltd; the Galbreath Company; and project management business of the Satulah Group Inc take place.	LaSalle Partners acquires COMPASS Management and Leasing, Inc and the US retail property management business of Lend Lease Real Estate Investments, Inc.	LaSalle Partners and Jones Lang Wootton merge to form Jones Lang LaSalle.	Jones Lang LaSalle continues to grow organically through the acquisition of carefully chosen companies who complement the existing culture and enhance the firm's ability to service clients.

Kall Kwik has undergone a radical transformation since it was founded in 1978. It is no longer the familiar high street shop for everyday copy and print requirements. It now serves the communications requirements for businesses across the country with design to delivery™ (D2D) solutions. With nearly 160 locations, which generate revenue of over £65 million a year, Kall Kwik's D2D proposition is a huge expansion beyond printing and copying to include creative design, direct mail, exhibition and advertising services and marketing solutions.

Market

In the UK, over £1 billion is spent every year on design, printing and copying services. Generally described as the 'print on demand' sector, Kall Kwik is the biggest player, with a market share of seven per cent. It is a large and highly fragmented sector, with Kall Kwik competing against a wide range of other service providers, ranging from traditional small quick printers, to larger commercial printers, design and direct mail agencies as well as other marketing agencies.

However, in another sense, Kall Kwik is unique having no direct competitors as no other network player can consistently offer such a broad and integrated range of design and print-based solutions.

Adding value beyond just printing services is an important factor in this market, and is something

that Kall Kwik has skillfully tapped into. Research undertaken by Cap Ventures reveals that for every £1 spent on print, businesses normally spend at least £6 on the design and fulfilment of the printed material.

Marketing, sales, training and human resources departments are often the main clients of the sector, requiring corporate brochures, product and sales literature, direct mailers, display materials, reports, training course manuals and presentations. High-profile, blue chip clients, such as David Lloyd Leisure, QMH Hotels, ICI Dulux and Vauxhall Rental account for a significant part of Kall Kwik's annual turnover.

Achievements

Kall Kwik's biggest achievement has been in making on-demand print equally accessible to

small businesses and corporate users. It has succeeded in providing its business customers with a complete marketing package, adding value for the biggest multinationals or smaller companies.

In a challenging and rapidly changing market, Kall Kwik has also achieved strong growth through nimble and well-timed diversification. For example, its Corporate Brands team, which works in partnership with national corporate clients with dispersed locations to provide complete marketing solutions for design, print and fulfilment, has grown rapidly, attracting business from major names such as Wimpy Restaurants, QMH Hotels, ICI Dulux and Vauxhall Rental. 2006 was in fact a record year with a number of new clients coming on board, including Sky Business, De Vere Group and Saab Rental.

Kall Kwik's success can also be attributed to its franchise-based business model, with Kall Kwik UK providing intensive marketing, training and operational support to its franchisees to ensure all services and products are delivered to a consistently high standard.

Kall Kwik UK has consistently been recognised as a leader in the franchise field, winning a host of awards, such as the British Franchise Association's Franchisor of the Year Award in 2005. Many of its franchisees have also won awards, such as Kall Kwik in Edinburgh winning BFA Franchisee of the Year 2003 and Cornhill Digital Business Centre being named Franchisee of the Year in the Start-Up Awards 2004. Significantly, Kall Kwik is the first brand to be recognised within both the franchisor and franchisee categories.

Kall Kwik has also won accolades for the quality of its communications, winning Marketing magazine's 'Connections 2000' award for best use of an intranet.

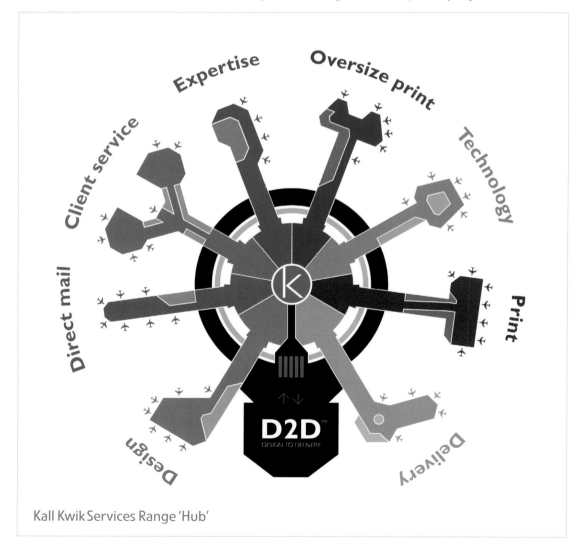

Kall Kwik Services Range 'Hub'

Product

Kall Kwik offers its business customers a complete range of print-based services for all of their communications needs. It describes this integrated service package as design to delivery.

Design to delivery is essentially an inclusive service, offering unlimited access to eight key product fields: design; direct mail; client service; expertise; oversize print; technology; print; and delivery. The strategy was developed in response to client requirements and market trends that highlight a gap in the marketplace for an accessible and single-source provider of design-led communications.

Design is where the whole process begins, and Kall Kwik has a rapidly expanding network of design agencies, employing over 200 designers. This is more than any other private sector company and reflects the businesses' ability to offer creative solutions to every project it works on, be it a promotional postcard or a hoarding-sized poster.

Direct Mail has always been a staple of Kall Kwik's offering, with locations able to manage the whole process, from co-ordinating a campaign to getting it out of the door. As well as its creative design skills, Kall Kwik has the technology to offer digital personalisation and can improve targeting even more by sourcing mailing lists.

Print services are at the heart of Kall Kwik, with the business committed to continuous innovation in the fast-changing and high-tech print sector. Careful pre-planning means that Kall Kwik can help choose the most cost-effective option from a wide range of techniques and processes, from on-demand digital, to litho print, personalised communications and custom finishing. It is also an expert in jumbo-sized print for exhibitions, banners, signage, advertising, display stands and posters.

Recent Developments

Responding to the strong demand for its design services, Kall Kwik has recently supported franchisees who wish to develop a second income stream from high-end creative design. There are 35 k designgroups around the country, structured as a confederation of local design studios, each with a shared approach to business design and common mantra of 'accessible creativity'.

Set up to offer an intimate local design service, but with all the resources of a national organisation, k designgroup's teams can take on a wide range of projects, including logo brand design, advertising, business branding, marketing, graphic design, and multimedia (including web design). The concept has proved popular with large and small clients, with k designgroup creating design solutions for the NHS, Vodafone and English Courtyard.

Another important recent development is the launch of Kall Kwik's new website (kallkwik.co.uk). A new clean design, detailed information about services, case studies, the ability to get an online estimate, and a service allowing clients to email files ready for printing,

are just some of the site's new features. Following the launch of the site in August 2006, Kall Kwik has seen a big increase in the traffic and enquiries it generates.

Promotion

Kall Kwik is known for its proactive and well-targeted marketing, reflecting its ability to serve its clients' own marketing objectives.

As it is a franchise-based business, Kall Kwik's franchisees initiate promotion in support of individual locations, albeit in accordance with guidelines from Kall Kwik UK.

Direct mail is Kall Kwik's preferred promotional medium, with mailers, awareness cards and 'D2D' magazine distributed to clients and prospects. The business uses the Mtivity marketing asset management system to enable individual franchisees to select and personalise their marketing materials.

Kall Kwik also uses the internet to advertise its services. Google's 'pay-per-click' advertising service is another valuable online marketing tool. Some other tactical advertising is carried out in regional and national press.

Local promotion is important, with high quality display materials, merchandising and corporate attire all supporting the corporate image.

The company also teams up with key partners, such as Canon and Pitney Bowes, to undertake joint advertising. Forming a strategic marketing

alliance, this can be an effective way to cut through to the business audience.

Franchisees can also use sales support literature, such as brochures, electronic presentations and press releases to communicate their services.

Brand Values

The Kall Kwik brand personality is unpretentious and aims to be 'on the wavelength' of its clients. It is professional, with a touch of design flair, and aims to help its clients 'look the business'. The company has a vision to make Kall Kwik the leading and most innovative national branded design to delivery network, enabling business to business communications with continuous profitable sales growth.

Ultimately, Kall Kwik aims to satisfy the need to make business to business communications stand out in a crowded, competitive marketplace. This profound satisfier is expressed through the tagline 'look the business'.

www.kallkwik.co.uk

Things you didn't know about Kall Kwik

Kall Kwik was hired in the final episode of the BBC television series 'The Apprentice' to undertake a design and print job that was 'make or break' for the candidates.

Kall Kwik has been a finalist in the British Franchising Awards for five years out of the last six.

Kall Kwik arranged for its Putney operation in south west London to print the 'Feed Me Better' campaign petition that was handed to the UK Prime Minister by TV chef Jamie Oliver.

1978	1979	1999	2005
The company is founded by Moshe Gerstenhaber, who purchased the master franchise from the US Kwik Kopy organisation.	The first Kall Kwik opens in Pall Mall, London.	Kall Kwik UK is acquired by Adare Group, the leading provider of print, mailing and data management solutions throughout the UK and Ireland.	Kall Kwik UK is named as the British Franchise Association's 'Franchisor of the Year'. Kall Kwik launches D2D.

LandSecurities

As the leading commercial real estate brand for more than 60 years, Land Securities has focused on delivering a customer offering which provides its occupiers with quality accommodation and unparalleled levels of customer service. Three signature qualities exemplify the Land Securities brand: expert – recognisably an expert in commercial real estate; progressive – genuinely changing in a changing world; and accessible – easy to talk to and do business with.

Market

Land Securities is the UK's leading real estate investment trust (REIT). Its national portfolio of commercial property, worth many billions of pounds, includes some of Britain's best-known retail outlets, including Birmingham's Bullring and Gunwharf Quays in Portsmouth, as well as London landmarks such as the Piccadilly Lights and Westminster City Hall. Land Securities has a multi-billion pound development programme with projects in Exeter, Bristol and Cardiff city centres as well as key sites in central London. It is also one of the leading names in property partnerships and through urban community development is involved in long term, large scale regeneration projects in the South East.

Leading competitors in the market are institutional investors such Prudential Property Investment Management, Legal and General, Standard Life and Morley Fund Management, quoted competitors such as British Land and Hammerson, together with private commercial companies such as The Crown Estate and Grosvenor.

Achievements

The Group's investment portfolio is now valued at in excess of £15 billion making it the world's third largest REIT, while the property outsourcing

business generated £96.6 million of profits in Land Securities' 2006 financial year.

The Group's achievements have been recognised by the numerous accolades it receives, which have included the prestigious 2006 Estates Gazette Property Company of the Year and 2006 Property Week Property Company of the Year. It has received recognition with the PricewaterhouseCoopers 2006 Building Public Trust Award for 'telling it as it is', while its website was recognised as the Best Corporate Website at the Corporate Communication Magazine Awards.

Its highly acclaimed Cardinal Place development received both the best office and retail

development, from the British Council of Offices and BCSC respectively, winning the Supreme Gold at the 2006 BCSC Awards.

It is a member of the FTSE4Good and the Dow Jones index, which acknowledges commitment to corporate responsibility, and in 2006 Land Securities was awarded a BiTC 'Big Tick' for its Environmental Initiatives. It has recently received Investors in People Accreditation across its entire business.

Product

Land Securities operates wholly in the £500 billon UK commercial property market and is the largest quoted property company in Europe measured by market capitalisation, which at £10.93 billion represents 20 per cent of the UK quoted property sector. Its business model is diversified, focused on retail property, London offices and property outsourcing. In the core markets of retail property and London offices, the Group provides about 5.8 per cent and four per cent respectively of the market floorspace and it is recognisably the market leader in property outsourcing by number of contracts. Within its core market segments Land Securities, activities

1944	1950	1968	1982	1987	1994
Harold Samuel, Land Securities' founder and chairman, buys Land Securities Investment Trust Limited, which at this point owns three houses in Kensington together with some Government stock.	Shares purchased for 44p in 1945 are now worth £6.15. The following year, Associated London Properties, is purchased for £2 million. This marks the first big take-over by the company.	In Britain's biggest property deal at this time, Land Securities takes over City Centre Properties which has assets of £155 million.	The name of the company is changed from The Land Securities Investment Trust Limited to Land Securities plc.	The total income of the Group exceeds £200 million and the portfolio valuation tops £3 billion.	Following the recession, the portfolio increases in value to over £5 billion.

Retail In 2006 Land Securities' shopping centre footfall was up 1.9% while Footfall National Index was down 2.1%

include property management, investment, development and the provision of property related services.

Recent Developments

Over the past few years Land Securities has developed a reputation for innovation and progression, both through the introduction of new products and services such as property outsourcing and Landflex, a tailored leasing product for London office occupiers, but also through the introduction of new customer focused initiatives such as a unique customer portal and customer call centres for its property outsourcing clients. This innovation and progression is also reflected in its financial strategy with the Group introducing a world-leading debt structure, enabling it to finance the business flexibly and at a lower cost of debt than its competitors.

In 2007 the enormous progression the Group has made was reflected by the introduction of a new visual identity, the culmination of a major brand review and audit carried out in the previous year driven by a requirement to clarify the Group's brand architecture and modernise its brandmark. The refreshed visual identity, which included a new 'cornerstone' logo and colour palette was designed to promote the brand's signature qualities as well

Accessible
We make it easy to talk to us, and to do business with us. Anywhere.

as to create clear space between Land Securities and its competitor set.

At the same time the review created clarity in terms of the Group's brand architecture with new marketing straplines created for each of the Group's business units: Land Securities – Retail Experience for its Retail business; Land Securities – Capital Commitment for its London Portfolio business; Land Securities – Trillium Property Partnerships for its outsourcing business and Land Securities – Changing Horizons for its Urban Community Development activities.

Promotion

Land Securities' first ever Group advertising campaign was launched in January 2007 across the national press, trade and investment media and included an online campaign. This milestone event was timed to introduce its new visual identity as well as to promote the Group's conversion to Real Estate Investment Trust. This campaign is to be followed swiftly by targeted advertising campaigns from its Retail and London Portfolio Business unit.

At the same time the Group continues to have an active media and investor relations programme, while also investing heavily in activities specific to its property portfolio. Each of its 30 retail outlets run consumer specific marketing campaigns, focused on increasing the number of visits to a specific destination. These campaigns use local above-the-line advertising as well as community focused promotional events to attract visitors to the centres.

At the same time, as a result of Land Securities' extensive development pipeline in major city centres, it also runs an active community engagement programme to ensure the smooth running of these activities with minimum disruption to its communities. These change management programmes use a number of promotional mechanisms including advertising,

websites, newsletters, public relations and community liaison managers.

The Group continues to sponsor conferences relevant to its core activities, examples of which are its major schools art and story project with the Prince of Wales Arts and Kids Foundation, its sponsorship of the Local Government Association Conference in 2006 and the Property Management Awards.

Brand Values

Land Securities brand values are excellence – striving to achieve the very best; customer services – it never forgets that its customers are the source of its strength; innovation – new ideas inspiring the Group to new heights; integrity – people trust Land Securities; and respect for the individual – everyone has the power to help, to grow, to influence, to contribute.

These values are reinforced by the Group's Values into Action initiative which recognises and rewards employees and key stakeholders whose behaviour reflects the core values.

www.landsecurities.com

Things you didn't know about Land Securities

Lord Samuel, Land Securities' founder, coined the phrase 'Location, location, location'.

Some of Land Securities' famous properties include, the Piccadilly Lights, Home Office, New Scotland Yard and Bullring, Birmingham.

The first episode of BBC's 'Hustle' was filmed in Land Securities' Landflex building – 'Empress State' – before its fit out began for the Metropolitan police.

Land Securities manages over 70 million sq ft of property (equal to over 1,000 football pitches).

Over 300 million customer visits are made to its shopping centres each year.

It has a two customer call centres which respond to thousands of property related customer service enquiries every year.

2000
Land Securities' purchase of Trillium sees it enter the new property outsourcing market. Pre-tax profits rise by 11.7 per cent to £327.7 million and the portfolio is valued at £7.5 billion.

2005
Land Securities acquires Tops Estates – a quoted shopping centre company – and LxB, an out of town retail specialist. Its portfolio is valued at £14.5 billion.

2006
Land Securities enters into a joint venture with the Mill Group and acquires Secondary Market Infrastructure Fund marking its entry into the primary and secondary PPP markets.

2007
Land Securities adopts real estate investment trust status and unveils a new identity.

LG Electronics was established in 1958 as the pioneer in the Korean consumer electronics market. Since then it has become a major global force with more than 64,000 employees working in 76 countries. In 2006, it was on track to report sales of US$43 billion.

Market

LG Electronics competes on a truly global scale, operating production and sales offices on every continent, and with 75 per cent of its sales outside Korea. North America is its biggest overseas market, accounting for 23 per cent of sales, with 19 per cent coming from Europe.

The company is active in a host of consumer-facing and business electronics segments, but in the business to business sphere, LG is particularly strong in plasma display panels, with a 27 per cent share, and also in air conditioning, where it is market leader. It has also dominated the optical storage market – including re-writable CD Roms and DVDs – for the last eight years. In mobile communications, LG ranked fourth in global mobile handset sales in 2005, and it is market leader in home cinema systems and DVD players.

Achievements

LG has grown exponentially in recent years, recording an annual growth rate of 21 per cent since 2001. It is now the global leader in several key electronics categories and has recorded many important industry firsts, going back as far as the 1950s and 1960s, when it produced Korea's first radios, black and white television sets and refrigerators. Then, it spearheaded Korea's emerging electronics industry, and it continues to lead the way. More recently, it developed the world's first 76 inch plasma TV, the world's first DVD Combi Home Theatre and first Super Multi DVD Recorder. It has also revolutionised washing

machine design, with its new Steam Direct Drive design, using 35 per cent less water and 21 per cent less energy.

The company is also at the forefront of home appliance networking, allowing appliances such as washing machines, air conditioning, televisions, refrigerators and cookers to be remotely controlled via computer.

LG has scooped numerous industry awards for its cutting-edge products and innovation. In 2005, it received the highest number of awards at the Consumer Electronics Show (CES), with 16 Innovation Awards. During the year it also received Most Promising Vendor of the Year Award at the Frost & Sullivan Asia Pacific Technology Awards.

In 2006, LG's slim LCD monitor with f-Engine, won both the iF design award and the red dot

design award, proving the strength of the company's Digital Display business. LG's mobile handsets have also scooped countless accolades, most recently winning the iF Design Award, red dot Design Award, and the President's Award for Good Design in Korea.

The company has also led the way in Corporate Social Responsibility, implementing a wide range of CSR programmes around the world. These include a 'Fight Against Cancer' campaign in France, the 'Thai Forever' anti-drug campaign, and 'LG Screen Connects You & Me' in China.

Product

The company is active in several key areas of the electronics market, principally digital appliances, digital displays, digital media and

1958	**1959**	**1960s**	**1978**	**1988**	**1991**
Goldstar, the forerunner of LG Electronics, is established.	The company develops Korea's first radio.	Technological developments include Korea's first refrigerator, black and white TV, air conditioner and washing machine.	Exports surpass US$100 million – a first for Korea's electronics industry.	Production subsidiaries in the UK, Thailand, Mexico and Philippines are established.	Goldstar invests in Zenith Electronics Corp in the US and agrees to jointly develop HDTV.

mobile communications. From washing machines and refrigerators, televisions to laptop computers, optical drives to air conditioning systems, and mobile phones to vacuum cleaners, LG's product range spans consumer and business to business sectors. In the B2B sphere, LG is perhaps best-known for its air conditioning products, making super-slim indoor units under the Art Cool brand name, and heavy-duty industrial units for commercial use.

Its digital display products, such as plasma televisions and display screens, and also LCD televisions and computer screens, have further cemented LG's position as a leading partner to business clients. Notebook computers, wall-mounted HD-ready projectors and satellite navigation systems also boost LG's credentials as a leading technology supplier to the business community.

Recent Developments

LG recently underlined its reputation as one of the world's leading innovators of LCD and Plasma televisions, by unveiling a 100 inch liquid crystal display (LCD) TV. This made it into the 2007 Guinness World Records Book for being the world's largest. It is approximately 1.5 times bigger than the largest currently available LCD TV (82 inches), and is similar in size to the largest plasma display TV currently available.

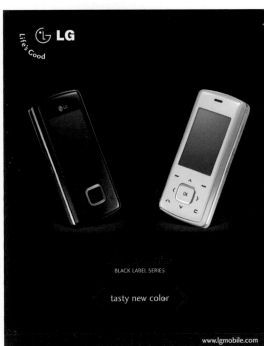

Other recent innovations include the introduction into the UK of the first five Mega-Pixel digital camera phone, the LG KG920. This outperforms even the latest digital cameras available in the UK market. In May, LG unveiled the AN110, the world's first wall-mounted projector which has HD-ready big-screen capabilities.

Apart from constant product innovation, LG has also undergone a radical shift in corporate strategy, recently launching a drive to increase sales and its brand profile through the launch of the 'Blue Ocean Management' campaign. Underlying this is a strong commitment from the global brand to becoming a top three consumer electronics player by 2010.

Specifically, LG plans to double its sales volume, profit and shareholder benefit by 2010 with 30 per cent of its sales volume and 50 per cent of its profit being derived through so-called 'Blue Ocean' products. The criteria of these products are growth potential (based on sales performance), market leadership (based on market share) and their contribution toward profit.

Promotion

To engage with customers around the world, and bring the brand to life against a backdrop of engaging activity, LG Electronics has implemented a programme of high-profile sponsorships. On a global scale, one of its main partnerships is with the International Cricket Council, which it has sponsored since 2002. The ICC World Cup in the West Indies in 2007 provides a major international stage to showcase the LG brand and connect with a global audience. Another global sponsorship asset, and a valuable channel for connecting with a youth audience, is LG's partnership with the world's largest extreme sports championship, Action Sports.

On the domestic front, LG's highest profile sponsorships are in the English Premier League. From the start of the 2006/07 football season, LG became the official supplier of mobile phones to Arsenal FC, complementing its existing sponsorship of Fulham FC as consumer electronics provider.

Other sponsorships include a range of relationships with British Gymnastics, as a national sponsor for the last seven years, and also in the past with snooker, rugby, motorsport, Formula One and the MTV Europe music awards.

The company also makes extensive use of above-the-line advertising to sell specific

products, such as a recent £2 million ad campaign to back the launch of its Chocolate mobile phone. The work encompassed TV, press and print executions.

Shows and live events also play an important part in LG's marketing strategy, especially when it comes to connecting with business audiences. It invests in having a considerable presence at the world's premier electronics events, such as CeBit, 3GSM, and the Ideal Home Show.

Brand Values

LG has four cornerstone values: Trust, Innovation, People and Passion. These link into the central promise of the LG brand: 'to provide tangible innovations that enrich the lives of our customers'. LG's products also carry this promise to the consumer, by aiming to be easy to use, reliable, simple in design, but delivering an enriching experience.

As well as these product benefits, LG also acts as a responsible and caring corporate citizen, building relationships with the local communities it works in and striving to sustain the environments it operates in.

Another core value of the LG brand is to have a pioneering spirit, transforming vision into reality and acting with boldness and fearlessness in accepting technological challenges. Reflecting this, LG Electronics believes in the dictum 'No Success without Challenge'.

www.lge.com

Things you didn't know about LG

LG launched the world's first internet-enabled refrigerator, in 2000.

The LG name evolved from 'Lucky Goldstar' the company's name prior to 1995, and from 'Goldstar' before that.

As well as electronics and telecommunications, LG is also active in chemicals, energy, finance and services.

In the 1960s, LG was the fist Korean company to export consumer electronics products (radios) to the US.

Among LG's many firsts, were Korea's first washing machine and in-room air conditioners.

1995	1999	2002	2005
The company changes its name to LG Electronics and completes acquisition of Zenith Corp in the US.	LG Electronics forms a joint venture with Philips, creating LG-Philips.	LG introduces the world's first commercalised home networking system.	The world's first Digital Multimedia Broadcasting notebook PC is unveiled.

LLOYD'S

Lloyd's is the world's leading specialist insurance market. It is not an insurance company, but an insurance market of independent businesses, offering an unrivalled concentration of specialist underwriting expertise and talent. Business comes into Lloyd's from over 200 countries and territories, and includes 89 per cent of FTSE 100 companies and 86 per cent of Dow Jones companies.

Market

In 2006 Lloyd's had the capacity to underwrite £14.8 billion worth of business. Lloyd's underwrites significant amounts of business for the worldwide insurance industry, as well as private individuals. Just under half of their business is for UK listed and other corporate clients.

Lloyd's is at the centre of the London insurance market, with 18 of the world's 20 largest reinsurance groups also having a physical presence in London. This is also the capital of the world's maritime insurance sector, accounting for two thirds of the global market.

But this is only part of the global picture. New competitor markets are on the rise, such as Bermuda, as well as other reinsurance markets in the US and Europe. All have to compete with alternative techniques for transferring risk, and deploying and redeploying capital, supported by an army of analysts and consultants.

Although Lloyd's has a record of tradition and expertise, it has to stay modern and offer a world class service to remain competitive.

Achievements

Lloyd's has been around for more than three centuries, helping communities and businesses to survive major world crises from the San Francisco

earthquake of 1906 to the terrorist attacks of 9/11. During that time, many aspects of Lloyd's changed, but its priorities and values have remained consistent.

This incredible history and reputation mean that Lloyd's is a truly famous global insurance brand.

It has earned this reputation through the expertise of some of the world's best underwriters and some of the most innovative insurance products available – on a daily basis. It's an offering that few can rival.

Lloyd's also has a global network with which few can compete, underwriting in more than 200 countries and territories around the world. This global status, like its track record of paying claims when disaster strikes, has been built up over the past 300 years.

Key to Lloyd's dependable reputation is its financial solidity. The market's ratings have remained stable since 2001, with an A Rating from

the ratings agencies Standard and Poor, AM Best and Fitch.

Product

Like any market, Lloyd's brings together those with something to sell – underwriters who provide insurance coverage – with those who want to buy – brokers, working on behalf of their clients who are seeking insurance.

Lloyd's is structured as a society of corporate and individual members, who underwrite insurance in syndicates. Lloyd's insurance policies are backed up by the chain of security which is made up of different components, one of which is capital provided by the members to support their underwriting. In recent years, the make-up of Lloyd's underwriting membership has gone through a major change; today most of the capital supporting underwriting in the Lloyd's market comes from corporate bodies, while

1688	1871	1887	1904	1906	1928
Edward Lloyd opened a coffee house in Tower Street, London. A clientele of ships' captains, merchants and ship owners quickly grew, with Lloyd's coffee house recognised as the place for obtaining marine insurance.	Lloyd's is incorporated by an Act of Parliament.	The first non-marine policies are underwritten at Lloyd's by Cuthbert Heath.	The first Lloyd's motor policy is issued, followed seven years later by the first aviation policy.	San Francisco earthquake claims are met by Lloyd's underwriters, establishing Lloyd's reputation in the US.	King George V opens the new premises of Lloyd's in Leadenhall Street.

private individuals or 'Names' as they became known supply only 10 per cent of the market's capital backing.

A member or a group of members form a syndicate. A syndicate's underwriting is managed by a managing agent, who employs underwriters to accept or decline risk. There are 64 syndicates operating within Lloyd's, covering many specialist areas, including: marine; aviation; catastrophe; energy; professional indemnity and motor.

Businesses from all over the world can come to Lloyd's to find insurance, often for highly complex risks. There are 162 firms of brokers working at Lloyd's, many of whom specialise in particular risk categories.

Lloyd's underwriters are renowned for devising tailored, innovative solutions to complex risks. As a result, Lloyd's covers the world's most demanding and specialist risks – from insuring oil rigs, man-made structures and major sporting events.

Recent Developments

Following the Asian Tsunami and Hurricane Katrina, 2005 was one of the worst years on record for natural disasters. Hurricane Katrina alone is estimated to have cost the insurance industry £14 billion (Source: BBC News, 14th September 2005). Lloyd's syndicates paid claims of more than £3 billion during the year. Due to its disciplined approach to underwriting their loss was restricted to £103 million.

With the need to understand and anticipate major risk trends, Lloyd's launched the 360 Risk Project in 2006. Its aim is to generate discussion on how best to manage risk in today's business environment. By tapping into the concentrated expertise and knowledge within the Lloyd's market – combined with the views of experts from the insurance, business, political and academic worlds – Lloyd's aims to stimulate practical, thought-provoking discussion about issues such as natural catastrophes and climate change.

As part of this project, Sir Trevor McDonald OBE moderated at the Lloyd's live debate on climate change. The 200 plus delegates included business leaders, government officials, leading scientists and academics.

Promotion

Since 2004, Lloyd's has been working on a brand strategy that more clearly defines its values and develops a more systematic approach to communications. Previously, it had taken more of a 'one-size-fits-all' approach, but now it aims to build a more targeted strategy, communicating and delivering a more tailored approach to franchisees, capital providers, and key stakeholders.

An important part of this is to promote a high level of awareness internally and externally of what Lloyd's is, how it works, what it stands for and what makes it different. In all of this, Lloyd's speaks with the voice of a market leader – bold, confident and with flair.

Brand Values

The Lloyd's brand is a massive asset, not just for the market itself, but for all the businesses associated with it. Today it is recognised all over the world as a leading global market which is able and trusted to take on some of the world's toughest risks.

It is a highly distinctive brand, known for its traditions, its unique way of doing business, and its ability to meet highly specialised requirements.

The core brand idea for Lloyd's is encapsulated in the phrase: Constant Originality. Constant conveys its good faith, security, reliability whilst Originality conveys Lloyd's creativity, individuality, authenticity and adaptability.

www.lloyds.com

1958
Lloyd's transfers to the new Lime Street building, officially opened by HM Queen Elizabeth, The Queen Mother.

1986
The current building at One Lime Street, designed by Richard Rogers, is opened for Lloyd's by the Queen.

1998
Government announces independent regulation of Lloyd's by the Financial Services Authority, effective from midnight on 30th November 2001.

2002
Lloyd's Members approve the proposals of the Chairman's Strategy Group. These outline major changes that will transform Lloyd's into a modern, dynamic marketplace attractive to capital providers and policyholders.

Things you didn't know about Lloyd's

Lloyd's provides insurance for eight of the world's top pharmaceutical companies and 48 of the world's top banks.

Each day, around 4,000 people visit the Lloyd's building.

In 2005, a Lloyd's underwriter designed a policy to protect an individual's chest hair.

Lloyd's paid out an insurance policy for Rolling Stones guitarist Keith Richards when he injured his finger while on tour in the 1990s.

Lloyd's offers hole-in-one insurance, which protects golf tournament organisers against the rare event of a player hitting such a shot and claiming the large prize that has been offered for such an acheivement.

Lloyd's provides cover against the Academy Awards being cancelled from terrorist threat to fire. In 2004 Lloyd's also insured the £27 million worth of jewellery worn by the stars at the Oscars.

The Lutine Bell, synonymous with Lloyd's, has hung in four successive underwriting rooms and is traditionally rung for major ceremonial occasions – once for bad news and twice for good.

Michael Page

INTERNATIONAL

As a world leader in the recruitment of qualified and skilled professionals for organisations across a broad spectrum of industries and professions, Michael Page International has been one of the fastest-growing brands in this increasingly competitive market. From a small London consultancy, it has grown to become a renowned international company based in 19 countries, with 122 offices and over 3,000 staff.

Market

Recruitment consultancies continue to play a vital role in keeping the wheels of industry turning; acting as the intermediary between companies and prospective candidates. Identifying and finding suitably qualified people for job vacancies, either for permanent or contract positions, is a highly valuable service for employers, and also for the appointees whose careers progress as a result.

Today, the labour market is highly complex. The rise of home-working, an ageing labour force and the increasingly globalised nature of modern business all make finding the right people for the right job a more challenging goal.

Recruitment consultancies' knowledge and connections can boost their clients' business by optimising their biggest overhead and most important asset: their people.

Although recruitment spending is closely linked to the health of the economy, which explains a slight slowing in growth between 2004 and 2005, spend on services is set to double in the UK over the next 10 years. Currently, in the UK, the recruitment industry generates annual revenues of over £23 billion.

Achievements

Michael Page International has grown into one of the most widely recognised brands in the global professional recruitment industry.

The Group boasts a client base including all of the companies in the FTSE 100 Index and over 80 per cent of the companies included in the FTSE Eurotop 300 Index, serving their needs with a database of over 1.8 million suitably qualified candidates around the world.

After 30 years of operation, Michael Page International can lay claim to a considerable number of industry 'firsts', including being the first executive recruitment firm to be floated on the London Stock Exchange and the first to develop an international computerised applicant network. The company has continued to invest heavily in the development of IT systems, gaining recognition as the most innovative in the business.

Michael Page International has won numerous awards including 'Best Accountancy/ Financial Recruitment Firm' at the 2003 and 2004 Recruiter Awards, being rated one of 'Britain's Top Employers' by The Guardian as well as one of the '100 Best Companies to Work For' by The Sunday Times in 2006.

Product

The product of Michael Page International is based on 'The 4Cs': consultants, candidates, clients and care.

The company believes that professional consultants are

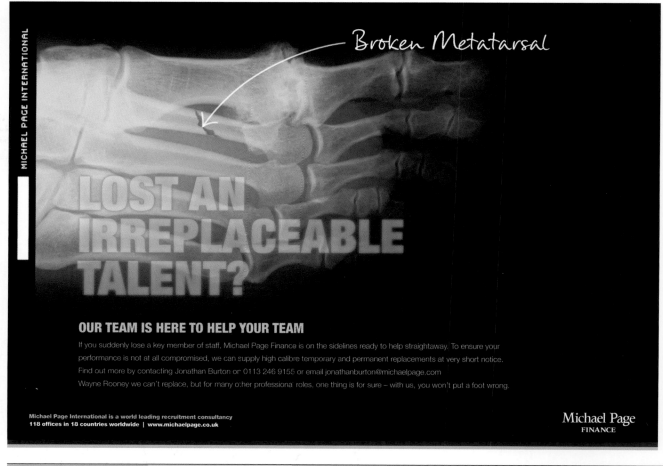

MICHAEL PAGE INTERNATIONAL

Broken Metatarsal

LOST AN IRREPLACEABLE TALENT?

OUR TEAM IS HERE TO HELP YOUR TEAM

If you suddenly lose a key member of staff, Michael Page Finance is on the sidelines ready to help straightaway. To ensure your performance is not at all compromised, we can supply high calibre temporary and permanent replacements at very short notice.

Find out more by contacting Jonathan Burton on 0113 246 9155 or email jonathanburton@michaelpage.com

Wayne Rooney we can't replace, but for many other professional roles, one thing is for sure – with us, you won't put a foot wrong.

Michael Page International is a world leading recruitment consultancy
118 offices in 18 countries worldwide | www.michaelpage.co.uk

Michael Page
FINANCE

1976	1985	1986	1988	1992	1997
Bill McGregor and Michael Page, who came from the oil and brewing industries respectively, establish Michael Page International in London.	Michael Page International opens its first overseas office in Australia and in the same year, establishes Michael Page City, providing specialist services to the banking and financial markets.	With a network of offices throughout the UK and continental Europe, Michael Page becomes the largest advertiser in the Financial Times – a position it has held ever since.	The company is admitted to the Stock Exchange, allowing further expansion, as Michael Page International opens offices in Germany.	Michael Page International launches the sub-brand Accountancy Additions, and a specialist Public Sector division in the UK.	The first generation website, www.michaelpage.co.uk is launched.

key; without them nothing can be achieved. This is reflected in the organic growth of the company, whereby nearly all the current management is the result of internal promotion.

Many candidates come to the company's door by way of referral or recommendation, or often, already have a history of being placed into previous roles via the consultancy.

Michael Page International also recognises that by having a pool of quality candidates, clients will be drawn to the consultancy. Coupled with this, a personal service is offered to all clients, whereby consultants take the time to find out how they can provide a bespoke recruitment solution.

Finally, the company prides itself on the care and consideration it takes in its work.

A vital aspect of the company's product offering is that it has focused on developing specialist consultancy teams to recruit for the disciplines in which they are often personally qualified.

It means the company has bankers recruiting for banks, salesmen recruiting sales professionals and so on. This strategy has helped Michael Page International achieve an unrivalled level of expertise and market penetration, with the company now structured into 13 specialist divisions.

These comprise: Accounting, Tax & Treasury; Banking & Financial Markets; Marketing; Retail & Hospitality; Sales; Legal; IT & Technology; Human Resources; Engineering & Manufacturing; Procurement & Supply Chain; Consultancy; Secretarial and Property & Construction.

Recent Developments

Michael Page International continues to expand its terrestrial network, with new offices in Dubai, Dublin, Johannesburg and Mexico – with more office openings planned for 2007.

2001
Michael Page opens in Tokyo followed two years later by an office in Shanghai.

2006
New offices are due to open in Dublin, Johannesburg, Dubai, Mexico and Russia by the end of the year.

The company has also launched the third generation of its website, allowing users to conduct faster, more detailed and accurate searches. The site is also an important tool for clients, with many of the company's leading clients having a branded presence on it. Since its launch, visitors to the UK portal have increased by 13 per cent, with an average of 210,000 visitors and 30,000 applications made per month.

Recently, the company has accelerated initiatives to embrace diversity, ensuring that all of its communications fairly reflect society. It is also combating age discrimination by ensuring that language used in job descriptions is appropriate and in line with the new age discrimination laws.

In 2006 Michael Page International committed itself to raising a substantial sum for Breast Cancer Care, setting £120,000 as a target. Many staff members participated in a variety of sponsored events, including the New York Marathon and a Pro-Am Golf Tournament.

Promotion

Michael Page International is a market leader in the classified advertising pages of the national and trade press worldwide. In the UK it is the industry's biggest advertiser, significantly ahead of its nearest rival. It also holds a leading position in Australia, France and the Netherlands.

The company's global office network, which has established close relationships with local organisations, also promotes the recruitment services of Michael Page International to a wide audience.

Sponsorships of events and professional conferences are another important promotional tool, as well as providing corporate hospitality for clients and candidates, for example the Michael Page International day at Ascot.

Its website is another useful communications tool. As the website grows, the company will forge further alliances with other high quality brands to ensure that Michael Page International continues to be promoted to a well-targeted international audience.

Brand Values

The quality and expertise of its consultancy and support staff are the best expression of

the brand values of Michael Page International. The company's policy is to recruit and train its staff to be the best in the business – to be passionate about their work and consistently make the best matches possible between candidates and clients – and above all, to uphold the philosophy of 'The 4Cs'.

Michael Page International is identified as a specialist brand with individual businesses operating in specific markets and disciplines. It has developed into a global brand, which sets common standards of service excellence, entrepreneurial spirit, continuity and operational effectiveness.

www.michaelpage.co.uk

Things you didn't know about Michael Page International

Every year since 1992, Michael Page International has been the largest recruitment advertiser in the FT. In 2000 it accounted for more than double the volume of advertising of the next three recruitment advertisers.

Every nine minutes Michael Page International helps professionals by placing them into new roles.

Throughout 2006/07, Michael Page is aiming to raise £120,000 for Breast Cancer Care.

MINTeL

Mintel is a global supplier of consumer, media and market research. For more than 30 years, its wide-ranging products have provided unique insights that have a direct impact on its clients' success. Mintel's leading analysts are world-renowned experts in diverse areas such as leisure, consumer goods, retail, financial services, sales promotion and social trends. Mintel's reach spans all corners of the globe with a presence in continental Europe, North America, Latin America, Australia, Israel, China and South Korea.

Market

The world of research is now unrecognisable compared to the market back in 1972, when Mintel was first established, and for many years this industry was largely associated with uninspiring raw data. But as the client base shifted from research and development to marketing departments, clients demanded so much more than simply pages of statistics. Today's market looks very different and Mintel now provides innovative ideas and analysis in an easily digestible format, enabling clients to hit upon that 'one big idea' that will set them apart from their competitors.

The ease of accessibility is key for all clients. Mintel led the way, being the first market research company to make its information accessible online. Extensive commitment to the instantaneous delivery of information has given Mintel's clients immediate access to exclusive global research, with all products available through the industry-leading website, www.mintel.com. Traffic to the group website is testament to Mintel's success, with hits now exceeding 4.5 million a year.

The market research industry has evolved rapidly in recent years and

there is little doubt that this trend will continue. Market research now forms the foundations of sustainable growth and profitability, making it a hugely exciting and challenging area to work in.

Achievements

Mintel has been a Business Superbrand for more than six years and aims to be consistently ahead of client demands and the competition.

Mintel's greatest achievement is that the company has successfully retained the entrepreneurial family culture of its early days, despite growing its workforce to more than 400 full-time and 1,000 associated employees globally.

A comprehensive people strategy has been implemented to cover every stage of the employee lifecycle, from hiring the best talent through to training and growing employees' skills across the group. A number of sales and research academies have now been set up in the company's head offices to help employees improve their career prospects. Mintel also offers a wide variety of courses on anything from languages to media training.

The company's commitment to environmental issues and charities continues. Mintel and its employees regularly organise events to raise money for charity, while at the start of 2006 the company set up a 'Green Team' to promote an environmentally friendly work ethic.

Product

Mintel's product portfolio is the result of years of client feedback and the innate ability to sense exactly what the market needs.

1972	1984	1997	1998	1999	2001
Mintel is established in London, providing food and drink research in the UK.	The first edition of Mintel's flagship report, British Lifestyles, is launched.	Mintel becomes the first research supplier to provide instant access online.	A US office is opened in Chicago. Mintle GNPD goes online.	Mintel Comperemedia is launched in the US.	Mintel acquires CIG and publishes its first European and US reports.

insight + impact

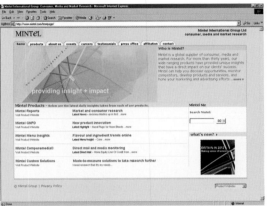

providing insight + impact

>> Evening Standard >>

ANOTHER MINTEL EXCLUSIVE

The acquisition of Cosmetics Research in 2005 added an important higher-end cosmetics focus to the Mintel GNPD, while Mintel Comperemedia has recently been expanded to capture email advertising.

Promotion

Media coverage is an integral part of Mintel's brand promotion and strong ties with journalists mean Mintel's research boasts daily coverage across all media. These include the FT, The Wall Street Journal, BBC News, The International Herald Tribune and Marketing, to name but a few.

Mintel has also formed successful affiliations with trade associations and industry bodies around the globe, including the Institute of Food Technologists (IFT), the British Retail Consortium (BRC) and la Fédération des Industries de la Parfumerie (FIP).

Passion for education is demonstrated by Mintel's sponsorship of the CIM awards and by the company's close relationship with the world's leading educational establishments, which now rely on Mintel's information to educate the business leaders of tomorrow.

Brand Values

Mintel believes that every member of its team is a brand ambassador. Furthermore, every contact Mintel makes with a client should leave them with a consistent message of how Mintel can help them make informed business decisions.

Mintel's brand values have been condensed into one simple phrase: insight + impact. The company provides insight into its clients' markets, consumers and products, questioning the status quo and ultimately having a positive impact on the clients' profits. Equally, internally everyone aims to find insight in everything they do and ensure that their work makes a real impact on their clients' business.

The continuing support and loyalty of its clients, many of whom had their first Mintel experience while studying at university and have maintained that relationship throughout their working life, is an integral part of its branding success.

www.mintel.com

From the newest marmalade in Guatemala, to the latest pizza sauce from the Philippines, the Mintel Global New Products Database (GNPD) is the premier global consumer packaged goods database. Mintel GNPD highlights over one million products featuring information such as ingredients, packaging and pricing details, allowing clients to monitor competitor offerings and uncover emerging opportunities in over 50 countries.

Mintel Comperemedia monitors marketing campaigns received by consumers in their mailbox and email inbox each day. Mintel uses an extensive panel of households in both the US and Canada and covers top financial service providers, the largest telecommunication operators and national airlines.

Mintel Menu Insights allows clients to see what flavours, ingredients and food combinations are big hitters on US restaurant menus, enabling clients to pre-empt what consumers will be looking to reproduce in their own kitchens.

The flagship product, Mintel Reports, gives a comprehensive exploration into a variety of consumer markets. Topics such as the emergence of ethical foods, the impact of terrorism and natural disasters on holidays, and the rise of the MP3 player are just some of the issues that were examined in 2006.

For those looking to capitalise on grassroots trends, such as using mobile phones as virtual wallets or iPod vending machines, Mintel Custom Solutions provides bespoke, cost-effective research solutions to all information needs. This service can also source anything from

collagen-filled soup from Japan to a pet nail polish from the US and get it onto your desk in a timely fashion.

Recent Developments

Constant innovation and improvement now underpin the streamlined structure and product portfolio offered by Mintel.

Mintel Oxygen is the new online delivery platform for Mintel Reports, focusing on exclusive opinions from Mintel's authoritative analysts. Succinct, relevant and actionable analysis, together with forward looking insights and opinions minimises the clients' work by highlighting major market trends and future developments that are set to have an impact on their business.

2004	2005	2006	2007
Mintel Menu Insights is launched.	Mintel acquires Cosmetic Research.	Mintel Comperemedia launches its email panel.	Mintel Oxygen is launched.

the nec
birmingham

The NEC Group operates five of the UK's leading exhibition, conference, music and event venues including the National Exhibition Centre in Birmingham. Every year some 4.5 million people visit its venues to do business, learn or be entertained.

Market

According to the Association of Exhibition Organisers (AEO), the UK exhibition industry attracts over £9 billion in annual expenditure. This is a buoyant market, with clients spending 45 per cent more on conferences and exhibitions in the UK between 2003 and 2004 than ever before.

The AEO estimates that the UK exhibitions and conference industry contributes £9.3 billion to the economy, supports 137,000 jobs and attracts 17 million visitors per year.

The NEC Group is a leading player in this thriving market. According to the AEO 100, which ranks the UK's leading conferences, exhibitions and venues, the NEC in Birmingham is the top UK venue for both trade and consumer exhibitions. By city location, Birmingham came top for holding the most trade exhibitions.

Achievements

The NEC's venues play host to some of the UK's best known events such as Crufts, BBC Gardeners' World Live and The Clothes Show, as well as hundreds of business exhibitions such as Spring Fair – the UK's largest trade show. The NEC Group also hosts some of the UK's biggest live music and sport events in its two arenas, brings major national and international conferences to the UK, and plays host to high profile TV events, including auditions for ITV's 'X Factor' and the BBC Sports Personality of the Year. The latter was held live at the NEC in 2006 – the first time the show has been outside London in its 53-year history.

The NEC Group as a whole continues to thrive with a record 26 new exhibitions won by the group in 2005/06. This was its best ever year for new business wins. The group was also boosted by its

International Convention Centre (ICC) – also located in Birmingham – being awarded the title of 'Best UK Conference Centre' by readers of Meetings and Incentive Travel magazine in spring 2006. The ICC famously hosted the G8 Summit in 1998, as well as many global conventions.

Product

The NEC Birmingham is The NEC Group's flagship exhibition venue, with 200,000 sq m of space in 21 interconnected halls. It is Europe's busiest exhibition venue, staging around 200 exhibitions per year, 70 per cent of which are trade fairs and 30 per cent public shows. The NEC is often described as an 'exhibition village', with its own road network, four on-site hotels, a lake, 22,000 car parking spaces and its own security, traffic and fire-fighting forces.

NEC Group's other venues include the ICC, The NEC Arena and The National Indoor Arena, all of which are located in Birmingham.

To maximise the effectiveness of these world-class venues, the NEC Group also provides a host of services for its customers such as: operational management services; event management; audio-visual and presentation facilities; internet, telephony and WiFi services through Event IT; floral arrangements; exhibition

1959	1970	1971	1976	1980	1989
The Pollitzer Committee investigates the lack of a quality exhibition venue in Britain.	Plans for a Birmingham venue start to take shape. A company is formed to mastermind the proposal, and is named National Exhibition Centre Ltd.	The Secretary of State for the Environment grants outline planning approval for the National Exhibition Centre in Birmingham.	The NEC is opened by The Queen, offering 89,000 sq m of exhibition space.	The NEC Arena is opened, and is one of the first large-scale concert venues in the country. Queen is the first act to perform there.	Three further halls are opened at the NEC, increasing the space to 125,000 sq m.

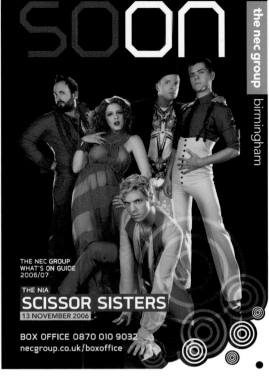

stands; hospitality or gifts; rigging and other technical services.

Recent Developments

During 2006, the NEC underwent the most dramatic change in its 30-year history. A new board was recruited, including a new chairman and chief executive, and a £40 million budget agreed with Birmingham City Council to implement an ambitious three-year programme, which includes the development of new brand identity and a refit for the NEC.

The entire environment is being redesigned, using bold colours and design ideas to reflect an exciting environment. It is however not just the physical look of the NEC that is changing. The board is also transforming the culture of service. An example is the courtesy bus drivers. Never before

invited to think about the service they provide, they have been encouraged to write their own script for the short journey from the car parks to the venue.

Eventually this positive, vibrant and charismatic environment will extend across other aspects of the business including the website, marketing collateral and promotional material.

The NEC has also revolutionised its approach to working with event organisers, taking a more engaged, market-aware, flexible and partnership-oriented approach.

The early signs are that the reinvention of the NEC is working well, with independent research conducted amongst organisers and visitors showing an average 80 per cent satisfaction score with organisers in 2006, against a target of 70 per cent. The research also revealed an average 4.14 out of six for visitor satisfaction. The new approach has also helped boost the business, with the NEC winning 20 new shows in the last six months of 2006.

Promotion

Integral to the reinvention of the culture and identity of the NEC is a transformation of its marketing. This is designed to reflect the vibrancy of events held inside the venues, as well as the £40 million investment being made in them.

This is the result of a change in mindset. Whilst the company used to see visitors as the show organiser's responsibility, with the venues regarded as 'sheds for hire', the new NEC board sees the business differently. As host to some of the UK's biggest events and live shows, the NEC now regards itself as, literally, being in 'show business', and wants its brand to reflect that.

To do this, the NEC's marketing now highlights the variety of its calendar of events, positioning

the venue as the place where new and exciting products are launched, ideas are shared or deals are done.

For the ICC, the marketing challenge is less about attracting visitors and more about illustrating the premium calibre of the venue and its events. To convey this, the NEC has devised a 'Bland is banned' campaign, which is a confident statement of the ICC's brand values of excellence and innovation.

Brand Values

The reinvention of the NEC brand is all about making it bolder, livelier and more engaging. The NEC Group's mission is to set the stage for some of the UK's best-loved shows, some of the world's most important business events and the very best in live music.

It brings millions of people together every year to learn, do business and be entertained.

www.necgroup.co.uk

Things you didn't know about NEC Birmingham

The NEC Group generates £1.3 billion for the economy every year and supports 22,000 jobs across the West Midlands

The NEC's 21 halls cover 200,000 sq m – that's the equivalent to 26 full-size football pitches.

The box office sells two million tickets every year. Its busiest day on record was Friday 2nd December 2005, when Take That tickets went on sale. The box office took over 300,000 phone calls, with 135,000 taken in the first hour.

Many animals come through the venues' doors every year – including 20,000 dogs at Crufts, 1,500 horses at Horse of the Year Show and 1,500 cats at the Supreme Cat Show.

In 1976 the NEC held 28 exhibitions, which were attended by 1.3 million visitors. Today, four million visitors attend around 600 exhibitions, conferences, concerts and other events.

1991	1991	1993	2006
The National Indoor Arena (NIA) is officially opened by Olympic gold medallist Linford Christie. The Sports Council awards a grant of £3 million towards construction.	The International Convention Centre (ICC) is opened for business on 2nd April.	A £106 million expansion adds four more halls to the NEC, taking the total exhibition space to 158,000 sq m.	The NEC celebrates its 30th anniversary. The NEC Group announces the appointment of a new chief executive, Paul Thandi.

NOKIA

Since the 1990s, Nokia has focused on superior design and innovative technology to become the world's leading mobile communications company. Its clear leadership in the mobile phone arena has allowed Nokia to constantly challenge traditional concepts of the mobile phone – this evolution has led to the manufacture of cutting-edge mobility products which in turn has resulted in many businesses enabling its employees to operate efficiently outside of traditional working hours and office locations.

Market

Traditionally it has been the IT, Utilities and Telecoms sectors that have driven the adoption of enterprise mobility technologies. However, in recent years the benefits of enterprise mobility have been more broadly recognised by a wider business community spanning all sectors. In 2005, 28.5 million smartphones were sold globally. In just one year the demand for these devices has almost doubled with over 90 million units sold in 2006. Nokia remains the industry leader with 44.5 per cent of the global market share (40 million units sold in 2006).

Achievements

Nokia is well positioned to provide mobility solutions for both large and small businesses, delivering significant operational efficiencies, return on investment and enhanced mobility. Some of these companies are below:

For the Honda Racing Formula One team Nokia and Avaya collaborated to provide a cost efficient IP telephony platform connecting 500 staff using Nokia S60 smartphone. The Honda team, located all across the world in the field, trackside or at the 86,000 sq m complex at headquarters, can seamlessly communicate in real time and work together. Honda realised a

30 per cent reduction in its telephony costs using the new solution.

Uniter Group provides its customers with bespoke office equipment (technical) support. With strict service level agreements in place to help ensure service calls occur within a clearly defined period, Uniter Group required a mobile solution for its field service engineers. Uniter Group deployed Nokia Intellisync Mobile suite, including Nokia Intellisync Wireless Email, Nokia Intellisync Data Sync, and Nokia Intellisync Device Management. The solution offers Uniter group a comprehensive synchronisation with service management information, as well as reducing mobile costs and the ability to adapt capabilities as the business evolves.

Like many growing businesses, A.T. Kearney professionals faced a growing volume of communications from current and prospective clients. Due to frequent travel, the firm's executives and consultants had difficulty managing this growing wave of messages, leading to lost business opportunities. As a result, A.T. Kearney's executives and consultants needed wireless access to email and personal information management (PIM) applications. A.T. Kearney deployed more than 575 handset devices that used Nokia Intellisync E-mail Accelerator and Systems Management client

software to provide its mobile professionals with wireless access to emails and PIM information.

As well as providing B2B mobility solutions, Nokia's business specific Nokia Eseries product range has seen significant success within the media. To date the Nokia E61 has been awarded ZDNet's Editor's Choice award, Computer Shopper's Best Handset 2006 award, BusinessWeek's 'worth watching' accolade and both Performance and Hot List awards from PC Plus.

Product

Today's business person doesn't just need a phone; they are often looking for tools which can support all their communication needs. Businesses likewise need to offer mobile tools to employees that fit the needs of the individual in order to

1987	1994
Nokia Mobira Cityman 900 – the first and original hand-held mobile phone – is launched.	The Nokia 2100 series becomes the first digital hand portable phones to support data, fax and SMS.

boost their productivity, while also supporting integration and security concerns of IT.

Nokia offers a wide range of business devices, which include communicators and messaging products. Each device is optimised for different types of users and all feature Nokia's familiar and easy-to-use interface. Now companies can choose from a variety of devices to meet specific employee needs.

Generally, mobile workers can be broadly grouped as follows:

Knowledge workers – such as consultants, or sales and marketing staff, who are typically equipped with a laptop and a mobile phone.

Skilled and process workers – such as field support and service workers who may be equipped with one or more industrial terminals, tablet PCs, PDAs, laptops or mobile phones.

To address the different needs of these mobile workers, Nokia offers a range of enterprise specific devices in different form factors.

The Nokia Eseries promises to provide a complete mobile work solution, featuring: fast and secure data connectivity for remote access to corporate information; the ability to send and receive email with attachments; access to popular office applications and advanced voice features.

Nokia's enterprise solutions are designed and developed to appeal to both business and IT management and the professional end-user. These solutions are fuelling the next phase of Enterprise Mobility with initiatives to help businesses with more strategic mobility deployments.

Recent Developments

In February 2006, Nokia completed its acquisition of Intellisync, a leader in platform-independent wireless messaging and applications for mobile devices. By combining the existing Nokia offerings with the synchronisation and device management solutions from Intellisync, Nokia is now able to connect nearly any device using any type of software to any application or network.

The Intellisync solution is unique in that it is both software and device agnostic. This has and will continue to enable businesses to deploy creative new mobility solutions while maintaining its investments of its legacy devices. Nokia believes that with these extended capabilities from Intellisync it will help businesses move from opportunistic point solution purchasing to more strategic mobility deployments. These new mobility services provisioned by Nokia include:

Wireless Email and Personal Information Management (PIM) Synchronisation – users can send and receive email, view attachments, respond to meeting requests, create new contacts, and manage subfolders while on the road. This data is being synchronised with the email server and desktop machine in the office at all times.

Comprehensive Security and Device Management – Nokia Intellisync Device Management features drive administrative efficiency (automating over the air upgrades and backup), reducing the strain on the IT department, and security by allowing businesses the control to lock down handsets and manage the flow of information.

Efficient File and Web Content Distribution – Nokia Intellisync File/Data Sync automates the distribution of important documents to a dispersed mobile workforce, ensuring that all employees are armed with the same up-to-date information when in the field.

The acquisition and development of the Intellisync solution has meant Nokia is now able to provide a full range of end-to-end mobility solutions.

Promotion

Since the launch of the first hand-held mobile phone in 1987, Nokia has been a technology trailblazer. Nokia handsets were the first to feature text messaging, to access internet-based information services and to include integrated cameras. Today, Nokia is leading the charge into the business arena with its world-class range of products incorporating new technologies such as UMTS, HSPDPA and WiFi. However, Nokia has applied the same enthusiasm for innovation in its collaborative projects as it does in its product development. To follow are just some of the examples where Nokia has engaged other world-leading providers of mobility solutions:

Oracle and Nokia teamed up to deliver improved customer service through integrated mobility applications. The alliance allowed users of the Nokia 9300, Nokia 9300i and Nokia 9500 communicator devices to use one device to access

all critical business applications as well as voice communications.

Avaya extended Enterprise Mobility to Nokia Series 80 Smart Phones. The flagship IP telephony software, Avaya Communication Manager, now supports the popular Nokia Series 80 smart phones, such as the Nokia 9300 and the Nokia 9300i smart phones and the Nokia 9500 Communicator.

Alcatel and Nokia announced a collaborative effort to mobilise business communications with the inclusion of Nokia Eseries, a range of business class devices and Nokia Intellisync Call Connect into the Alcatel IP Communication server.

Cisco's Unified CallManager and Cisco Unified CallManager Express are comprehensive IP over WLAN business voice communications solutions. With Nokia's software client installed on Nokia Eseries dual mode devices, calls can be routed over the IP network, leveraging investments in Cisco Unified WLAN and Cisco IP Communications solution, and delivering advanced business voice features to end-users.

Brand Values

Nokia is about connecting people – to the people that matter to them and the things they find important. In business this means keeping an open dialogue and exchange of information between the office and employees. Nokia develops mobile devices and solutions that not only support the needs of the business but also the working preferences of each employee. Nokia is dedicated to enhancing people's lives and productivity by providing easy to use, secure products.

www.nokia.co.uk

Things you didn't know about Nokia

Nokia is named after the river Nokia in Finland.

When Nokia was founded in 1865, Nokia initially manufactured paper, then card, then moved on to rubber.

The world's first transportable phone, the Nokia Mobira Talkman, came complete with a 10kg charging box the size of a suitcase.

Nokia is the only Telecommunications provider able to offer businesses with a holistic end-to-end mobility solution.

2001	2004	2005	2006
The first Nokia camera phone is launched – the Nokia 7650.	Nokia announces the first handset in the Communicator range – the Nokia 9500.	Nokia brings its first 3G device to market – the Nokia 6630. Nokia Eseries family of devices launches to the business community.	Nokia completes its acquisition of Intellisync, a leader in platform-independent wireless messaging and applications for mobile devices.

The O$_2$ brand launched in 2002. Since then O2 has grown dramatically, becoming the UK's largest mobile phone operator with 17 million active customers. O2 has stood out with an award-winning marketing strategy that has made existing customers more loyal and attracted a large volume of new customers. In January 2006 this success was reflected in the £18 billion paid for the O2 group by the Spanish telecoms group, Telefónica.

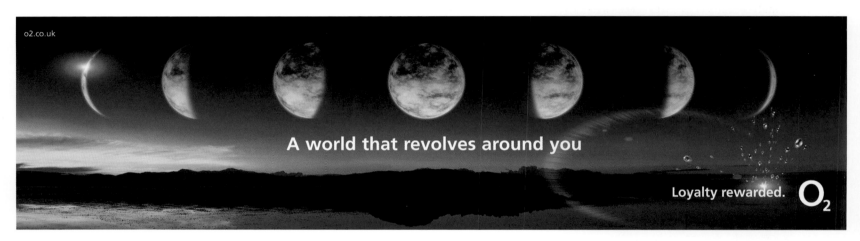

o2.co.uk

A world that revolves around you

Loyalty rewarded. O$_2$

Market

O2 is one of five licensed operators in the UK's very competitive mobile communications market, which places a strong emphasis on the delivery of new products and services to make quick gains and short term differentiation. O2 has lead the way with a customer-centric strategy, putting the customer at the heart of everything it does and only delivering products and services that are based on customer needs. O2 attaches great importance to, and places much of its marketing effort into, keeping existing customers loyal in a market with notoriously high churn rates.

Whilst voice services remain important in the use of business mobiles, customers are increasingly demanding new mobile data services. As well as the increased use of text messaging, the market is also seeing rapid growth in other areas of mobile data such as mobile email, coinciding with the growth in picture messaging (MMS) and music in the consumer market.

Achievements

O2 has already notched up an impressive list of achievements within its four years of trading.

Research shows strong brand awareness is being translated into purchase intent as O2 is top for network consideration (Source: Millward Brown Oct 2006).

By staying true to its customer-centric strategy O2 has overtaken the competition in many areas and is now number one in the business market with the largest share of business accounts (Source: SME GfK NOP data for Oct 2006).

In addition O2 has received a number of high profile accolades within the telecoms and marketing industries. In November 2004, O2 picked up one of the most coveted prizes in the advertising industry: the IPA Advertising Effectiveness Awards Grand Prix. Furthermore, in November 2006 O2 received another IPA award, this time the IPA Gold Award. This is the first time that a brand has picked up the top two IPA awards, showing the strength of O2's consistent and fresh advertising.

Product

Most mobile operators aim to attract high value business customers and to encourage them to take up mobile data solutions. However it's still critical that customers are comfortable and confident using their mobile before they take on more services.

That is why, in 2004, O2 put significant investment into its network and into its service for small business and corporate customers, all of whom can speak to a person in the UK, 24/7, and have their queries answered so they can make the most of their mobile.

Within the business market, mobile internet and mobile email are key applications and O2 offers

the latest technology. Through O2 Connection Manager businesses are able to work remotely through WiFi and GPRS.

Following its launch in 2001 BlackBerry® has gone from strength to strength. BlackBerry enables users to send and receive email whilst on the move without ever having to dial up to receive messages. O2 was the first mobile network to launch the BlackBerry Pearl™ in October 2006. A top of the range product offering stylish looks with the usual BlackBerry capabilities, the launch of this device continues the trend in the convergence of data and voice services.

The O2 Xda range also continues to expand. A winner of many accolades, including What Cellphone 'Award of Excellence 2004', this is a personal handheld device that combines an advanced mobile phone and touch screen PDA into one device. The Xda has been key to O2's drive to get business customers using mobile data, and since the first Xda was launched in 2004 newer and faster Xda devices have been rolled out, providing different functionality for different business requirements. In November 2006 the latest Xda device, the Xda Orbit, was launched coming complete with Microsoft® Windows Mobile® and GPS.

2002	2003
Following the demerger of mmO2 plc from BT to create a wholly independent holding company, the UK brand BT Cellnet relaunches as O2.	O2 launches its first insight led business advertising campaign with the '2 min challenge' – a pledge to find the right mobile solution for its time poor SME users in under two minutes.

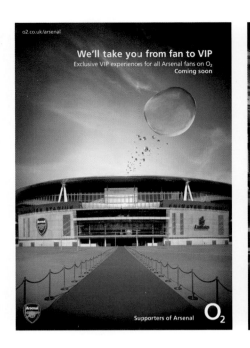

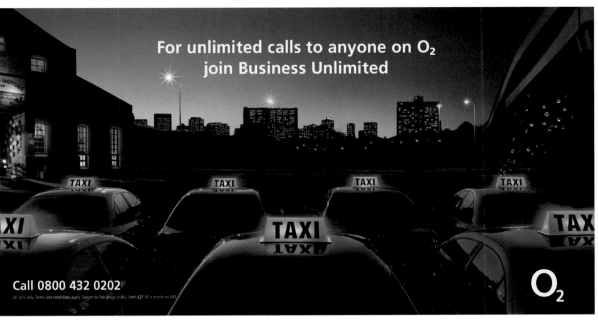

Recent Developments

Trust is all important for businesses whose day to day workings hinge on telecoms solutions that are efficient and reliable. Gaining trust takes time and, most importantly, proof. The O2 strategy is to focus on consistently delivering tangible substantiation that O2 understands, and can deliver on, business needs.

An example of this in the business market was the 'one call for service' campaign in July 2005 that reassured customers that any query could be resolved with only one phone call from them.

Recognising that value is important to business customers, as well as strong and reliable service, O2 launched its Business Unlimited tariffs in 2004, usurping the competition with unlimited calls amongst other O2 account users. Although Vodafone had launched Intercall, a tariff that offered free calls on the Vodafone network within accounts, Business Unlimited gave unlimited calls to anyone on O2; not only calls to colleagues for free but also to suppliers, customers, friends and family.

O2 continues to set its sights high and aims to become one of the best loved brands in the business market. The first step towards this was

taken in September 2006 as O2 launched its 'Signs' campaign – the first real business campaign aimed at creating an emotional affinity with business customers by showing an understanding of their businesses and reinforcing the key service messages of No IVR, 24/7 service and UK based business advisors.

Promotion

Since its launch in May 2002, O2 has moved rapidly to generate strong awareness of the O2 brand, with an emphasis on reaching the high value, technology-accepting business and personal customers that it most wants to attract. One of O2's key strengths is its striking brand identity – with its recognisable blue grading and bubble properties – which is consistent across all customer touch-points. The O2 brand aims to provide a serene and calming antidote to the 'shouty' sales messages that flood the market.

In the business sector O2 has run both product-based and service-based advertising. A continued support of data lay behind the new BlackBerry Pearl campaign as O2 was the first brand to promote this product in the UK, aiming to

drive greater data penetration amongst its customer base.

Behind this activity ran the well established sponsorships of the England rugby team and Arsenal FC. The 'End of Season' campaign that promoted Arsenal's move from Highbury was built on creating better customer experiences as O2 developed unique events like the fans' five-a-side on the hallowed Highbury turf. The idea of treating O2 customers like natural VIPs will continue to run into 2007 with the Rugby World Cup in August. These sponsorships continue to drive awareness and credibility within the corporate market.

Brand Values

Almost five years after launch, the O2 brand possesses a fresh and distinctive personality, resting on four core values. First, O2 is positioned as a bold company that is full of surprises. Secondly, O2 aims to be clear and straightforward – a company with the ability to communicate complex technologies and propositions in a way that is simple and easy to understand. Thirdly, it is an open and candid brand: it is fresh in a way that entirely sets it apart from its key competitors. Finally, O2 endeavours to be a trustworthy brand – responsive in listening to the needs of its customers, and honest in both its branding communications and its conduct as a company. Above all else, O2 is an enabling brand which constantly invites its audience to try new things with its consistent 'see what you can do' message.

www.o2.co.uk

Things you didn't know about O2

O2 Airwave is a secure digital radio network dedicated for the use of the UK's emergency services. As part of HMG Critical National Infrastructure it is designed to stay working during major incidents (like 9/11) when mobile and fixed telephony networks may fail.

As a mobile partner to Live8 in summer 2005, O2 helped to organise the biggest text lottery in history. Customers sent in 2.1 million texts for the chance to win tickets, generating over £3 million in revenue for the cause.

O2 customers send one million text messages per month.

2004	2005	2006	2007
O2 signs a long term strategic agreement with NTT DoCoMo to exclusively launch the i-mode® mobile internet service in the UK and Ireland.	O2 overtakes Vodafone to become the UK's biggest mobile network, with 16 million active users.	O2 de-lists, from the London Stock Exchange, on completion of the take-over by Telefónica S.A. It also posts its best-ever quarterly customer growth in the UK.	The O2 is scheduled to open in the summer as Europe's premier music and entertainment destination.

With almost 100 branches, Office Angels is the UK's leading recruitment consultancy specialising in secretarial and office support staff. Each week, it finds 8,000 people short-term assignments and places more than 9,000 people in permanent jobs every year. Its clients include 90 per cent of The Times Top 100 companies.

Market

The UK recruitment market is dominated by temporary and contract business, accounting for 86 per cent of revenues. According to the REC Annual Recruitment Industry Survey, temporary and contract recruitment services generated revenues of £20.27 billion in 2004/05, which marked an 11 per cent fall on the previous year. The permanent recruitment market, also according to the REC, was worth £3.21 billon over the same period.

The international recruitment industry is a market closely linked to the strength of the economy and trends in labour supply and demand. As such, factors such as the rise in home and freelance working, and people working for longer, all affect it. Other economic trends, such as the influx of well-qualified workers from new EU Member States, also play an important part.

The market is highly fragmented, incorporating a number of very large companies and a huge array of small to medium-sized firms. Office Angels is the market leader in secretarial and office support staff.

Achievements

Office Angels is consistently regarded as one of the UK's best employers, priding itself on the training and development of its people. This was underlined in 2006 when, for the second year running, it was voted the eighth best company to work for, in The Sunday Times '100 Best Companies to Work For' survey.

Based on employees' views, the company's success in the survey reflects its efforts to listen to its people and to create a strong and supportive organisational culture.

Office Angels has also led the way in championing diversity in the workplace. In 2003 it joined Race for Opportunity (RFO), a government-backed initiative amongst UK organisations committed to race and diversity issues. Every year, Office Angels is involved in the RFO's benchmarking programme and, in 2006, Office Angels received an RFO silver certificate in recognition of its achievement.

In addition, Office Angels has increased its investment in initiatives to benefit the community, recently donating used computers to Computer Aid International, the charity which sends PCs to schools and community organisations in the developing world.

Office Angels has been praised for its progressive approach to age diversity. In its position as an Age Positive Employer, Office Angels acknowledges that today's workforce is made up of a diverse range of age groups and therefore embraces a non-discriminatory approach to recruitment.

Product

Office Angels' areas of expertise enable clients to use one supplier for all their office support requirements. Both assignment and permanent staff are assigned across a range of secretarial, administrative, financial, call centre and customer service positions.

All Office Angels' consultants undergo intensive training and development to ensure they are equipped with the skills to work in the 'people business'. The result is a highly motivated workforce, as is reflected in the company's high position in The Sunday Times '100 Best Companies to Work For' ranking. In the survey, employee feedback showed that 92 per cent of employees said that they had fun with their colleagues and 82 per cent feel 'part of the family'.

Office Angels provides its services to jobseekers free of charge and each candidate follows a thorough and formal procedure from registration through to assignment, which includes an in-depth interview ard skills evaluation.

To assess candidates' skills, Office Angels uses a skills evaluation system, which allows consultants to assess the fundamentals, like PC skills, but can also create tailored tests to reflect a client's

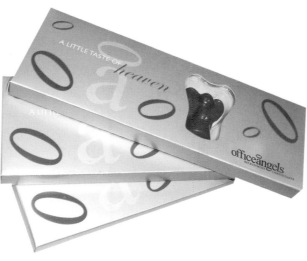

exact requirements. It also provides online training courses.

Through working closely with candidates and providing them with continued support, Office Angels lives by its belief that it is in the business of finding 'jobs for people' rather than 'people for jobs.'

Integral to Office Angels' commitment to its assignment staff is its ongoing candidate care programme. Initiatives such as regular social and networking events, Angel of the Month and Year awards, pension schemes, competitions, training and free Friday lunches help ensure that candidates are rewarded for their dedication and professionalism. All of these initiatives do not go unnoticed, with employee feedback showing that 81 per cent believe it rewards good performance and 82 per cent saying the company appreciates when a good job has been done.

At www.office-angels.com – Office Angels' website – candidates are able to register quickly with the branch of their choice and view all current vacancies. This facility is not, however, a substitute for the personal, one-to-one service that remains the cornerstone of the Office Angels philosophy.

Recent Developments

In 2006, Office Angels celebrates its 20th anniversary. To mark this, the company conducted research to see what mid-noughties office workers have in common with their famous predecessors from the 1980s, The Yuppies.

The survey found that Young, Upwardly Mobile Professionals have morphed into Gadget Obsessed, Status Symbol Infatuated Professionals – otherwise known as 'Gossips'. These UK workers were asked to identify essential office status symbols.

In the survey, almost 70 per cent of office workers said micro gadgets are the ultimate office status symbol, including an iPod nano, Blackberry, PDA and laptop memory stick.

Office Angels also launched its Ascent Management Training Scheme and each year 12 talented individuals are selected to join the programme. The year-long scheme exposes Ascent Trainees to every aspect of the business, including professional training in the necessary skills to run a business. At the end of a minimum training period of 12 months, the trainees should qualify as Branch Managers – leading teams, winning new business, overseeing marketing and setting and achieving targets.

Promotion

Office Angels have developed a highly effective marketing strategy which aims to capitalise on the brand's position as an industry leader. Activity encompasses press, outdoor and radio advertising, direct mail, event marketing, public relations, sponsorship, corporate social responsibility,

internal communications, research, the internet and an extensive programme of client and candidate care.

The business also has regular link-ups with leading consumer brands for local and national promotions including Filofax®, Liptons, TK Maxx, Canderel, Nestlé and Clairol.

Office Angels gains further brand exposure by conducting regular research studies and publishing reports on a range of employment-related issues, including flexible working, employee benefits and managing communications in the modern office. These regularly attract wider media coverage in the consumer and trade press.

The company's highly effective PR strategy scores some impressive results, giving it a higher media profile than any other recruitment consultancy. In 2005 alone, Office Angels generated over 900 media hits, reaching 390 million people.

Brand Values

The maverick style and personality of the Office Angels brand attracts clients and candidates alike. It has a passion for recruitment and is dynamic and forward thinking. Its clients are not industry or sector specific as they buy 'personalities' rather than 'processes' and therefore want an attentive, personal service. Clients are also keen to discuss issues, as they have the assurance that the Office Angels name signifies that there will be a real difference in the service they receive.

www.office-angels.com

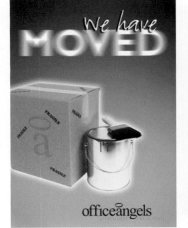

1986	2003	2005	2006
Office Angels is founded and the first office opens in London.	Office Angels joins Race for Opportunity (RFO), a government-backed initiative amongst UK organisations committed to race and diversity issues.	Office Angels is voted as one of The Sunday Times '100 Best Companies to Work For' and is featured at position number eight.	Office Angels celebrates its 20th anniversary.

Things you didn't know about Office Angels

Research conducted by Office Angels in a poll of 1,500 UK employers showed that 93 per cent of managers nominated trust as the single most important trait in their assistants. The second sign of secretarial excellence is the ability to organise, nominated by 88 per cent of managers.

Working closely with the Royal National Institute for the Blind (RNIB), Office Angels has introduced technical testing equipment that blind and visually impaired candidates can use to give them access to work opportunities with its clients.

Each year the 600 staff of Office Angels nominate a charity to be the main focus for fund-raising activities.

Office Angels has a broad spectrum of candidates, of which one in four are male and one in five are over 45.

prontaprint

trusted to deliver, every time.

Prontaprint has maintained its position at the forefront of the print-on-demand market through investment in the very latest digital technology. The brand is continuously evolving – developing new opportunities for both clients and Franchisees.

Market

In an age where design and print technology is rapidly developing, the business print world demands the very latest digital know-how the minute it hits the market.

Prontaprint is exploiting its commercial design and print expertise, concentrating on tailored communications for business clients – and the number of centres with turnover in excess of £1 million is growing rapidly.

Prontaprint is committed to taking a completely client-focused role to ensure that the network is in a strong position to capitalise on major changes within the B2B market. Understanding clients' businesses is crucial to satisfying a greater proportion of their needs. Delivering exceptional standards of client care and relationship management are key to the total service offering.

In recent years, clients have increased in-house capabilities, becoming digitally enabled and web-smart. In response, Prontaprint has adapted

and introduced new products and services including affordable short-run, full colour digital printing, large format digital colour printing, variable data printing, scanning, archiving and retrieval as well as web-based print solutions.

Achievements

Established over 35 years ago, Prontaprint has a fully integrated European network of over 175 digitally linked centres across the UK and Ireland and employs over 1,100 people with an annual turnover nearing £50 million.

The company is a founder member of the British Franchise Association (BFA) and played a crucial role in establishing a regulatory body for the Franchise industry. It remains a strong supporter of the BFA and was appointed to the board in 2005.

Prontaprint is also affiliated to the British Print Industry Federation and the British Association of Printers and Copy Centres, the Institute of Printers and XPLOR International (the Electronic Document Systems Association).

It also has a strategic global alliance with Sir Speedy, the premier US based quick print franchise. The alliance enables Prontaprint to offer clients central purchasing and digital transfer of documents to more than 1,600 locations in over 28 countries, for local printing and distribution.

Furthermore, it was the first national print-on-demand network to sign a formalised licensing agreement with the Copyright Licensing Agency.

This allows licensed copying of specified material within agreed limits. Prontaprint is therefore able to offer clients advice on copyright issues and help protect businesses from potential copyright infringements.

Product

Prontaprint offers a comprehensive portfolio of business communication solutions to businesses of all sizes including design, print, display, direct mail and finishing services.

Its centres feature the latest digital black and white, colour and high volume print equipment with both digital and traditional print capabilities.

The company is committed to an ongoing programme of investment in the latest digital technology to improve and develop its products and services. This allows clients to order what they require, whenever they require it, and reduces the need to hold stock, minimises wastage and requires less up-front investment.

1971

The first Prontaprint centre is opened in Newcastle-upon-Tyne, aiming to overcome high prices, large minimum orders and long lead times associated with commercial printers.

This forms the basis of Prontaprint's ethos – high quality design, print and copying at affordable prices, with rapid turnaround times, excellent client care and one-stop-shop approach.

With many documents now produced digitally, clients' original designs can be easily enhanced, updated, and amended. Work can also be securely stored electronically at Prontaprint centres, where it can be easily accessed.

Prontaprint's scan to archive system enables the conversion of paper documents into digital images, accessible from anywhere in the world. Clients have instantaneous access at their fingertips, coupled with robust file security and integrity of data – enabling the easy transfer of files to approved recipients.

The versatile nature of the Prontaprint digital network means that material can be supplied to one centre and sent out digitally across the network to be produced at different centres simultaneously, simplifying distribution and increasing capacity and efficiency. This not only saves the client time and money with reduced wastage and storage costs but also improves competitive advantage by enabling clients to respond to market opportunities quickly.

Prontaprint has recently become one of only a handful of businesses in the UK to install the latest image personalisation technology, enabling clients to reach their target audience on an individual level by allowing the personalisation of messages on correspondence such as direct mail and invitations.

Recent Developments

Proud of its heritage, Prontaprint remains focused on consistently evolving the brand to meet changing client needs in the commercial design and print market.

With a corporate client base including British Airways, NEXT, Hush Puppies and Dixons, Prontaprint is rolling out a new brand positioning to develop this market further with an investment of over £3 million following almost two years of research.

The new brand positioning was initially piloted at seven Prontaprint centres across the country, chosen to represent a cross section of the print market in terms of size, offer and service. The six-month trial delivered a sales growth seven times higher than the rest of the network.

The roll out includes a new corporate identity, learning and training for Franchisees and their staff and enhanced business services. A powerful new positioning statement – 'trusted to deliver, every time.' – has been introduced, alongside the strong use of illustration and a warm aubergine corporate colour to reinforce the human face of the brand.

Promotion

Prontaprint has been transformed from a high street print and copy shop into a key player in the B2B Print-on-Demand sector through continual investment in the development and promotion of its brand on a local, national and international level.

It has maintained its market-leading position through a sustained and structured approach to business planning, sales and marketing strategy at both macro and micro levels.

Marketing activity is based on extensive client feedback and market research. Independent in-depth surveys of existing, lapsed and potential clients help to identify changing factors of importance among small, medium and large businesses when buying print and related products and services.

Results provide Franchisees with a greater understanding of buyer behaviour as well as identifying new market opportunities.

Prontaprint believes that consistent and regular external sales and marketing activity is central to the ongoing profitable growth of each centre. This activity is focused on the acquisition, retention and development of business clients.

It also provides Franchisees with a wide range of central sales and marketing tools and resources to enable them to grow their businesses locally coupled with external sales support.

Brand Values

Prontaprint has four key brand values – Close, Connected, Can-do and Collaborative.

'Close' focuses on building long term relationships with clients on a one-to-one level. This is achieved through close contact with clients and close understanding of their needs.

'Connected' refers to Prontaprint's powerful network of talented and experienced people as well as the use of technology. Prontaprint harnesses these connections to ensure clients get the best results with their business communications, on time, every time.

'Can-do' reflects the business culture of getting things done. Whatever the job, large or small, Prontaprint aims to go the 'extra mile', ensuring it is 'trusted to deliver, every time.'

Finally, 'Collaborative' reflects that talking to its clients is the start of a two-way conversation, rather than a one-way sales pitch. By working in partnership with clients and each other, Prontaprint consistently guarantees distinctive design and solutions.

www.prontaprint.co.uk

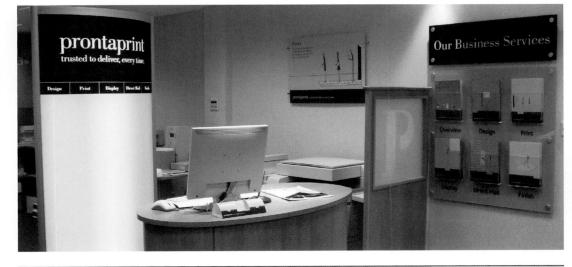

Things you didn't know about Prontaprint

Prontaprint was the first print brand to be acknowledged as a Business Superbrand.

Prontaprint is currently rolling out a new brand positioning, following an investment of over £3 million and almost two years of research into the market, brand development and training.

The first Prontaprint Franchise Agreement was signed over 30 years ago in 1973 – since then the business model has gone from strength to strength.

1973	**1980s**	**1996**	**2000s**
Following the signing of the first Franchise Agreement, the Prontaprint business model goes from strength to strength.	The company continues to expand widely across the UK, as well as into international markets.	Prontaprint becomes part of Adare Group.	Prontaprint now has the largest network of digital design, print and copy centres in the UK and Ireland.

⟳ Rentokil Initial

Rentokil Initial is one of the leading business services companies in the world. Some 70,000 employees provide a wide range of support services such as pest control, parcel delivery, interior landscaping, catering, cleaning, washroom services and facilities management. In over 40 countries, the 'Rentokil' and 'Initial' brands have come to represent consistent quality of service.

Market

Both Rentokil and Initial compete in multiple markets around the world. Their commitment to meeting the needs of customers rests on well established country operations, backed by the strengths of a worldwide organisation – including cutting-edge research and development.

Rentokil is the leading provider of pest control and specialist hygiene services. As well as protecting businesses and homes against the traditional 'pests' such as rodents, cockroaches and flies, Rentokil technicians also treat microbiological risks and treat buildings for woodworm and dry rot. Preventative treatment and swift response to any problems are particularly important for businesses that prepare or handle food, such as food manufacturers, catering companies and grocery retailers.

Initial provides a wide range of services, from cleaning and catering, to textiles and washroom services. From multinationals to small and medium-sized businesses, from retail parks to high street shops, and from major hospitals to community dentist surgeries, Initial's over-arching aim is to provide the support services that enable effective business environments.

Achievements

Rentokil is consistently recognised for its contribution to health and safety. It was named as

Company of the Year by the Society of Food Hygiene Technology during its 25th Anniversary awards and has been recognised with the prestigious RoSPA Gold Medal Award for Occupational Health and Safety over the last six years.

Rentokil has also received significant awards for its work to protect the environment, including a major commendation on behalf of Business Commitment to the Environment.

The quality of Initial's services has been recognised by a host of accreditations. Many of its service providers are accredited to the operational quality standard ISO 9001 as well as the environmental quality benchmark, ISO 14001.

The Rentokil Initial group is also leading the way in Corporate Social Responsibility, being in the top 100 of the UK's Business in the Community Index and, for the second year running, features in the

Dow Jones Sustainability Index. All over the world, Rentokil Initial contributes to the local communities in which it works. For example, in Australia, it is an active supporter of a range of community programmes, including sponsorship of the Daintree Rainforest Rescue. In South Africa, it established the Zenzeleni Trust, an initiative to contribute to the fight against HIV/AIDS, and in the UK, it is among the few organisations to gain a national contract with the Government's Learning and Skills Council to deliver Vocational Qualifications, Apprenticeships and Basic Skills – including adult numeracy and literacy.

Product

In pest control, Rentokil's technicians and support staff can offer unrivalled expertise and a professional attitude, supported by the most comprehensive range of safe, effective and

1902	1903		1906
The discovery of a strain of bacteria lethal to rats and mice, known commercially as Ratin, is made.	Mr A P Bigelow introduces a towel rental service for businesses in London, with the unique selling point that each towel is marked with the customer's initials.	This forms the basis for the name of the company – 'Initial Towel Supply Company'.	A London sales office to sell Ratin is opened.

humane products. Rentokil also offers a range of DIY products through hardware stores, garden centres and grocery retailers. While these cannot offer the level of protection of a professional service programme, they provide a solution that can deal with light residential infestations.

Rentokil Hygiene offers air and water treatments – helping the recovery of 'sick' buildings, while its special disinfection service offers an 'emergency service' for businesses.

Initial is a multi-service brand encompassing a range of services which help to create effective environments everywhere.

Initial Cleaning and Facility Services offers a variety of critical building or office support services, such as office cleaning, retail cleaning, factory cleaning, window cleaning, IT hygiene, waste management, facility management and maintenance. These services and more are provided by Initial to ensure the smooth and healthy running of businesses.

Initial Washroom Services provides a comprehensive range of washroom products and services to keep washrooms looking good and staying hygienic.

In continental Europe, Initial Textile Services meets customer needs for workwear, linen and floorcare – cleaned, repaired and delivered back on the peg.

Recent Developments

For customers in the food and catering sector who require very high levels of protection from pests, Rentokil's PestNetOnline has become a market-leading service. This is an online reporting system for tracking pest risks and escalating problems if

an infestation occurs. The success of PestNetOnline has led to the introduction of a complementary service, Pestconnect. This is the first remote pest detection and treatment service on the market, identifying a problem as soon as it occurs and alerting the Rentokil technician so that it can be treated before it becomes a threat.

Another important development came in June 2006, when, after two years of investment, Initial officially launched Initial Integrated Services. This is a fresh approach to facilities management, delivering multiple workplace services through a single provider.

Meanwhile the Rentokil Initial group continues to grow its business, recently making new inroads into the fast growing economies of China and Vietnam.

Promotion

The internet is a vital tool in Rentokil Initial's global promotion strategy, specifically tasked with building relationships with its business customers. To this end, the group recently launched two new global online hubs, www.rentokil.com and www.initial.com. These are being backed up by almost 100 new local websites launching in 2006/07. This is one of the largest business to business web development projects in the world.

The www.rentokil.com site features a host of vital information and support tools for customers, even down to a section on the lifecycles of annoyingly persistent pests.

The launch of www.initial.com ensures two-click access to the right service in the right country for Initial's customers and prospects. This is an important step towards providing the multi-service brand with a world-class online facility.

The new online hub will ensure that essential information about Initial's services is accessible in real-time and with local language options wherever required.

Brand Values

As a service business, the ethos of Rentokil Initial is about people serving people. Ever since the foundation of Rentokil and Initial, the same commitment to expertise and personalised customer service underpins the business around the world.

The Rentokil brand is synonymous with expertise in Pest Control. However, it also represents trust – the trust that customers have in Rentokil technicians to protect them from pest problems with efficiency and professionalism.

Initial enables effective environments everywhere. Its people are trained to deliver personal service use cutting-edge technology and to respond to customer needs while simultaneously helping to protect the planet. As a global provider servicing local needs, it is responsible for healthy, safe and representative business environments, worldwide.

www.rentokil-initial.com

Things you didn't know about Rentokil Initial

The European Textiles operation washes 93,500 tonnes of linen every year, equivalent to the weight of 316 Boeing 747 airliners.

Initial Retail Cleaning has over 1,000 scrubber dryers, which can clean a floor area the size of 400 soccer pitches daily.

At Victoria Station in London, Initial Cleaning clears up every day after commuters, removing half a kilo of chewing gum and five tonnes of rubbish.

Each night, the group's parcel delivery services collects on average 340,000 parcels from its network of branches and delivers them next day at their allocated times. The business has a reliability rate of over 98 per cent.

1925
Rentokil Ltd is officially registered, named after 'Ento-Kill Fluids' used to kill woodworm.

1927
Initial is floated on the stock market.

1969
Rentokil Group Ltd is listed on the London Stock Exchange – one of the largest new issues of shares the City had seen.

1996
Rentokil acquires the Initial brand and services, and in October, Rentokil Initial is born.

RIO TINTO

As one of the biggest names in the mining industry, Rio Tinto produces a broad range of metals and minerals, sold in a variety of markets with differing characteristics and pricing mechanisms.

Market

Markets for metals and minerals reflect business cycles in the global economy. Metal prices, for example, are set every day by the London Metal Exchange, and these provide the basis of prices for metals sold all over the world. Fluctuations in prices inevitably affect Rio Tinto's financial results, though the company in recent years has enjoyed record profits due to buoyant markets.

The big story in the global mining industry is China's phenomenal appetite for minerals – especially iron ore, copper and aluminium – as the country rapidly undergoes its own industrial revolution. In 2005, China accounted for 15 per cent of Rio Tinto Group sales. This has come from minimal levels only a few years ago and now represents growth at a time when demand elsewhere in the world has been relatively subdued. The indirect effect of China's mineral supply and demand on global markets is considerable.

Achievements

Rio Tinto owns long life operations producing coal, copper, gold, aluminium, industrial minerals and iron ore. In addition, it continues to research and develop new projects, and has a clear and focused

exploration programme to seek out opportunities for further expansion.

When we go shopping, almost everything we buy can be traced back, either directly or indirectly, to the mining industry – and often to Rio Tinto itself. The company provides the minerals and metals that are the building blocks of everyday life, including iron, copper, aluminium, titanium dioxide, borates, gold, diamonds, coal, uranium, nickel, zinc, silver, lead and salt.

Rio Tinto is also a significant energy producer, providing low-sulphur steam coal to power stations that supply homes, businesses and industries in the US, Australia and Asia. It provides metallurgical coking coal to iron and steel mills in Asia and Europe. It also mines the uranium oxide that, when enriched into fuel rods, enables nuclear power stations to generate electricity in Europe, the US and Asia-Pacific. Growing internet use and more sophisticated forms of consumer electronics are increasing the demand for power in the developed world, as is electrification in developing countries.

Rio Tinto is investing heavily in what it sees as a strong outlook in demand for metal and minerals. A robust pipeline of development projects is in place on four continents representing capital expenditure of about US$5 billion.

Product

Rio Tinto's mines provide some of the world's most vital materials, from the superstars of the commodities industry – like iron, copper, silver, diamonds and gold – to little-known yet vital substances like ilmenite, rutile, zircon, bauxite and boron.

Ilmenite, for example, with its ability to scatter light, imparts brilliance and opacity to paints, plastics and paper. Rutile is used in the manufacture of titanium metal, which is used to make jet engines. Zircon is a mineral used in the production of ceramic tiles and sanitary ware. Refined to zirconia, it is used in advanced ceramics,

1873	**1905**	**1962**	**1960s-1980s**	**1988**	**1995**
Rio Tinto is founded to reopen an ancient copper mine in Rio Tinto, southern Spain, which the Spanish Crown is willing to sell to provide money for a country weakened by 50 years of civil strife.	The Consolidated Zinc Corporation is created to treat zinc-bearing mine waste at Broken Hill in New South Wales, Australia – later expanding into mining and smelting there and in the UK.	Rio Tinto plc is created, after which it embarks on a number of new mining projects, extracting copper in South Africa, uranium in Namibia, and copper and tin in Portugal.	Rio Tinto develops significant interests in cement, chemicals, oil and gas, as well as manufactured products for the construction and automotive industries.	A major strategy review leads the company to refocus on its core mining and related activities. In the late 1980s and early 1990s it sold off non-core businesses, while acquiring more mining interests.	Rio Tinto's exploration and technology efforts are refocused to guarantee efficiency and exploit the Group's full potential.

Diamonds

Rio Tinto has created an impo...
international diamond trade. R...
offer diamond products across...
champagne and cognacs of Ar...
to the spectacular whites of D

Technology

Rio Tinto's Technology group an...
shareholder value by working wit...
units to secure technical optimis...
best practice, develop strategies...
improvements, and ensure that t...
a source of long term competitivi

Aluminium

Bauxite, the natural ore used to m...
abundant mineral in the earth's cru...
into alumina which is smelted into...
material, aluminium has firmly est...
most useful and important metals

Global business, local neighbour

We set out to build enduring relationships with our neighbours
that are characterised by mutual respect, active partnership,
and long term commitment.

computers, spacecraft, clothing, jewellery and electronics. As an ingredient of TV screens and computer monitors, it protects us from harmful x-rays. Rio Tinto is one of the world's leading suppliers of these vital minerals.

Bauxite is refined into alumina, which is smelted into aluminium. Rio Tinto is a major producer of all three.

The Group is also a top supplier of boron. Boron-based minerals are called borates, a vital ingredient of many home and garden products. Rio Tinto's Borax mine in California's Mojave Desert is the world's largest borates mine.

Rio Tinto's gold production comes mainly as a by-product of copper mining. The Group produces seven per cent of world copper, ranking it fourth in the world, and four per cent of mined gold, making it the fifth largest producer.

Gem diamonds share the stage with gold as a luxury commodity. With the opening of the Diavik diamond mine in Canada in 2003, Rio Tinto is able to offer diamond products across the colour spectrum, including the most spectacular flawless whites.

Rio Tinto is the world's second largest producer of iron ore with production of about 125 million tonnes per year. In energy, Rio Tinto accounts for seven per cent of traded thermal coal and 13 per cent of uranium, ranking the company fourth and third respectively in world terms.

Recent Developments

Rio Tinto invested US$2.5 billion in the growth of the business in 2005.

A project to enlarge the Bingham Canyon open pit at Kennecott Utah Copper in the US was approved in February 2005. The East 1 pushback is expected to extend the life of the open pit to 2017. Capital expenditure on the project is budgeted to be US$170 million.

Rio Tinto committed US$290 million to further expand existing Hamersley Iron mines in Western Australia. In October, Rio Tinto announced that it will spend US$1.35 billion on

further expansion of Hamersley's Yandicoogina mine and Dampier port.

Approval was given for construction of a US$775 million titanium dioxide project comprising a US$585 million mineral sands operation and port in Madagascar and a US$190 million upgrade of Rio Tinto's ilmenite smelting facilities in Canada. First production from the Madagascar operation in the Fort Dauphin region is expected in late 2008 and the initial capacity will be 750,000 tonnes per year of ilmenite. The ilmenite will be smelted at Rio Tinto's facilities at Sorel in Quebec.

The Argyle diamond mine block caving project was approved in late 2005 at a cost of US$910 million, and Rössing Uranium's open pit is to be enlarged with the addition of mining equipment for a total incremental and sustaining capital cost of US$112 million.

Promotion

Rio Tinto recognises the importance of maintaining a spotless reputation, while being seen as a leader in the field of sustainable development. All activities linked to this area are grouped under one line manager, the head of Communications and External Relations – who reports to the chief executive.

The department's communications are primarily aimed at shareholders, opinion leaders and key media. Among other duties, it conducts corporate

auditing and reviews for 'The way we work', Rio Tinto's statement of business practice. This statement is crucial to the company's conduct, as it describes the manner in which it works closely with local communities and adopts safety and environmental policies that go beyond requirements. 'The way we work' has been translated into more than 20 languages to spread the word, including Oshidonga (Botswana), Farsi (Iran), Welsh, Japanese, Russian, Chinese, Indonesian and Zulu.

In addition, the communication unit works closely with Rio Tinto's health, safety and environment (HSE) department, which plays a key role within the Group. Building from a foundation of compliance with existing health and safety rules, Rio Tinto seeks to improve its performance by setting targets, implementing effective management systems, and operating the best possible practices. Its goal is zero injuries in the workplace and the elimination of occupational disease.

Brand Values

The company's strategy has been substantially unchanged for well over a decade. The underlying principle is simple: it is in business to create value for its shareholders, in a responsible and sustainable manner.

In order to deliver superior returns to its shareholders over many years, it takes a long term, responsible approach to all its activities. It helps meet the global need for metals and minerals that contribute to improved living standards, as well as making a direct contribution to economic development and employment in those countries where it invests.

Rio Tinto seeks world class, large-scale, low-cost operations. It does not invest on the basis of product or geographical location. Instead, it looks for projects that will create shareholder value and generate strong cash flow, even when prices are depressed. By consistently pursuing this strategy over many years, Rio Tinto has established a spread of commodity exposures that serve this goal well.

www.riotinto.com

A WORLD LEADER
in mining

Rio Tinto is a global leader in finding, mining and processing the earth's mineral resources. We supply a broad range of essential minerals and metals, helping to meet global needs and contributing to improvements in living standards.

We produce aluminium, copper, diamonds and gold, energy products (coal and uranium), industrial minerals (borax, titanium dioxide, salt, talc, and zircon), and iron ore. Rio Tinto Group companies in more than 40 countries employ 32,000 people and own assets worth US$30 billion.

We take a long term approach, concentrating on the development of first class orebodies into large, long life, efficient operations capable of sustaining competitive advantage.

Besides the quality and diversity of our assets, we depend on the skills of our people and on our commitment to be a global partner and local neighbour with those who share in our activities.

To learn more about Rio Tinto, visit www.riotinto.com

RIO TINTO

Rio Tinto plc
6 St. James's Square
London SW1Y 4LD
United Kingdom
T: +44 (0)20 7930 2399
F: +44 (0)20 7930 3249

Rio Tinto Limited
Level 33, 120 Collins Street
Melbourne
VIC 3000
Australia
T: +61 (0)3 9283 3333
F: +61 (0)3 9283 3707

2000	**2004**
Rio Tinto completes US$4 billion worth of acquisitions, covering aluminium, iron ore, diamonds and coal, adding further strength to an already exceptional base of resources.	The Group sells off non-core assets for US$1.2 billion and makes investments of approximately US$4 billion in development projects.

Ryman
the stationer

Ryman sells a range of over 3,000 commercial stationery products from its chain of over 90 high street stores. Its products are mainly targeted at the small office and home office market.

Market

Ryman is the only specialist commercial stationery retailer operating in the high street. Others tend to compete in the wider personal, home and student sector, selling games, books, CDs, magazines and other non-stationery items. However, in the face of this diversification, Ryman has continued to build on over 100 years of service and a long-standing reputation as the UK's stationery specialist.

Continuously growing from its roots as the first self-service stationery shop, today Ryman is competing in an extremely competitive market, further intensified by direct mail companies such as Viking and out of town superstores such as Staples.

However, much of Ryman's success can be attributed to the speciality of products stocked, the breadth of services offered in-store and a professional, knowledgeable and highly trained customer service team.

According to Key Note research, the UK market for personal and office stationery is worth around £3 billion, made up primarily from core products such as paper and board, writing instruments, filing and storage solutions.

However, the stationery market is constantly changing and Ryman has reacted and adapted to factors influencing this market such as changes in the way we work and the tools we need to do so. Many predicted that the IT revolution and rise of the so-called 'paperless office' would torpedo demand for paper, pens and traditional office supplies. But, despite the growth of electronic information storage and trading, there seems to be as much demand for stationery as ever.

The computer-based office has led to a surge in demand for consumables such as ink jet cartridges, paper and storage devices, such as USB Memory sticks, CDs and DVDs. These are now available in a wide variety of options to suit a proliferation of PC and printer led uses.

With identity theft growing at a current rate of 165 per cent a year and costing over £1.3 billion a year, the business has seen a significant increase in sales of shredders.

Other factors keeping the sector buoyant include more students in higher education, lower unemployment and increasing numbers of people working from home.

Technological advances have also increased Ryman's scope of operations. Electronic

1893	1960s
Ryman is founded by Henry J Ryman, with the first store opening on Great Portland Street, London, where one of its major London stores still stands today. The first week's takings are £50.	Up until this point, the store chain is family owned.

developments – such as multi-function machines and mobile phones – are now areas of significant growth. However, this has further increased the number of Ryman's competitors, setting it against retailers such as Currys Digital and Argos.

Achievements

Ryman has managed to grow and prosper in a particularly difficult market. The high street has been under pressure from out of town shopping, mail order and, more recently, e-commerce, and, in addition, the market for paper products has been hit by high prices and IT-related uncertainty.

Given that background, Ryman is an impressive performer, with compound growth since 1995 of 80 per cent. Today, the business boasts a turnover of over £50 million. The secret of its success has been to invest in the key areas of its business – its people, information technology and the warehouse and distribution function.

It has also continually invested in updating and improving the fabric of its stores and diversified into new product areas – like new electronic developments – to react to changes in market conditions. A significant achievement in its sector was to become the first stationery retailer to sell mobile phones. An important element of its success is due to putting service and product knowledge at the top of the agenda, investing in people and promoting from within.

Product

Ryman sells everything an office could require – from writing equipment, paper and filing and storage solutions, to high-tech items such as mobile phones, printers and multi-function machines. It sells a full range of products needed to support most office machinery, including print cartridges, discs and storage devices. It also sells office furniture encompassing desks, chairs,

workstations and filing cabinets. Ryman has always been at the forefront of stationery innovation bringing colour to what is traditionally a very conservative area, often being the first to introduce products such as box files, ring binders and filing cabinets in a variety of shades.

As a specialist stationer, Ryman carries products not often found in a generalist stationery retailer. Furthermore, products are available with grades and sizings to suit specific needs. New product innovations are quickly embraced and Ryman strives to be ahead of the competition in all areas.

Ryman offers a full business service in a number of stores for photocopying, binding, laminating and faxing. Self service photocopying both in black and white and in colour are also available.

As well as the physical retail outlets, Ryman also sells these products via its website, www.ryman.co.uk, a mail order catalogue, Ryman Direct, and an office supplies directory, covering thousands of extra lines.

Recent Developments

The most significant development is the launch of the Ryman e-commerce website, selling the full range of its products. This is designed to support the high street retail offering, providing an alternative channel of sales and communication to Ryman business and home office customers.

Promotion

Ryman is a household name in the South East, but increasingly recognised throughout the country. The name is kept continually in front of the customer by regular, targeted promotional activity.

Ryman's promotional strategy is a combination of consistently offering value for money coupled with excellent service through ongoing multi-saver offers and regular price-led promotional activity. A typical Ryman promotion lasts between four to

five weeks; however, key selling times such as 'back to college' will last between eight to nine weeks.

National and regional press advertising is used to promote the new technology ranges such as mobile phones. The Ryman Direct catalogue is mailed regularly to the business market and the Ryman telemarketing team maintain contact with the large database of customers.

Since 1998 Ryman has sponsored a major football league – the Isthmian League – which is a feeder league for the main National Football leagues. All the Ryman League clubs are close to a Ryman store and strong links are being built between clubs and local stores. Hardly a day goes by, particularly between August and May, when Ryman is not featured in the sports pages of the National press as well as many local publications, TV and Ceefax/Teletext.

Brand Values

The Ryman brand values are quality, value, reliability and service. This has been developed and nurtured over 100 years and Ryman is an acknowledged specialist in its field.

These values have enabled Ryman to build and retain a loyal customer base. It is proud of its record for investing in its people, training them to be able to deliver the high standards of service, backed by expert knowledge of the range of products and their applications.

www.ryman.co.uk

Things you didn't know about Ryman

Ryman sells 100 million sheets of paper and two million pens every year. That's enough ink to draw along the length of the Great Wall of China almost 300 times.

At present there are 12 members of staff who have been with Ryman for over 25 years, 20 members of staff who have celebrated at least 20 years service and 52 members of staff who have been with Ryman for over 15 years. One member of staff has been with the business for 50 years.

Ryman sells over 80 different own brand cartridges and stores have a cartridge recycling point.

1993	1995	1996	1998
Ryman celebrates its 100th birthday at the Park Lane Hotel, Piccadilly, where six small businesses are shortlisted for the Ryman small business award for outstanding enterprise and innovation.	Ryman is acquired by Chancerealm Ltd, in which Theo Paphitis is the controlling shareholder.	The Ryman direct mail order catalogue is launched.	Ryman.co.uk e-commerce website is launched.

SAATCHI & SAATCHI

Saatchi & Saatchi is a worldwide creative company, whose fundamental focus is developing business-transforming ideas. Saatchi & Saatchi has 132 offices in 82 countries, and employs 6,500 people. It delivers world-class creativity in branded content, strategic innovation, shopper marketing, digital production, interactive, design, and of course, advertising. Saatchi & Saatchi is part of Publicis Groupe, the world's fourth largest advertising agency holding company.

Market
The global advertising market in 2005 was worth around US$400 billion, roughly one third of total paid-for communications spend. Global advertising spend is expected to have grown by six per cent in 2006, and is forecasted to grow another 5.8 per cent in 2007, according to Carat. Internet advertising is a key driver of this growth, increasing globally by 30 per cent year on year. In Great Britain, it is forecast to overtake newspaper spend by the end of 2007, and TV by 2010.

From a supply point of view, the market is dominated by a number of advertising agency networks, who are members of publicly quoted holding companies, such as Omnicom, WPP, Interpublic Group, and Publicis Groupe. Each of these groups own a number of competing global networks, and most have significant regional or local agencies, too. They also own companies offering a wide array of marketing services, such as media buying, PR, research, sales promotion, direct marketing and events.

Achievements
Saatchi & Saatchi has created some of the most famous and effective advertising ever run. Amongst its more iconic was the work which positioned British Airways as 'The World's Favourite Airline'. Indeed, since its inception, Saatchi & Saatchi has won countless local and international creative awards, across a wide range of clients and categories.

And it continues to do so. At the Cannes International Advertising Festival 2006, the agency was ranked number two network in the world and number one network in the world in combined Film, Press, Outdoor and Radio ranking. Its New York office won more Lions than any other US Agency and the network won a total of 37 Gold, Silver and Bronze Lions across all of the nine categories.

Also in 2006 the agency won substantial new assignments; business wins across the network include Sony Ericsson, Avaya, JCPenney, Emirates Airlines, Total and Société Général.

Product
Saatchi & Saatchi has moved away from an executional and advertising-centric model to a more holistic approach, adding strategic innovation, branded content and shopper marketing to its core advertising offering. Saatchi & Saatchi is now working with clients seamlessly across all these disciplines. In the process it has become more diverse in its paths to market; more entrepreneurial, emphasising unorthodox remuneration deals; and the end creative product is more multi-faceted, embracing long-form movies, documentaries, digital image banks, mobile soap operas, virals, interactive posters and long copy press ads.

1970	1975	1979	1982	1989	1995
In the UK, Saatchi & Saatchi Company Ltd opens for business in Golden Square, London, with brothers Charles and Maurice Saatchi at the helm.	Saatchi & Saatchi merges with Compton UK Partners. The new group's largest agency operating subsidiary becomes Saatchi & Saatchi Garland-Compton, the fourth largest agency in the UK.	Saatchi & Saatchi Garland-Compton becomes the largest single agency in UK with billings of £67.5 million.	Saatchi & Saatchi Company plc buys US agency Compton Communications Inc and in doing so becomes one of the top 10 worldwide agency networks.	Saatchi & Saatchi Advertising Worldwide becomes the first advertising agency to advertise in central Europe following the fall of the Berlin Wall.	Maurice Saatchi leaves as Chairman of Saatchi & Saatchi Company plc; Saatchi & Saatchi plc changes its name to Cordiant plc.

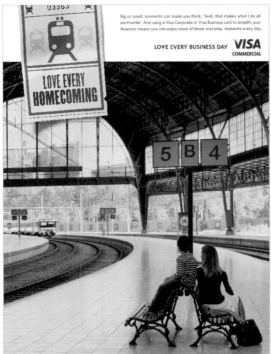

To inspire this explosive creativity, Saatchi & Saatchi now delivers a far richer array of relevant insights, through innovative research and proprietary knowledge generation. A good example of this is the CultGeist network. It is part research, part social network and part blog. It draws on emerging global trends via an internet-enabled community of over 2,000 young people at the cutting-edge of culture, across the globe, realising rich and detailed insights into emergent youth trends.

Recent Developments

In 2005 Saatchi & Saatchi looked at how change was redefining what its clients had to do to win in their markets. It concluded that its need for business innovation was as great, if not greater, than many of its clients. In addition, the rapid impact of new technologies, dizzying media fragmentation and the empowerment of the consumer had changed the very basis on which businesses connect with those consumers.

The agency understood that its core competence of creativity was a more valuable asset than ever. Its application, not only to communications, but to business, had become a source of genuine competitive advantage in any market, and sits squarely at the heart of any successful attempt to lead business transformation.

It also concluded that the strength of the agency came from its long history of big advertising ideas that had helped transform its clients' businesses. However it also knew that clients could no longer

afford to work with agencies that would tell them how to solve a problem before defining it. Therefore, the agency had to change.

Industry@Saatchi was founded from a recognition of the overwhelming importance to business leaders of corporate innovation. It was built around a deceptively simple idea: bringing creativity to the boardroom can help ambitious, visionary clients re-think their business ideas, create breakthrough thinking, and make change happen. Clients currently include PricewaterhouseCoopers, Diageo, Dr Martens and P&G.

Saatchi X was created for the highly competitive FMCG arena. This leading 'shopper marketing team' aims to use its market-leading insights and radical creative thinking to turn shoppers into buyers.

Many businesses have younger consumers who are particularly hard to reach by traditional means. In response, GUM@Saatchi was launched to offer brand-building creative to not only compel young people's attention, but even generate its own revenue stream by creating branded entertainment properties entirely rooted in modern culture. This comes in many forms including film, music, art, events, fashion or interactive, delivered via the mobile phone, the internet, a cinema screen, or an MP3 player. Because consumers will pay for content, branded or not, if the experience is rich and rewarding enough, GUM@Saatchi is able to agree radical IP and revenue sharing models with its clients, redefining current notions of ROI.

Promotion

Saatchi & Saatchi's own marketing is focused on a Business Development Unit, which looks after internal and external communication. It aims to harvest new client relationships, through a wide range of marketing activity such as PR, online, direct mail and marketing materials – from corporate brochures to one-off 'think pieces' to creative showcases. The department is also in charge of the agency's PR and building Saatchi & Saatchi's profile in the media from press to broadcast opportunities, including BBC TV's 'The Apprentice' and the BBC TV documentary 'Inside Saatchi & Saatchi'.

In addition the agency also produces a range of materials to keep existing and prospective clients informed of the agency's developments. These include the website, showreels, case histories as well as developments on key accounts and recent press coverage.

Brand Values

Saatchi & Saatchi's mantra is 'Nothing is impossible'. Indeed, it is carved into the stone on the top step of its offices in Charlotte Street, London.

Its mission is to fill the world with 'Lovemarks' – brands that inspire loyalty beyond reason. Kevin Roberts, Global CEO has written and lectured extensively about the 'future beyond brands'.

www.saatchi.co.uk

2000	2002	2004	2006
In September Saatchi & Saatchi is acquired by Publicis Groupe SA.	The merger of Publicis Groupe and Bcom3 creates the fourth biggest communications group in the world.	In June, Thompson Murray, US best-in-class shopper marketing agency, is acquired. Combining with the existing retail marketing unit, Saatchi & Saatchi X is formed.	The agency premieres a feature length documentary, produced entirely by its branded content division, Gum@Saatchi, on behalf of its Sagatiba Cachaça client, at the Cannes Film Festival.

Things you didn't know about Saatchi & Saatchi

Saatchi & Saatchi was the first ad agency to launch itself with the publication of a house ad, in The Sunday Times on the 13th September 1970.

Saatchi & Saatchi was the first agency to produce an 'over the wall' poster when communism collapsed in Eastern Europe (Saatchi & Saatchi negotiated space for the first advertising in the Eastern Bloc).

Saatchi & Saatchi was the first agency to produce a live interactive cinema campaign which was for British Airways.

Saatchi & Saatchi was the first ad agency to drop the word 'advertising' from its name, to signal a fundamental shift to being an Ideas Company.

The Samsung Group is now one of the largest global corporations. From its beginnings in South Korea, it now operates worldwide across a multitude of sectors as diverse as finance, chemicals and heavy industry. At the forefront of this well known brand is Samsung Electronics, a subsidiary of the wider Samsung Group and currently one of the world's most dynamic and successful organisations.

Market

Over the last decade, Samsung Electronics has morphed from a small-scale manufacturer with a developing brand, to become one of the world's strongest and most powerful technology companies. Boasting a vast product portfolio, Samsung's success can be largely attributed to its strength in three areas – memory chips, liquid crystal displays and handheld telephones. Samsung is a leader in all of these spaces, commanding an 18 per cent share of the thin-film transistor (TFT) market and a 12.6 per cent share of the mobile handset market, as well as being a market-leading producer of three types of memory – DRAM, SRAM and flash.

Achievements

Samsung has evolved into a group of companies spanning multiple industries with widespread success. Coherently structured, streamlined, globally focused but responsive to the needs of local markets, the group's core businesses of electronics, finance, trade and services delivered sales of US$140.9 billion and a net income of US$9.4 billion in 2005.

The last 12 months have been a year of milestone product launches for Samsung which has seen its efforts recognised by a number of awards. Over 100 Samsung products have received the electronics industry's most influential design awards. This total is the best ever annual showing for Samsung. The prestigious International Forum Design (iF) organisation bestowed 25 iF Design Awards on Samsung products in 2006, doubling the 12 awards given to Samsung last year.

Product

Samsung is divided into several different affiliated companies, with Samsung Electronics the best known and most profitable. It manufactures a wide range of products, including audio/visual, computer-related and telecommunication products, as well as home appliances and various components.

Recent Developments

2006 has been another momentous year for Samsung in terms of innovation. Samsung's continued investment in research and development has long been a hallmark of the company. This focus, involving an investment in 2006 of US$6.1 billion, is centred around 16 research centres located in eight countries worldwide. Some 27,000 researchers work to ensure that Samsung remains on the cutting-edge of innovation.

The fruits of Samsung's research and development process resulted in a number of world firsts in design and technical innovation during 2006. The launch of the Ultra Edition range of mobile phones saw Samsung introduce the world's slimmest ever phone with a profile of just 6.9mm. The introduction of the Ultra Edition 8.4 3G handset was also the slimmest of its kind, dispelling the myth that 3G handsets have to sacrifice design for functionality.

Innovation is not, of course, exclusive to mobile phone handsets. Samsung built on its reputation to be first to market with cutting-edge technologies with the launch of the first ever Blu-ray disc player available to consumers. The launch of the player responded to growing

consumer demand for playing and recording high-definition content, which far surpasses the video quality DVD can handle. Samsung's focus on research and development allowed it to answer a market need faster than any of its competitors.

Other innovations include the arrival of the K5 MP3 player which combined Samsung's lauded MP3 designs with those of a mini-boom box by incorporating built-in speakers. Despite being a fraction of the size of the smallest stereo system, the speaker design delivers the same quality of sound.

Promotion

Research and development, alongside product design, have yielded dramatic results for Samsung

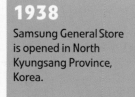

1938	1950s
Samsung General Store is opened in North Kyungsang Province, Korea.	Samsung becomes a producer of basic commodities such as sugar and wool.

imagine bringing life to your living room with full HD Blu-ray

Your heart stops. You're overwhelmed by a cascade of colour as the light hits the water. He's 3 feet away. Has he seen you? Thankfully you're watching Samsung's new Blu-ray BD-P1000 player. Offering the sharpest picture quality available courtesy of High Definition 1080p (or 'progressive', meaning full quality resolution) with unbelievable clarity around the edge of moving images. It also features an HDMI digital output, a 10 in 2 Multi-Memory Card Slot for viewing high quality still images and backward compatibility with DVD/CD with the option to upscale DVDs to 1080p. Samsung's New Blu-ray disc player. Seeing is believing.
www.samsung.com/uk/blu-ray

Samsung **Blu-ray** BD-P1000 Player

SAMSUNG

imagine an LCD TV
that's as brilliant off as it is on

With its fluid form and sleek design, you will admire the striking new Samsung R7 LCD TV before you've even switched it on. And when you do switch it on, you won't be disappointed. With a sensational 12.8 billion colour palette and integrated Freeview tuner, it takes entertainment to a new level of brilliance.
www.samsung.com/uk

Samsung **R7**

SAMSUNG

in recent years. The company has supported and assisted development with an aggressive marketing campaign. Five years ago, Samsung pledged to re-position its brand perception, aligning itself with premium, cutting-edge products. The policy has paid off – according to an influential survey of the world's most valuable brands by BusinessWeek and Interbrand, Samsung is now ranked 20th with a value of US$16.2 billion, an increase from US$3.2 billion in 1999. Samsung is now the most valuable consumer electronics brand in the world.

Sponsorship has played a large part in increasing visibility of Samsung's brand. There have been fewer high profile sponsorship deals than that between Samsung and Chelsea Football

Club in the UK. Samsung became the club's official sponsor in a five-year partnership which marked the biggest ever sponsorship deal signed by Chelsea and the second largest by Samsung, after its sponsorship of the Olympic Games.

The 2006 World Cup marked a key milestone for Samsung, with the R7 range of LCD TVs becoming Europe and the UK's number one choice. According to GfK research, Samsung's market share in the first half of 2006 was 20 per cent (value and units).

All of this adds up to a stellar performance by the Samsung brand. From the prestigious Olympic partnership to its compelling product offering, Samsung is one of the world's fastest moving and most innovative companies in business today.

Brand Values

Brand value has been a critical performance indicator for Samsung for a number of years and a major area of focus for its marketing strategy. This focus has resulted in the impressive top 20 ranking in the 100 most influential brands by BusinessWeek and Interbrand.

The Samsung brand is based around core values of technology, design and innovation and is associated with premium, cutting-edge products.

Samsung is striving to use its brand to continually position itself as a leader in the digital convergence revolution, and an innovative provider of consumer electronics that people instantly recognise and desire.

www.samsung.co.uk

SAMSUNG

imagine
the world's slimmest
mobile phones

The **Ultra** Edition

SAMSUNG

1960s
Samsung expands overseas – one of the first Korean companies to do so. It also penetrates the communications sector, successfully establishing a newspaper and broadcasting company.

1970s
The foundations for the present day Samsung are laid. Investment grows its strengths in the semiconductor, information and telecommunications industries.

1993
Chairman Kun-Hee Lee's vision and introduction of 'New Management' acknowledges the need to transform the company in order to keep pace with a rapidly changing global economy.

2000
A 'Digital Management' approach is adopted to ensure that Samsung maintains a leading position in the Information Age.

Smith & Nephew is a global medical technology company, employing over 8,500 people in 33 countries. Celebrating its 150th anniversary in 2006, Smith & Nephew has a long history of medical innovation, from the beginning of creating a better tasting cod liver oil to advanced designs in orthopaedic implants. Today, it has revenues of over US$2.5 billion and is the UK's largest medical technology company.

Market

The global medical technology market is vitally important, not only in helping to push the boundaries of medical knowledge and healthcare, but also aiding people to recover faster and saving costs for healthcare providers.

Smith & Nephew is a leader in the UK medical technology market, and one of the biggest companies in its field in the world. It is the global market leader in the £860 million market for arthroscopy equipment (allowing the minimally invasive surgery of joints) and is also the world leader in the £2.2 billion market for wound management, providing products to treat hard-to-heal wounds. The company is also one of the fastest-growing companies in the £7.7 billion orthopaedic market, providing hip and knee implants along with trauma products primarily to help heal severely broken bones.

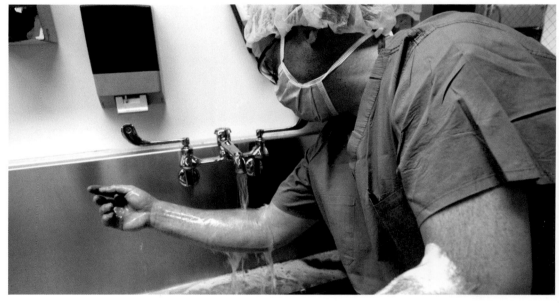

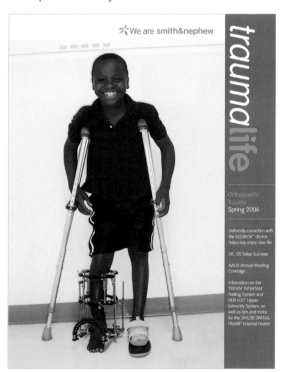

As the world's population ages and technological advances allow patients to live longer and healthier lives, these are all high growth markets. In addition, the growing problem of obesity is also fuelling demand for medical technology, as it brings forward the need for joint replacements. However, as in any high-tech industry sector, competition is intense and market players have to constantly keep at the forefront of innovation to stay ahead.

Achievements

Smith & Nephew has a track record of bringing innovative new products to market that help improve people's lives. Its ground-breaking innovations stretch back over many years. For example, in the 1920s and 1930s, it created ELASTOPLAST and Plaster of Paris bandages. In 1956, Richards Medical Company (acquired later by Smith & Nephew) invented the RICHARDS Adjustable Hip Screw, the first-ever compression hip screw that opened the door for more people having successful hip fracture operations. In 1987,

it introduced the GENESIS Knee System, providing the world's first 'modular' system for replacement knees. Following a decade of development, OXINIUM Oxidised Zirconium, a revolutionary material, was introduced for use in knee and hip implants which provided improved wear characteristics. In 2006, it launched the JOURNEY Bi-Cruciate Stabilised Knee System, which helps provide a more natural knee movement. In addition, there have been many more innovations from Smith & Nephew that have had a significant impact on medical science and patients' lives.

The company now has one of the fastest-growing orthopaedic businesses in the world. In wound management, Smith & Nephew's products treat the largest number of wounds of any company in the sector. Its full portfolio is unique, with competitors tending to have a focus on one type of product. The company's strength comes from being able to transform technology into affordable and high quality products that reduce the cost of treatment and speed the healing process.

1856	1896	1914–1918	1928	1930	1974
Thomas James Smith opens a pharmaceutical chemist shop in Hull.	Horatio Nelson Smith, the founder's nephew, joins the firm and becomes known as T.J. Smith and Nephew. He begins to develop medical dressings.	To fulfil the needs of the war years, staff numbers increase from 50 to over 1,200.	The company begins developing ELASTOPLAST.	Plaster of Paris bandages are launched.	The Smith & Nephew Foundation is established to become the central co-ordinator for all Smith & Nephew charitable work.

In Smith & Nephew's endoscopy business, where it has established a 29 per cent arthroscopy market share, the company is pioneering new minimally invasive techniques, devices and services that are beyond the capabilities of its competitors. For example, it is applying techniques it has mastered in treating knee, shoulder and small joints, to develop and commercialise new ways to treat hip injuries.

The company has won numerous awards for its work, including the ASM International 2005 Engineering Materials Achievement Award for its OXINIUM technology. This is the brand name for oxidised zirconium, a strong, hard-wearing material that dramatically improves the life-span and performance of orthopaedic knee and hip implants.

Product

Over seven years ago, Smith & Nephew completed a major transition, from being a multi-faceted business with a mixture of professional and consumer brands, to have a specific focus on advanced medical devices. In the process, it sold its consumer brands and underwent a total brand and identity reinvention.

Today, Smith & Nephew divides its business into four divisions: orthopaedic reconstruction; orthopaedic trauma; endoscopy; and advanced wound management.

The orthopaedic reconstruction business, provides joint replacement systems for knees, hips and shoulders. The introduction of Smith & Nephew's proprietary OXINIUM technology has driven growth in recent years, as has other leading-edge technology, such as its BIRMINGHAM Hip Resurfacing System (BHR). Ideal for younger people with hip osteoarthritis, BHR helps patients make a much needed return to an active lifestyle. Another innovation in reconstruction is the LEGION Revision Knee System – the only revision system available to patients sensitive to conventional metal implants.

The Orthopaedic Trauma business makes products for treating complex broken bones. In this area, Smith & Nephew is also achieving strong growth through innovation, particularly with the introduction of the PERI-LOC Locking Compression Plating System, designed for leg bone fractures. It helps reduce operating time and the invasiveness of the procedure.

In Endoscopy, Smith & Nephew's full line of devices and techniques for minimally invasive procedures includes endoscopes, cameras, light systems, radio frequency wands and instruments for removing and repairing damaged soft tissue. It also designs and installs specialist Digital Operating Rooms for endoscopy procedures.

Recent innovations in Endoscopy include the GLIDER Articular Cartilage Probe, using radiofrequency energy for smoothing diseased cartilage tissue. Smith & Nephew's Wound Management Business creates a range of products that help doctors and nurses treat wounds such as pressure sores, burns and complex surgical wounds. As well as providing the industry's only full portfolio of wound management products, the company offers comprehensive education programmes for medical staff – training over 150,000 clinicians every year. Products include the ALLEVYN and ACTICOAT dressing ranges. ALLEVYN dressings are the biggest-selling wound care dressing in the sector and saw revenues increase by 13 per cent in 2005. The ACTICOAT product range is also growing fast, with 2005 income up by 25 per cent.

Recent Developments

In addition to the developments already highlighted, during 2006, Smith & Nephew received FDA approval for its EXOGEN 4000+ bone healing system.

The successful ALLEVYN range was enhanced with the introduction of new and improved ALLEVYN Adhesive Dressings and Sacrum Dressings, delivering three times the previous products' fluid handling capacity. The launch of both EMPERION Modular Hip and LEGION Revision Knee systems, helped address the demands of revision hip and knee surgeries.

Smith & Nephew also expanded through the strategic acquisition of Osteobiologics Inc, which markets bone graft substitutes for repairing defects in cartilage and filling holes in bones.

Promotion

Smith & Nephew's brand promotion focuses on its healthcare customers, such as surgeons and nurses. It is a complex sales environment, where surgeons or nurses are the decision-makers, but hospitals, health authorities or private insurance companies are the purchasers. While professional advertising, brochures and the use of the internet are used to promote the brand, Smith & Nephew relies heavily on its sales force to develop close relationships with customers.

Professional literature plays an important role, and is organised into three different groups. Sales literature gives an overview of the features, benefits, and needs of the products. 'Proof' pieces are more clinical in nature, giving evidence of the effectiveness of the products, while 'Use' literature provides instruction for use.

The company takes care to carefully ensure a consistency of brand communication. A brand extranet, with a full library of guidelines, and an extensive image library, is invaluable in helping the different business units maintain a consistent look and feel, but also achieve a more culturally sensitive and localised interpretation of the brand.

The company also invests substantially in internal promotion, using publications, posters, and programmes to regularly promote the brand to employees. A wide range of activities include bringing in actual patients, whose lives the company's technology have helped improve, to meet employees, and giving awards to employees who best represent the values of the brand.

Brand Values

The Smith & Nephew brand is all about 'helping people regain their lives'. With this at the core of everything it does, it aims to ensure that its focus each day is on making someone's life better.

The values that guide Smith & Nephew's business, in the products it designs and the communications it creates, are Performance, Innovation and Trust. In delivering these values it behaves with a distinctive personality, expressed by its people and its communications. These are: Responsive; Confident; Energetic; Honest; and Personable.

www.smith-nephew.com

1986	1994	2000	2006
The orthopaedic specialist Richards Medical Company is purchased for £201 million. Making Smith & Nephew a major force in the US, this is the company's largest single acquisition to date.	Smith & Nephew opens an office in China.	Smith & Nephew sells its consumer products business, including ELASTOPLAST and the UK distribution business for Nivea.	US Food and Drug Administration approves the BIRMINGHAM HIP resurfacing system for use in the US.

Tarmac

Founded on the strength of a single patent and with a nominal capital of £25,000, Tarmac has grown to become an international operation, involved in a wide range of activities, serving over 21,000 customers, employing more than 12,000 people with an annual turnover of more than £2 billion.

Market

Tarmac is the leading supplier of building materials in the UK, providing solutions in all areas of everyday life, for everyone.

Indeed, Tarmac products have exceptionally wide ranging applications. They are used in the UK building industry from being required in the construction of homes and office buildings to football pitches and stadiums. However, Tarmac products can also be found in everyday products such as toothpaste and paper.

Achievements

Tarmac understands that every one of its customers and their project requirements are different. It therefore draws upon its wide range of resources and skills, depending on each customer's specific needs.

Tarmac's materials have been used, at some stage, in the construction of all Britain's main roads. More recently Tarmac helped to create the new Millennium Stadium in Cardiff, the M6 Toll Road, the Emirates Stadium, Ascot Racecourse and Terminal 5 at Heathrow airport. In addition, Tarmac has recently started supplying materials for the first stage of development for the London Olympics in 2012.

Caring for the environment is, and will remain, an important part of Tarmac's commitment to ensuring a sustainable future in the areas where it operates. Proof of its success is its achievement of ISO 14001 environmental certification at more than 73 per cent of its industrial sites, with an aim to achieve 100 per cent by the end of 2007.

Tarmac takes social responsibilities extremely seriously and makes employee safety its overriding concern. Indeed, it was awarded the industry Quarry Products Association annual health and safety award in 2005. Tarmac also achieved, through a targeted campaign, an 83 per cent improvement in lost time injury frequency rate so that by 2005 over 92 per cent of units were lost time injury free. This meant that during 2005, 92 per cent of Tarmac's units experienced no accidents that led to time off work.

Tarmac invests continually in operations and training to help meet its customers' needs, to give it the resources to provide market-

1905	1918	1938	1956	1974	1980s
Tarmac is officially launched by the Wolverhampton MP, Sir Alfred Hickman. It was developed from the TarMacadam Syndicate Limited, which was formed two years prior to this.	After Word War I, demand for metalled roads in the UK starts to take off. Tarmac acquires slag tips and roadstone quarries and sets up works around the country.	Tarmac begins to diversify into civil engineering. The company becomes involved in building not only roads and bridges but, with the onset of World War II, defensive works, military-strength roads and airfields.	Tarmac is awarded the prestigious contract to build Britain's first stretch of motorway.	A Housing Division is created which evolves into a network of housing companies throughout the UK. The housing boom of the 1980s saw it become the nation's largest house builder.	Tarmac is involved in the landmark construction of the M25 and the Channel Tunnel. It also begins to diversify into new areas – manufacturing bricks, tiles, building blocks and concrete products.

leading products and to deliver high quality, straightforward, reliable services.

Tarmac also aims to develop its business in a sustainable way to provide a safe, healthy environment for its employees, and to demonstrate environmental excellence in all its operations.

Product

Although well known as a supplier of asphalt, Tarmac also provides ready-mixed concrete, primary and recycled aggregates, asphalt, contracting services, mortar, blocks, pre-cast concrete, flooring and industrial products. It also works hard to help its customers to reach their environmental targets by providing recycled, as well as primary materials for their projects.

Recent Developments

Tarmac operates with an eye to the future, focusing on providing sustainable building solutions that take into account the changing world and climate.

TermoDeck – a heating, cooling and ventilation system – uses the thermal mass of concrete floors to cut energy use for heating and cooling buildings by up to 50 per cent.

One of Tarmac's recent developments is its porous pavement system, which allows rainwater to permeate through the surface and be stored for other uses. This was developed in response to the increasing issues of flash flooding and the need to save water.

Promotion

Tarmac's corporate advertising focuses on creating awareness around the company's full product and service offering with individual product and sector promotional activities complimenting this work.

Tarmac's famous seven T's corporate identity, designed in 1964, was updated into its present

form in 1996 and its application is now governed by stringent corporate guidelines. These guidelines provide the company with a consistent corporate identity and ensure that Tarmac's brand is protected.

Brand Values

Tarmac aims to be the first choice for building materials that meet the essential needs for the development of the world in which we live.

To ensure that this objective is met, Tarmac follows its brand values of being Reliable, Responsive, Understanding and Straightforward. Tarmac believes that this helps it to carry out its

work, day in and day out, and guides it in its dealings with customers as well as in its internal communications. Tarmac also aims to be ready, reliable and rock solid.

Tarmac's broader vision is 'to work together to build a better world' and this is demonstrated in the way in which it manages the impact of its operations on the environment, local communities and employees. Tarmac takes this role very seriously by consulting with the public, investing in restoration projects and listening to the needs of its customers.

www.tarmac.co.uk

Things you didn't know about Tarmac

Tarmac is named after its own invention – the road surfacing material Tarmacadam.

Tarmac was 'called up' to widen and strengthen roads in the south of England to carry D-Day invasion traffic.

Crushed limestone, extracted by Tarmac, is used for a diverse range of applications including paving, water purifying and light bulbs, as well as chewing gum and toothpaste.

Tarmac used recycled romance books to provide an important part of the sub base of the M6 toll road.

Tarmac has planted 111,645 trees and 14,188m of hedgerows in the last five years.

1999	2000	2004	2006
Tarmac is demerged from its construction services business to form two separate listed companies – Tarmac plc and Carillion plc.	Tarmac is acquired by its present parent company Anglo American plc which is one of the world's largest mining and natural resource companies.	Tarmac's largest single investment project is completed – a larger, more efficient cement plant reducing CO_2 emissions.	Tarmac enters Turkey and Romania.

With more than 200,000 students, it is the largest university in the UK. Its UK students give it an overall satisfaction rating higher than students at any other university, and it is ranked fifth among UK universities for teaching quality. This pedigree makes the University an invaluable partner for the business community, with more than 50,000 companies and organisations having sponsored their staff to take Open University (OU) courses.

Market

A mission of openness to all who wish to study, regardless of age or previous qualifications, is at the heart of the University's activity. The University, which was founded on the belief that communications technology could bring high-quality degree-level learning to everyone, has helped millions to realise their full potential through flexible education programmes.

Some people study with the OU to improve their careers; others to seize learning opportunities previously denied them; still others for pleasure. It remains the university of choice for busy professionals, allowing them to study without disruption to their careers. Some 70 per cent of students remain in paid work throughout their study.

Vocational programmes are a key plank of the University's activity. The OU Business School, for example, is among the largest business schools in Europe and among the largest MBA providers in the world. Indeed, about 75 per cent of FTSE 100 companies have sponsored – or sponsor – their staff on OU courses.

Extensive programmes in computing and technology, health and nursing, education and social care also see thousands of graduates updating their skills and bringing them to their own professional sectors. Ten per cent of UK social workers and five per cent of nurses and teachers are trained by the University.

Collaboration with the Forces gives thousands of Forces personnel access to the OU programme. Similarly, a partnership with unionlearn, which aims to help unions to become effective learning organisations, offers learning opportunities to trades union members across the UK.

Outside the UK, the University continues to build partnerships with businesses and higher education institutions across the world – a reflection of the increasingly globalised nature of modern business. Long-standing programmes that serve thousands of professionals and bold new

schemes combine to ensure the OU's international agenda continues to bring advantages both to those countries and institutions benefiting from the University's expertise, and to the OU's own students and staff.

For example, a global academic alliance between The Open University and NIIT – Asia's largest education provider – makes available a series of undergraduate computing courses from the University to students enrolled at NIIT education centres in parts of Africa and Asia.

Elsewhere, the University is working with educators, donor organisations and governments from countries across Africa to improve health services and education through a series of targeted programmes. TESSA – the Teacher Education in Sub-Saharan Africa programme – is providing

Annual Report 2005/2006

changing lives
changing society

online training that enables the extension of basic education.

Achievements

Less than four decades since its launch in 1969, The Open University is widely respected as one of the finest teaching universities in the world. It is ranked fifth for teaching quality of all UK universities, according to The Sunday Times University Guide 2006 and – according to the results of the National Student Survey of 2006 – its students gave the University an overall satisfaction rating higher than any other university's; the OU was awarded the same accolade in the 2005 survey.

One of the key factors in its reputation for teaching is the University's internationally-

1966	**1969**	**1971**	**1973**
Labour's manifesto for the 1966 General Election contains a commitment to establish the University of the Air. Labour wins the election and in 1967 detailed work on planning the University began.	The Open University is formally opened.	The first students begin work on the first of the University's courses.	The University's first degree ceremony is held.

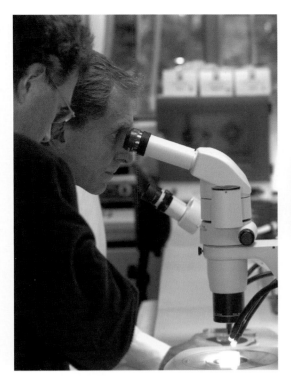

renowned research. The Open University researchers work closely with industry to meet its research and development needs, and with governments and public services to help to develop and explore the impact of new policies and practices.

Innovation and research activity has received a significant boost with £2 million funding from the Higher Education Innovation Fund Awards, which will be used to support knowledge transfer outside the academic world.

The explosion of new media means that it is possible to reach and engage students, to bring learners and teachers together, in previously unimagined ways. The OU remains committed to harnessing new technologies that will enable it to deliver the very best learning experience to a potentially worldwide audience.

At the heart of that work remains a commitment to openness to all who want to study and achieve their potential – and to distribute to the wider public Open University materials and knowledge. The long-standing partnership with the BBC helps to meet the second of those aims. Peak-time series funded by the University, such as 'Rough Science', bring new audiences to the University. Co-production partnerships, such as 'Coast', 'The Money Programme' and 'Child of our Time', do the same.

OpenLearn, which makes some of the University's educational resources freely available on the internet, is the University's latest achievement in delivering on a belief that location and personal circumstance should be no barrier to study. The project has made hundreds of hours of learning materials and collaboration tools available for students and educators free of charge.

The University is also leading the way in improving the accessibility of learning materials and services for students with disabilities. It has more than 10,000 disabled students – a number larger than the total campus population at some universities.

Underpinning its major role in developing best practice in higher education, the University is one of only two in the UK to have been awarded the leadership of four nationally important Centres for Excellence in Teaching and Learning; the project has attracted funding of £12 million over a five-year period.

Other developments include the signing of a 22-year deal with Cranfield University to deliver postgraduate education to Services personnel through the Ministry of Defence College of Management and Technology.

A collaboration project in which the OU and the University of Manchester – Britain's two largest universities – are partners will see combined degree programmes being offered internationally.

Partnership activity also extends to nursing. The first graduates from the University's Pre-Registration Nursing Programme have gone straight into employment as registered nurses in the NHS. The programme is the result of a partnership between the University, healthcare employers and NHS regional workforce confederations.

Product

The Open University's portfolio features supported open learning courses at all levels of higher education – from Openings introductory programmes through to postgraduate masters and doctorate programmes. More than 600 courses are offered in subjects including arts and humanities; business and management; education; environment; health and social care; information technology; law; mathematics; modern languages; science; social sciences; and technology.

The volume and complexity of the information that reaches homes and workplaces means the University has to respond more quickly than ever to provide courses that are topical and relevant and that equip learners to play an active role in shaping the future. A growing number of courses aim to help a wide audience understand and

engage with the big debates and issues of the day. Recent topics include ethics, Islam, information security and financial literacy.

The University is also adding to its range of foundation degrees, which are targeted at professionals who are seeking formal recognition for vocationally-focused learning.

Professional development courses for employees are an important part of the portfolio. As well as sponsorship of individuals and tailored programmes for groups of colleagues, the University also offers CPD courses through its Centre for Continuing Professional Development. It offers short, tailored CPD courses in response to the needs of employers, professional bodies and other organisations for professional updating and career development of their staff and members.

Promotion

The use of communications technology in delivering material and services to students – where such technology best meets students' needs – means it is fitting that the internet and other e-tools are among the University's principal promotional tools. The student guidance site, for example, receives 70,000 page hits per week and the Open Library receives more than 2.5 million page views per year.

Brand Values

The Open University retains an ambition to continue to break down social and economic barriers to make higher education as accessible as possible. The development of an increasingly comprehensive and diverse range of courses that make lifelong learning relevant to everyone, whatever their previous experience or ambition, is part of this intent.

It is innovative, international, democratic and inclusive, and is driven by a goal to achieve ever-higher standards of academic excellence and achievement.

www.open.ac.uk

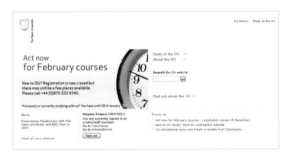

Things you didn't know about The Open University

Current and former students include Lenny Henry, Joan Armatrading and Matthew Kelly.

Almost three-quarters of OU students are aged under 44.

One-third of undergraduate students – on entry to the University – have fewer than two A-levels, the minimum requirement for entry at most other UK universities.

Thirty-five per cent of all part-time undergraduate students in the UK are studying with The Open University.

Twenty per cent of new OU students received financial help with their fees in 2005/06.

1983	1987	1998	2001
The OU Business School is opened.	Student numbers pass 100,000 for the first time.	The 25th anniversary of the first degree ceremony and the conferment of the University's 200,000th graduate are celebrated.	Student numbers reach 200,000 for the first time.

The Daily Telegraph

Renowned for delivering the highest standards of journalism six days a week The Daily Telegraph is the biggest selling quality daily newspaper in the UK. It is noted for its outstanding coverage of news, both home and overseas, and the stand-alone broadsheet business section is highly respected in the city and the wider business community. The newspaper's appearance is defined by its sophisticated use of traditional typography and strong photographs.

Market

The combined circulation of UK national Daily newspapers is 10.6 million, of which the four qualities account for 2.19 million per day on average. The Daily Telegraph takes 41.1 per cent circulation share of the quality market, 248,000 copies ahead of The Times.

According to ABC figures for November 2006, The Daily Telegraph achieved an audited average daily circulation figure of 901,238. Furthermore, the average daily readership stands at 2,150,000 adults (Source: NRS Oct 06, 12 month rolling data).

Achievement

The Daily Telegraph has won many recent awards. For example, in November 2006 Russell Taylor and Charles Peattie were awarded the Cartoon Art Trust's 'Best Strip Cartoon' award for Alex.

At the Association of British Insurers Media Awards 2005, Jessica Gorst-Williams won the Consumer Champion award. In addition, Alison Steed was named Personal Finance Journalist of the Year for the fourth consecutive year and Ian Cowie was voted Personal Finance Editor of the Year for the second year running. Ian was also given the Headlinemoney Award for Journalist of the Year and Pension Writer of the Year in 2005. The same awards highlighted Alison Steed as Protection Writer of the Year and Jenne Mannion as Freelance Journalist of the Year.

Product

October 2005 saw the launch of a separate stand-alone Business section in The Daily Telegraph. As the only remaining daily broadsheet newspaper, The Daily Telegraph invested in the new broadsheet product with a view to affirming its long-held commitment to providing quality business news, comment and updates.

The Daily Telegraph Business section is famous for its accurate, bold and insightful coverage, provided by an award-winning team of journalists. Led by Editor, Damian Reece, the Telegraph's big names in Business include Jeff Randall, Ambrose Evans-Pritchard, Christopher Hope, Edmund Conway, Ian Cowie, Richard Fletcher, Alistair Osborne and Russell Hotten. Regular contributions also come from leading business figures.

In the summer of 2006 The Daily Telegraph Business section's 'Fair Trials for British Business' campaign provoked 7,500 signatures of support and included some of the UK's leading business people, who agreed with the newspaper's view that loopholes in a law originally designed to combat

terrorism should not be used to pursue British business people whose extradition is sought by other countries. A letter was presented to the Home Secretary along with the signatures of support.

The Daily Telegraph Business section is renowned for breaking major news stories, such as the announcement in November 2006 of Sir Michael Grade's defection to ITV from the BBC. Jeff Randall, The Daily Telegraph Business Editor-at-Large, scooped the UK's three major television companies when he broke the story to broadcast media just in time for their 10 o'clock main evening news bulletins.

Even the BBC did not know about the story until Jeff broke the news, and the channel carried a live interview with him that night, as did Sky News.

1855	**1862**	**1897**	**1947**	**1987**	**1992**
The first Daily Telegraph & Courier is published, having been founded as a vehicle for its proprietor, Colonel Sleigh, to wage a vendetta against the Duke of Cambridge and his conduct in the Crimea War.	The Daily Telegraph's championing of charitable causes sees the newspaper raising £6,000 for starving cotton workers in Lancashire.	A young Winston Churchill reports from the North-West Frontier for the Telegraph.	In April, Telegraph sales exceed one million.	The Telegraph moves from Fleet Street to the Isle of Dogs.	The Telegraph leaves the Isle of Dogs for Canary Wharf.

one of the largest floorplates in England, covering 68,000 sq ft and accommodating a new 'hub and spoke' editorial system.

The Daily Telegraph launched its daily podcast in November 2005 and was the first British newspaper to offer a download of this type. It has since expanded the podcast format to include news, sport and comment, as well as covering major events such as the Budget.

Video highlights accompanying many major stories and events have also launched on Telegraph.co.uk, with some of the best Telegraph talent featuring in mini televised reports, accessed via the website.

As part of the drive to make news accessible to readers at all times and in a wide variety of formats, the Telegraph offers news alerts which can be delivered by email to desktops, by text to mobile phones or via a free Blackberry news service.

TelegraphPM – a 10 page up-to-the-minute summary of the day's news, business and sport – was launched in Autumn 2006. It is published online at 4pm and again at 5.30pm to include latest market reports, and is designed to be read on-screen or printed off to read on the journey home.

Promotion

The Daily Telegraph ran a successful campaign in 2006 promoting its Budget coverage with online advertising on the day of the Budget to drive users to the latest details and comment on Telegraph.co.uk. The campaign told readers not to wait until the next day to find out the essential details but to visit Telegraph.co.uk immediately.

The campaign also included a takeover of Yahoo!'s Finance channel, plus banner advertising across a number of different business networks, and PPC search marketing.

As a result, Telegraph.co.uk was the most visited newspaper website for budget coverage on Budget Day. The following day the campaign also generated an additional four per cent uplift in copy sales for a 16 page Budget analysis in The Daily Telegraph, demonstrating how web and newspaper coverage can work successfully in tandem.

Brand Values

The Daily Telegraph brand values are accuracy, honesty, integrity, quality and heritage.

Its brand personality is intelligent, British, trusted, good humoured, insightful and engaging.

1992. Held in great affection amongst the business community, Alex is much more than a cartoon, commenting on the wheeling and dealing of the business world and winning awards and accolades for his creators Charles Peattie and Russell Taylor.

A little later that evening Telegraph.co.uk published a video interview with Randall, with online analysis by Damian Reece and a profile of Sir Michael Grade.

The Telegraph multi-platform approach meant that the story broke with audio and visual that evening and was the headline story for the newspaper the next day. Online updates – with news, comment and share price reaction – followed, as did interactivity, with readers and users posting their views on the story.

One of the most popular features of The Daily Telegraph Business section has long been its Alex cartoon. Alex has been a stalwart of the Business section since his creators joined the Telegraph in

Recent Developments

In 2006 the Telegraph Media Group embarked upon a momentous shift in the way news is gathered and reported. Where previously stories were broken in the newspaper and subsequently published online, the newsroom has now adopted a multimedia approach to news using several publishing platforms, meaning that stories can be reported as they happen. In order to provide the state-of-the-art newsroom required for this cutting-edge approach to news provision, the Telegraph Media Group made a substantial investment in new offices in central London. The editorial floor is

www.telegraph.co.uk

1994	2004	2005	2006
The Electronic Telegraph becomes the first British newspaper to launch on the internet.	The Barclay Brothers buy The Telegraph Group.	The Daily Telegraph relaunches with a stand-alone broadsheet Business section and a separate compact Sport section. It also becomes the first British paper with a daily podcast.	The Group rebrands as Telegraph Media Group and moves from Canary Wharf into state-of-the-art offices on Buckingham Palace Road, London.

WEBER SHANDWICK
W O R L D W I D E

Weber Shandwick is the UK's, and one of the world's, leading PR agencies. Part of The Interpublic Group of marketing companies, its roots go back to the earliest days of PR, but in its newest incarnation Weber Shandwick celebrated its fifth anniversary in 2006. The agency puts its creative talent and communications expertise to work on award-winning campaigns for some of the biggest companies in the UK and internationally.

Market

The UK public relations market is growing in size and diversity, with an estimated 40,000 people now working in public relations in-house as well as in consultancies. It is also growing in terms of spend, with many companies and organisations switching marketing resources from traditional advertising to PR and other marketing disciplines, as well as investing in the asset of corporate reputation.

The key growth areas for public relations are healthcare PR, digital PR, corporate responsibility communications, multi-cultural communications, technology PR and corporate reputation management.

The consultancy sector varies from one-man bands to UK-only agencies and international players. Weber Shandwick is the UK's largest consultancy, employing around 350 people in the UK and some 2,000 internationally in a network of offices and specialist consulting groups. Internationally Weber Shandwick has 82 wholly-owned offices in 42 markets, and exclusive affiliate relationships boost that network to 121 offices in 76 markets.

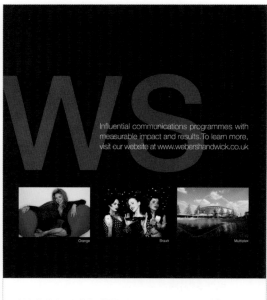

Achievements

Weber Shandwick has been recognised for its work by a range of organisations, from PRWeek magazine and the Chartered Institute of Public Relations, to the United Nations. Recent achievements include being named PRWeek's International Consultancy of the year for 2005/06 and The Holmes Report's European Consultancy of the Year for 2006/07.

The International Public Relations Association awarded Weber Shandwick Golden World Awards of Excellence for its work around the world with three honours in 2006. As well as winning the 'PR on a Shoestring' award for its pro-bono campaign for War Child, Weber Shandwick's UK-led campaign won the prestigious United Nations Award for raising awareness of the plight of thousands of children around the world affected by war. The team launched a CD with tracks from leading bands that became the fastest selling online album in history, and generated blanket media coverage. Last year, Weber Shandwick in Scotland won this award for its 'Save the North Sea' campaign.

Recent high-profile creative assignments for clients have ranged from: working with Tony Blair and a host of Asian Government leaders to highlight poverty and development opportunities in Asia; helping the International Osteoporosis Foundation change the way the disease is viewed by the public and healthcare professionals; and launching The Body Shop's Corporate Alliance Against Domestic Violence with Cherie Blair, to creating a multi-award winning Better Sex campaign for Viagra, putting

together burlesque, the boudoir, Braun and 60 consumer magazine writers to promote Braun's new beauty range; and helping Siemens to exceed sales targets of its Siemens CL75 Poppy mobile phone by launching it at London Fashion Week with British design duo Gharani Strok in front of Jemima Khan and 80 celebrities. Weber Shandwick's London consumer team also dramatically relaunched KFC's brand identity with the gigantic face of Colonel Sanders being built in the Nevada desert and making the new KFC logo visible from space.

Product

Weber Shandwick is a full service public relations agency. Its policy of recruiting the best media and PR professionals means the consultancy now possesses some of the strongest teams of experienced senior ex-journalists and industry-specific communications specialists in the business.

1974	1987
Shandwick International is founded in London with a single client and a global vision.	The Weber Group is founded in Cambridge, Massachusetts as a communications agency for emerging technology companies. In less than a decade it goes on to become a top 10 PR firm.

In the UK Weber Shandwick has six specialist practice teams in technology PR, healthcare PR, financial communications, corporate communications, consumer marketing and public affairs. Its office network gives clients access to UK-wide, pan-European and global audiences in all these sectors.

The UK business employs around 350 people across offices in London, Manchester, Glasgow, Edinburgh, Aberdeen and Belfast. Weber Shandwick also has an office in Dublin and an affiliate agency in Cardiff.

Globally the company is part of the extensive global IPG network with a strong PR presence across the US, Europe, Asia-Pacific and in the emerging economies of China, India, Russia and Brazil. In early 2006 the consultancy strengthened its presence in Europe by extending the network into Poland, Croatia, and Bosnia and Herzegovina. It has also announced new affiliate offices in Romania, Slovakia, Slovenia, Serbia and Montenegro, Latvia, Lithuania as well as Estonia and opened its first Nordic office in Sweden with local IPG advertising companies Lowe Brindfors and Storåkers McCann.

While Weber Shandwick's primary focus is public relations, the agency also works closely with sister companies McCann Eriksson (advertising), FutureBrand (branding consultancy), Jack Morton (event management) and Octagon (sports marketing) to deliver integrated communications for clients.

Recent Developments

In the past two years Weber Shandwick has invested in a range of niche consulting services including digital communications, youth marketing, crisis management, product placement, broadcast PR, financial services, consumer technology, and internal communications.

New launches include a corporate social responsibility and environmental communications practice, a new baby boomers marketing practice, O50, launched jointly with sister agency Futurebrand, and a cross-practice multi-cultural communications division to advise clients on using the media to communicate with the UK's ethnic groups.

SLAM, Weber Shandwick's lifestyle marketing practice, has also been relaunched as a boutique

'hotshop' specialising in celebrity, fashion and beauty, luxury, music and event PR.

Internationally, Weber Shandwick has significantly strengthened its position in Northern Europe and the future economic giants of Brazil, Russia, India and China.

During the past year the consultancy made some high profile new hires to head up its Broadcasting, Web Relations, Crisis and Issues Management services.

Promotion

A new strategic marketing team ensures that Weber Shandwick is always at the forefront of the PR industry in delivering its messages across key marketing platforms. These include: a new website featuring topical blogs with up to the minute opinions and comments from Weber Shandwick's experts; seasonal e-magazines showcasing Weber Shandwick's client work across all areas of expertise including thought leadership pieces from key strategists from around the world; and media events featuring the hottest media properties and politicians.

Brand Values

Weber Shandwick is one of the UK's leading public relations consultancies, with a deep pool of specialist talent and one of the strongest European and international networks. Weber Shandwick is a leader in the modern communications environment, and its client list reflects some of the top brands, companies and organisations in the UK and around the world. Public relations is a people business, and Weber Shandwick makes a significant investment every year in staff learning and development to ensure the consultancy continues to develop added-value services and

deliver real business results for its clients. Weber Shandwick is one of the biggest graduate recruiters in the UK public relations industry with a dedicated year-long programme providing training in media relations and creativity.

www.webershandwick.co.uk

1998	2000	2001	2006
Shandwick is acquired by The Interpublic Group.	Shandwick merges with The Weber Group.	BSMG Worldwide merges with Weber Shandwick.	Weber Shandwick continues to win awards and is recognised for its work across the European market earning the title of The Holmes Report's Pan-European Consultancy of the Year 2006.

Yellow Pages is part of Yell, a leading international directories business whose brands include the telephone-based Yellow Pages 118 24 7 and its online presence, Yell.com. Yell's overall business proposition is to put buyers in touch with sellers through a range of simple-to-use, cost-effective advertising solutions.

Market

Yell is the biggest player in the £4.4 billion UK classified advertising market (Source: The Advertising Association 2004). The highly competitive market consists of a range of media, including other printed directories, local and national newspapers and internet search engines.

Achievements

Since Yellow Pages was first published over 40 years ago, the directory has become a part of everyday life and both consumers and advertisers trust Yellow Pages to deliver the results they require year after year.

More than 28 million copies of Yellow Pages are delivered annually to UK homes and businesses, ensuring that Yellow Pages is the UK's most used classified directory (Source: Saville Rossiter-Base 2005/06).

Yellow Pages is a powerful medium, which is used more than one billion times a year, with seven out of every 10 'look-ups' resulting in a company being contacted and over half (57 per cent) of contacts resulting in a purchase (Source: Saville Rossiter-Base 2005/06).

Product innovation, value for money and advertising packages that deliver leads all contribute to ensuring that Yellow Pages stays ahead of its game in today's competitive market place.

Yellow Pages is also well known for its award winning, memorable marketing campaigns, which have contributed to keeping the directory at the forefront of people's mind for many years. As part of its commitment to excellence, Yell has achieved and maintained registration to ISO 9001, ISO 4001 and ISO 18001 – the international management, environmental and health and safety standards. Yell was also included in the FTSE4Good index for the first time in 2006 and the Dow Jones Sustainability Index for the third year running. This demonstrates Yell's commitment to responsible business practice.

In 2005 Yell was awarded Investors in People Champion status – one of only 24 companies in the UK who hold the title.

Product

Yell is committed to supporting the growth and development of businesses in the UK. It aims to understand, anticipate and meet the changing demands of advertisers and users and to take advantage of new technologies and communication methods in the development of world-class products and services.

Yellow Pages is ubiquitous, with huge reach. More than 95 per cent of UK homes have a Yellow Pages directory and it is used by 84 per cent of UK adults (Source: Saville Rossiter-Base 2005/06).

Yellow Pages directories offer advertisers sophisticated targeting geographically, socio-demographically and attitudinally. More than 100 area editions are published annually in the UK, and detailed demographic background information is available on the highest profile classifications.

Research shows that Yellow Pages is well ahead of the classified advertising competition on value,

1840s	1966	1973	1979	1993	1996
The forerunner of modern day directories emerges, with the publication of Kelly's London Post Office directories. These contained information on local gentry and traders, listed by county.	The UK's first Yellow Pages directory appears, bound into the standard Brighton telephone directory.	Yellow Pages is rolled out across the UK.	Yellow Pages becomes a registered trademark.	Talking Pages is launched.	Yell.co.uk is launched.

with the vast majority of advertisers saying they feel it offers good value for money (Source: Saville Rossiter-Base 2005/06). On average, Yellow Pages helped advertisers generate over £25 worth of new business for every pound spent on advertising (Source: Saville Rossiter-Base 2005/06).

Recent Developments

Yell is constantly looking at new and innovative ways to improve and enhance Yellow Pages, as well as extending into new areas to stay at the top of the increasingly competitive classified advertising market. In recent years many developments have been implemented, such as full-colour advertising, allowing advertisers more flexibility in the style of their advertisements. Furthermore, in 2004 Yellow Pages underwent a significant redesign in order to highlight to users 'added value' content within the directories.

Classification headings in Yellow Pages directories are reviewed regularly to ensure its users find what they need easily. There are currently 2,200 classifications in total. Alongside traditional classifications such as Builders and Plumbers, recent additions include DNA Testing, Talent Agencies & Management and Colonic Hydrotherapy, reflecting current social and market trends.

A new Insurance Guide was designed to be an easy-to-use way for Yellow Pages users to source all their insurance needs in one place. This was revamped in 2003 to include headings by product type.

In 2005 the Restaurant Guide was rolled out nationally and has recently been enhanced to include 48 headings ranging from Bistros & Bars to Nepalese cuisine.

Yellow Pages is also working in partnership with a number of organisations to ensure the preface has comprehensive information relevant to consumers. A new travel guide from Transport for

London is currently being rolled out across London directories. The London Central directory was the first to feature a striking redesign of the Yellow Pages front cover which clearly signposts the new and relevant information inside.

Brand Values

The Yellow Pages brand is built on its reputation for accessibility, trustworthiness, reliability and warmth. In keeping with the brand's friendly and helpful personality, Yellow Pages' involvement with charity and environmental projects reflects its concern with issues that affect individuals and communities throughout the UK. For instance, Yellow Pages has worked with Marie Curie Cancer Care since 1999, supporting the annual 'Great Daffodil Appeal', helping to raise more than £16 million to date for the charity. This equates to 90,000 nights of care by Marie Curie Nurses for terminally ill cancer patients and their families within the comfort and surroundings of their own home.

Yell is very aware of environmental and social issues and its impact on the wider community and is now working with 96 per cent of local councils to encourage the recycling of old directories.

Yell also runs the Yellow Woods Challenge, an award winning environmental campaign for schools, in partnership with the Woodland Trust and local authorities. Schoolchildren simply collect old Yellow Pages directories and compete with other local schools to win cash prizes for the most directories per pupil. For every pound awarded to schools, a matching pound is given to the Woodland Trust. Each participating school is given a free educational pack to help teach children about the importance of recycling, woodland conservation and the environment. Since its launch in September 2002, the campaign has involved 1.4 million schoolchildren and recycled more than 1.3 million directories.

www.yellgroup.com

Things you didn't know about Yellow Pages

New classifications introduced in 2006 included DNA Testing, Dog Walking, Reiki and Reproduction Furniture.

Yellow Pages can prove it works for free. Advertisers can have their own 0845 number which tracks how many calls each ad generates.

The most popular classifications for users are Restaurants, Insurance (all), Garage Services, Plumbers, Builders and Car Dealers - New (Source: Saville Rossiter-Base 1994-06).

Yellow Pages can be recycled into egg boxes, animal bedding, stuffing for jiffy bags, newsprint and cardboard.

In February 2005, Yellow Pages launched for the first time in Hull, completing its coverage of the UK.

2000	**2001**	**2003**	**2006**
Yell.com is launched, replacing Yell.co.uk.	Full colour advertising is launched nationally in Yellow Pages.

In addition, Yellow Pages Insurance Guide is launched. | Yellow Pages 118 24 7 is launched.

Yellow Pages Insurance Guide is revamped to include headings by product type. | TFL travel guide is launched across the London directories. |

Charities supported by the Business Superbrands

Army Benevolent Fund
www.armybenfund.org
Tel: 0845 241 4820
Registered Charity No: 211645

The Army Benevolent Fund is the Army's National Charity. Since the end of World War II the Fund has given financial support and practical advice to soldiers, former soldiers and their families in times of need. Around half of the money that the charity raises each year is given directly to individuals in need. The need can range from an electric wheelchair for a soldier's disabled son or a stair lift for an injured former soldier, to care home fees for a World War II veteran.

The rest of the money that the charity raises is divided between around 80 smaller charities that look after the special needs of the Army Community. These charities include the Army Families Federation, the British Limbless Ex-Service Men's Association, Combat Stress and the 'Not Forgotten' Association.

Supported by: General Dynamics UK

Ascension Eagles
www.ascensioneagles.com
Tel: 07866 612610
Registered Charity No: 1106766

From the 2012 London borough of Newham, Ascension Eagles (AEC) are Britain's best cheerleaders. The AEC programme builds leadership, teamwork, citizenship and community integration while teaching championship level cheerleading. Over the past decade, AEC has been recognised as one of the nation's most successful youth programmes. Founded in 1996 as a way to keep young people off the street, AEC involves 100 members (aged 6-24) in year-round activity and trains up to 1,000 other young people through outreach workshops. These record-breaking,

history-making champions have entertained 180 million worldwide and have an international reputation.

Supported by: ExCeL London

Brake, the road safety charity
www.brake.org.uk
Tel: 01484 559909
Registered Charity No: 1093244

Every day, nine people are killed on UK roads and 10 times as many are seriously injured. Many of those whose lives are tragically cut short are young – road crashes are the biggest killer of 15-24 year-olds. Brake is a national charity dedicated to preventing road death and injury and caring for people bereaved or injured in road crashes. Our work includes educating different road users – from children and their parents, to young people learning to drive, to professional drivers – through resources, training and events. We co-ordinate National Road Safety Week and provide free community training on different road safety topics, including family road safety and young driver safety, through the FedEx & Brake Road Safety Academy. Our BrakeCare division is the national provider of support for road crash victims.

Supported by: FedEx Express

Breakthrough Breast Cancer
www.breakthrough.org.uk
Tel: 020 7025 2400
Registered Charity No: 1062636

Breakthrough Breast Cancer is the leading charity committed to fighting breast cancer through research and education and has established the UK's first dedicated breast cancer research centre, in partnership with The Institute of Cancer Research. Breakthrough's scientific work ultimately aims

to eradicate breast cancer by discovering the causes of the disease, finding methods of prevention and developing new treatments, with results being translated as rapidly as possible into practical help for patients.

Breakthrough campaigns for policies that support breast cancer research and better services, as well as promoting breast cancer education and awareness among the public, policy makers, health professionals and the media.

Breakthrough is committed to a single vision – to work for a future free from the fear of breast cancer.

Supported by: Basildon Bond, Office Angels

Cancer Research UK
www.cancerresearchuk.org
Tel: 020 7242 0200
Registered Charity No: 1089464

Cancer Research UK is the world's leading independent organisation dedicated to cancer research. It carries out scientific research to help prevent, diagnose and treat cancer, through the work of 3,500 scientists, doctors and nurses across the UK. Its groundbreaking work, funded by the general public, is helping more people beat cancer every year.

Cancer Research UK has a major influence on the UK Government. Its unique position allows it to inform political debate, provide expert advice and influence healthcare policies. It works closely with politicians to make sure that the views of its supporters, scientists, doctors, cancer patients and their families are heard.

Supported by: Superbrands (UK) Ltd

Charities Aid Foundation
www.cafonline.org
Tel: 01732 520 000
Registered Charity No: 268369

CAF is an independent charity committed to effective giving. We have been working to help donors, both companies and individuals, to give more effectively, and charities to make the most of their resources for more than 80 years. For companies we provide solutions that encourage closer engagement with their communities. We work in partnership with organisations to design and develop Corporate Community Investment programmes that are based on effective and sustainable methods of giving. Through both our company giving and employee and customer engagement programmes, CAF provides companies with professional targeted assistance. For individuals, CAF makes it easy to find charities and donate to them tax effectively and for charities, CAF offers low-cost banking, as well as financial and training services to make donations go further.

Supported by: Samsung

ChildLine
www.childline.org.uk
ChildLine helpline: 0800 1111
Registered Charity No: 1003758

ChildLine is the free and confidential 24-hour helpline for children in trouble or danger across the UK. Trained volunteer counsellors comfort, advise and protect children and young people who may feel they have nowhere else to turn.

Since it was launched in 1986, ChildLine has saved children's lives, found refuge for children in danger on the streets, and given hope to thousands of children who believed no one else cared for them. ChildLine has now counselled nearly two million children and young people.

Children call ChildLine about a wide range of problems, but the most common problems are abuse (both sexual and physical), bullying, serious family tensions, worries about friends' welfare and teenage pregnancy.

ChildLine joined the NSPCC on February 1st 2006.

Supported by: BT

CHILDREN with LEUKAEMIA
www.leukaemia.org
Tel: 020 7404 0808
Registered Charity No: 298405

Leukaemia is cancer of the blood. It is the most common childhood cancer and is a devastating disease, killing one in four children who are diagnosed with it. The number of new cases is rising every year and we don't know why.

CHILDREN with LEUKAEMIA is Britain's leading charity dedicated exclusively to the conquest of childhood leukaemia through pioneering research into the causes and new treatments, as well as providing support for leukaemic children and their families.

Supported by: BSI

Combat Stress
www.combatstress.org.uk
Tel: 01372 841600
Registered Charity No: 206002

Combat Stress, The Ex-Services Mental Welfare Society, is the only charity to provide specialist help and care to ex-Servicemen and women who suffer from Service related psychological injury, caused through service to their country. We help veterans from the Armed Forces and Merchant Navy, from all ranks and all conflicts and of all ages through a nationwide network of welfare officers and three short stay remedial treatment centres in Surrey, Shropshire and Scotland.

The demand for our care shows no signs of abating; we take on over 900 new clients each year. We have never been busier and are already working with a growing number of veterans of the Iraq War and the conflict in Afghanistan to add to the list of the many men and women of less recent conflicts and peacekeeping operations who currently need our help and support.

Supported by: General Dynamics UK

COMIC RELIEF

Comic Relief
www.comicrelief.com
Tel: 020 7820 5555
Registered Charity No: 326568

Comic Relief was launched from the Safawa refugee camp in Sudan, on Christmas Day 1985, in response to crippling famine in Africa. The aim was to take a fresh and fun approach to fundraising and, through events like Red Nose Day, inspire those who hadn't previously been interested in charity. There have now been 10 Red Nose Days and three Sport Reliefs.

Comic Relief has worked with some of the biggest names in entertainment, sport and business and tackles some of the biggest issues facing people across the world. Their work ranges from supporting projects that help children who are living rough in India to community programmes helping the elderly across the UK. A number of high profile partnerships have brought in millions of pounds to help reach these aims but the biggest group of supporters remains schools.

Supported by: BT

Community Network
www.community-network.org
Tel: 020 7923 5250
Registered Charity No: 1000011

Community Network provides a telephone conference call service to other charities and not for profit organisations. As the pioneers of social telephony, the emphasis is on creating opportunities for social inclusion, breaking down the isolation many people suffer through age, frailty, mobility, location, transport or caring responsibilities. Community Network creates 'virtual' communities of interest using user-friendly affordable, accessible technology – using just a phone. Working in partnership with other agencies, including local Government, Community Network has developed projects such as: FriendshipLink, 'bringing' friends to your home by phone; FaithLink, allowing people to 'attend' religious services from their homes; telephone group book clubs; and 'respite care' groups for carers.

Supported by: BT

Dreams Come True
www.dctc.org.uk
Tel: 01730 815000
Registered Charity No: 800248

Dreams Come True was formed in 1988 with the express aim of helping fulfil the dreams of terminally and seriously ill children. We are a national charity helping children who have both life threatening and long term degenerative illnesses including Leukaemia, Cystic Fibrosis, Cancer and Muscular Dystrophy. We have helped over 3,000 children see their dreams become reality and with further support, can help even more.

Supported by: Mintel

Endometriosis UK
www.endometriosis-uk.org
Helpline: 0808 808 2227
Registered Charity No: 1035810

Every day two million women in the UK live with endometriosis.

Endometriosis UK, the leading UK endometriosis charity offers a number of key services that empower women with vital information and support including a free helpline and regional groups.

Despite being so common, there is no known cause or cure for this chronic disease and awareness and understanding is very low. Endometriosis occurs when cells from the lining of the womb grow in other parts of the body and, while these cells continue to respond to the menstrual cycle, they cannot escape from the body. This results in severe pain and much reduced quality of life.

Our mission is to improve the lives of all people affected by endometriosis and help them overcome the impact of the disease.

Supported by: Weber Shandwick

Great North Air Ambulance Service
www.greatnorthairambulance.co.uk
Tel: 01325 487263
Registered Charity No: 1092204

The Great North Air Ambulance Service (GNAAS) provides emergency ambulance provision for severely injured or ill people from the Scottish Borders to North Yorkshire, coast to coast. This service runs seven days a week, during daylight hours. Patient care is GNAAS's number one priority. This is why each member of the team is trained to such a high level, beyond NHS standard. Nearly all missions fly with a doctor on board, which gives the patients the gold standard of pre-hospital care. It is the only air ambulance charity to do this outside London.

Patients are airlifted to the most appropriate hospital for their needs; this differs from road ambulances who have to take the patient to the nearest hospital.

GNAAS receives no Government or lottery funding and relies completely on donations from the public. If the public stops donating, the service would be grounded, which sadly has happened in the past.

Supported by: Eddie Stobart

Hastings Half Marathon
www.hastings-half.co.uk
Tel: 01424 437001
Registered Charity No: 293745

The Hastings Half Marathon takes place in mid March each year. It is organised each year by The Hastings Lions Club, to raise money for needy causes and to promote the ancient town of Hastings.

Around 5,000 runners take part, with an additional 300 youngsters participating in a 2.5km Mini-Run. The event has strong crowd support and a lively atmosphere, with bands playing along the route.

The event has been voted 'The Best Half Marathon in the UK' by Runners World magazine for the fifth consecutive year. Many international athletes join their UK counterparts, with a particularly strong contingent coming from Kenya.

The event has raised nearly £2.5 million in its 22-year history with General Dynamics giving £1,000 to the first three charity teams to cross the finish line.

Supported by: General Dynamics UK

Help the Aged
www.helptheaged.org.uk
Tel: 020 7278 1114
Registered Charity No: 272786

Help the Aged is an international charity dedicated to creating a world where older people can live their lives free from poverty, isolation and neglect.

Its unique understanding of older people's needs enables it to raise public awareness of issues affecting older people in the UK and overseas, campaign for changes in policy and practice nationally and regionally, and provide practical support to help disadvantaged older people live independent lives. Independent of Government, it is funded by individuals, companies and trusts. The charity operates advice lines and a home safety and security service, gives grants to community groups, publishes a wide range of information and guidance, runs a nationwide network of charity shops, and delivers emergency relief and ongoing support following humanitarian disasters overseas.

Supported by: BDO Stoy Hayward

Hope and Homes for Children
www.hopeandhomes.org
Tel: 01722 790111
Registered Charity No: 1089490

Hope and Homes for Children (HHC) aims to give hope to the poorest children in the world – those who are orphaned, abandoned or vulnerable – by enabling them to grow up within the love of a family and the security of a home, so that they can fulfil their potential.

HHC works in 13 countries across Eastern Europe and Africa reuniting families, supporting young mothers who may otherwise abandon their babies and providing a vital lifeline for grandparent and child headed households affected by HIV/AIDS. We believe that, above all else, every child needs the loving care of a family.

We place particular emphasis on working with governments, local authorities and local communities to ensure that our programmes inform the development of future policy towards children in the countries where we operate. We are determined that our work should achieve long term impact on individual lives and on the future of entire societies.

Supported by: Lloyd's

WE ARE MACMILLAN. CANCER SUPPORT

Macmillan Cancer Support
www.macmillan.org.uk
Tel: 0808 808 2020
Registered Charity No: 261017

Macmillan Cancer Support works to improve the lives of people affected by cancer, providing practical, medical, emotional and financial support and pushing for better cancer care.

We offer a source of support, helping with all the things people affected by cancer want and need, and are a force for change, pushing for better cancer care.

Macmillan Cancer Support takes into account not just the medical needs of people affected by cancer but the social, emotional and practical impact cancer can have. We are there for people from the moment they suspect they have cancer, and for their families too.

We deliver our own services and work with other partners to develop new ones. Our largest partner is the NHS but there are others in the public, voluntary and private sectors of care too.

Supported by: Avis, General Dynamics UK, Lloyd's

Make-A-Wish Foundation® UK
www.make-a-wish.org.uk
Tel: 01276 405060
Registered Charity No: 295672

Make-A-Wish Foundation UK grants magical wishes for children and young people fighting life-threatening illnesses.

Make-A-Wish has no cures to offer and all too often some of our endings are sad, but during desperate times when there seems to be no hope, Make-A-Wish steps in to provide positive and uplifting relief. Most of all, a wish granted brings a time of magic and joy for the special children and families that we serve. Over 4,000 special wishes have been granted since 1986.

Supported by: Flybe

Marie Curie Cancer Care
www.mariecurie.org.uk
Tel: 0800 716 146
Registered Charity No: 207994

Marie Curie Cancer Care provides free high quality nursing to give terminally ill people the choice of dying at home, supported by their families. Every day 410 people will die of cancer in the UK. Most want to be cared for in their own homes, close to the people and things they love. This year Marie Curie nurses will make this possible for more than 18,000 cancer patients. But for every family that we help there are always others that we can't. We want to reach all of these families – making choice a reality for them all.

Supported by: Yellow Pages

Cruelty to children must stop. FULL STOP.

NSPCC
www.nspcc.org.uk
Child Protection Helpline: 0808 800 5000
Registered Charity No: 216401

The National Society for the Prevention of Cruelty to Children (NSPCC) is the UK's leading charity specialising in child protection and the prevention of cruelty to children.

The society has been protecting children from cruelty since 1884, when it was founded by Benjamin Waugh. It is the only children's charity with statutory powers enabling it to act to safeguard children at risk.

The NSPCC provides an independent campaigning voice for children. It works to influence Government on legislation and policy that affect the lives of children and families, and runs public education campaigns to raise awareness of, and encourage action to prevent, child abuse.

ChildLine joined the NSPCC on February 1st 2006.

Supported by: Basildon Bond, BDO Stoy Hayward, BT, Group 4 Securicor, JCB, Saatchi & Saatchi

Richard House
www.richardhouse.org.uk
Tel: 020 7511 0222
Registered Charity No: 1059029

Richard House Children's Hospice is a modern, purpose-built hospice in east London, created for children with life-limiting or life-threatening conditions.

No child or their family should have to face the trials of coping with a terminal illness alone. Richard House provides emotional support, relieves symptoms and pain, calms anxiety and helps a family to cope with the situation, while creating positive experiences along the way.

We offer a range of services including day care, residential accommodation, support in the home, and family support including befriending and bereavement services.

Many children in our care face complex disabilities and need constant attention and we can be a lifeline to families, helping them

make the most of the short but precious lives of their children.

Richard House is currently caring for over 150 children and their families. In 2007 Richard House will need to raise £2.9 million to be able to maintain its services.

Supported by: ExCeL London

SPARKS
www.sparks.org.uk
Tel: 020 7799 2111
Registered Charity No: 1003825

SPARKS funds pioneering medical research that has a practical, positive impact on the lives of babies and children.

Since 1991, SPARKS has funded over 160 medical projects in the UK, committing over £12 million to tackle conditions as diverse as cerebral palsy, meningitis, the dangers of premature birth, spina bifida, childhood arthritis and cancers.

In the UK, many important areas of paediatric research depend heavily on funding from charities like SPARKS rather than the public purse. It's this knowledge that motivates the dedicated SPARKS team.

Supported by: Deutsche Bank

 St GILES TRUST

St Giles Trust
www.stgilestrust.org.uk
Tel: 020 7703 7000
Registered Charity No: 801355

St Giles Trust helps disadvantaged people to maximise their potential. The people we support have multiple problems including homelessness, poverty, unemployment, health, disability and addiction. We work with 15,000 people a year.

Our focus is crime prevention and community safety. We offer a range of integrated services that enable disadvantaged people to escape the cycle of homelessness, poverty and unemployment and play a positive role in the community. Our services make contact with people in the community and on the streets, help them with housing and offer education and training to help them into employment.

We have 18 prison projects focusing on housing, education and employment. We also train prisoners to NVQ3 in Advice and Guidance (equivalent to 2 A-Levels) so they can advise fellow inmates. A new project called Straight to Work, which employs our former Peer Advisors to provide resettlement support to people leaving prison has just started.

Supported by: Lloyd's

War Child
www.warchild.org.uk
Tel: 020 7916 9276
Registered Charity No: 1071659

War Child works in countries acutely affected by conflict – Iraq, Afghanistan and the Democratic Republic of Congo – to protect street children, child soldiers as well as children in prison.

On the ground War Child's practical action, advocacy and awareness-raising can embrace giving grants to set up small businesses, encouraging a community into a more positive attitude to street children and attempting to change national Government policy.

In the UK and internationally, War Child works to build an informed culture, secure policy change and raise funds. Our target group is 16-30 year-olds, who we reach through www.warchildmusic.com, music concerts and other live events. In 2006 we released the fastest recorded and released album and won a UN award for 'outstanding achievement in public relations campaigns'.

Weber Shandwick has been helping War Child since 2005, and was especially involved in promoting the album Help: A Day in the Life.

Suppported by: Weber Shandwick

WOODLAND
TRUST

Woodland Trust
www.woodland-trust.org.uk
Tel: 01476 581111
Registered Charity No: 294344

The Woodland Trust is the UK's leading woodland conservation charity, owning more than 1,200 woods which are open free of charge for the public to enjoy. Our vision is to protect what we have, restore what has been spoilt and create new woods for the future, to make our countryside friendlier for people and wildlife.

The UK has only 12 per cent woodland cover compared to a European average of 44 per cent. To tackle this, the charity works with communities to plant millions of trees throughout the UK. It also campaigns for better protection of ancient woodland which is the UK's most precious wildlife habitat and home to threatened species such as the dormouse and red squirrel. Trees and forests also stabilise the soil, generate oxygen, store carbon, transform landscapes and provide one of the richest habitats for flora and fauna.

Supported by: Yellow Pages

Mallen Baker
Development Director
Business in the Community

Business in the Community (BITC), founded in
1982, is an independent business led charity
whose purpose is to inspire, engage, support and
challenge companies to continually improve the
impact they have on society.

Its president is HRH The Prince of Wales and it has
a current membership of over 750 companies.
This includes 71 of the FTSE 100 and 82 per cent of
the FTSE's UK leading companies in their sector.
Together BITC members employ 12.4 million people
in over 200 countries worldwide, including one in
five of the UK private sector workforce.

BITC's objective is to create a public benefit by
inspiring companies to improve the positive
impact of business in society and be a platform
for dialogue, collaboration and for sharing best
practice concepts.

BITC is the largest national network of its kind, with
over 100 partnerships across the UK and more than
60 international partner organisations sharing their
experiences from around the world with the aim of
translating policy into practice. Its strategy is driven
by over 200 business leaders from companies at
the forefront of socially and environmentally
responsible business practice.

Corporate Social Responsibility – the new minimum standard for Business Superbrands

By Mallen Baker

The owners of great brands understand that the value of the brand comes from the relationship it creates with the customer.

The terms of reference for that relationship are changing fast. The expectations of customers and society as a whole are changing with regard to what the minimum terms of trust are. And trust is essential for a good brand to flourish.

Corporate Social Responsibility (CSR) has become the broad heading to describe this new area. Whereas in its early days the term described the commitment of companies to invest in charitable or community causes, it has come to describe how companies resolve dilemmas around the way that they make their money. This is a much more difficult area, and one where it is easy to get things wrong.

CSR is fundamentally about relationships – the relationship between the companies or its brands and customers, suppliers, Government, employees and communities. That makes it by definition subject to change over time, and also at risk of inconsistent signals and unintended consequences.

The most trusted brands are those that have taken the initiative, positively building trust rather than waiting for the moment when they have to defend their reputation from attack.

Marks & Spencer, for instance, identified that its customers did not expect to have to decide on the details of what chemicals they would or would not accept in M&S products – they expected the company to do the research and then to do the right thing in its customers interests. In response, M&S gradually built its initiatives across its product ranges to the point where it was well placed to give its social and environmental commitments a much higher profile. Its 'Look Behind the Label' campaign has been an effective part of the new resurgent M&S refreshing its appeal, particularly to younger audiences that had not identified with the values of the brand previously. But it was only able to do this once its practice in this area was completely robust – the customer has, over the years, developed a fine nose for sniffing out false claims.

Of all the issues that have appeared on the horizon in recent years, the one that has grown to the point where no one can ignore it is that of climate change. Businesses that would formerly have been expected to be in denial over such a phenomenon have embraced it.

BP, for instance, having been an early mover in recognising the problem, has been one of the highest profile brands on the issue with its highly distinctive, provocative and thoughtful advertising. When John Browne coined the phrase 'Beyond Petroleum' he was neatly describing what, for an oil major, must be a 40-year journey. Even recent difficulties with its pipelines in Alaska have not been able to remove the brand advantage of having taken leadership on the issue from an early stage.

Action is not restricted to companies with a direct consumer role. ABB for instance, takes its role as one of the world's largest engineering companies to focus on a goal of enabling its customers to improve performance whilst lowering environmental impact. In order to achieve this, sustainability-based risks and opportunities are part of the company's approach to project management, including bid evaluation and mergers and acquisitions. It evaluates environmental performance of its products throughout their lifecycle and has an internal approval process to ensure that new designs meet this performance aspect.

Of course, amongst most markets likely to be challenged by climate change is the airline sector, which for various reasons is singled out in the popular consciousness and by politicians as having a heavy – and growing – footprint. Initial moves to encourage consumers to address this, such as the steps taken by British Airways to encourage its passengers to pay extra for a carbon offset for their journey, have not been widely taken up. More dramatic has been the gesture made by Sir Richard Branson who pledged all of the profits associated with the Virgin transport businesses to research into environmental technologies. This measure – rather more dramatic than BA's shareholders would be likely to tolerate – has nevertheless served to underline just how seriously businesses are taking the challenge.

Companies that have smaller footprints have begun to set themselves the target of

When it comes to green matters we develop grey matter.

Our investment in environmental and science education has helped inspire British school children for 37 years. Since 2003, teachers in over 700 UK schools have chosen to use our resource pack, which helps teach children about energy issues.

bp.com

beyond petroleum

achieving 'carbon neutrality'. BSkyB, for instance, one of the media companies that has done the most in developing its approach to CSR, was an early adopter. HSBC have also made the pledge, and others are likely to follow. Notwithstanding that the whole process of becoming 'carbon neutral' is one of heated debate, the policy intention behind the statement is clear.

Often the real environmental and social impacts come not from the operations of the companies themselves, but by the impact of their products as used by their customers. Everybody knows that the motor car is one of the greatest sources of polluting emissions. Companies such as Toyota have built market-leading profiles through embracing the opportunity to invest in the technologies of tomorrow to produce less polluting products. The Toyota Prius has in itself almost become an icon for the popularisation of alternative technology cars. It may not singularly explain why Toyota has accelerated fast past its US rivals GM and Ford, still locked in the gas-guzzler era, but it has certainly shown that the commitment to invest in alternatives

can be part of the strategy of a financially successful business.

This is not necessarily new. 3M, which is often feted for its remarkable approach to constant innovation within its product range, put its '3P' approach (Pollution Prevention Pays) at the heart of that innovation over 25 years ago. Not only has this helped it to produce products that have, over time, removed chemicals of concern to be replaced by more benign alternatives, it has also focused on minimising the energy and waste from its production processes to achieve major cost savings.

Others have had to innovate in order to survive rapidly changing expectations that have already become quite critical. Walkers, for instance, has had to develop a whole new type of vegetable oil and invest in boosting its production in order to produce crisps that address some of the growing obesity and health concerns.

This growing interest by consumer-facing companies leads to new opportunities for B2B firms. For instance, German chemical group BASF as the largest chemicals manufacturer in the world, now focuses on innovation as a way to help its customers to achieve sustainable development. Over the last 10 years BASF has been helping its customers to evaluate products and processes with eco-efficiency analysis. To date, over 250 BASF products – ranging from vitamins to solvents – have undergone eco-efficiency analyses. Every new product introduced by BASF is now required to undergo this process.

Not all of the social and environmental responsibilities of businesses start and finish with those aspects that the company can control. Much of the bad press out there about individual companies and brands attaches to what happens in the supply chain. Customers and NGOs make no distinction. If a supplier abuses human or labour rights, it will be the buying company and the big brand that gets the attention.

Nike of course was the first one to be hit hard by this. Once a scandal has become associated in the public mind with a brand, it can be very hard to shake. The company is now rated to be one of the best in the world for dealing with its huge and diverse supply chain, and talking transparently about its problems. There are still, however, a lot of people out there for whom the brand remains synonymous with the sweatshop. Once lost, a reputation is hard to rebuild.

Again, being proactive is the best approach. Companies such as B&Q – part of Kingfisher – Waitrose and Boots the Chemist, have had a vigorous approach to building responsibility into their supply chain for some years. B&Q started tackling sustainability issues over 15 years ago, recognising that the sourcing of timber would inevitably become a big issue in the future. Measure its success in the absence of scandal.

Some brands have made their commitment to social responsibility a key part of their market definition. The Co-operative Bank,

The Body Shop, Ben & Jerry's ice cream, innocent smoothies – all of these have become known for aiming for the highest standards and attracting the positive loyalty of consumer activists. They are niche brands, but the best of them have shown that it can be a profitable niche.

On the flip side, there are some companies that those activists just love to hate. Nestlé recently introduced its Fairtrade coffee 'Partners Blend' to the fury of some, but with the support of groups such as the Fairtrade Foundation that has the aim of increasing the percentage of the market committed to Fairtrade products and recognises that in order to achieve that you have to win over the major players.

For many businesses, however, the real benefit of a focus on CSR is not to do with the external rewards, but the internal. Those companies that treat their staff well within a high performance culture describe benefits

such as the ability to attract and retain top talent, and generally improving workplace morale and motivation. Global brands such as Microsoft® – seen as controversial by some because of the sheer scale of its success in dominating its market – ranks consistently highly in different parts of the world as having great workplace cultures. And this doesn't have to be solely a big boys club – smaller companies such as Happy (formerly Happy Computers – a computer training company) rate very highly on the scale of employee satisfaction and retention by taking a flexible approach to employee conditions and encouraging them to volunteer in the community.

There is no magic bullet in CSR that guarantees success purely because of good intentions – just as there isn't in any other aspect of how brands are created and promoted. But in building trust with customers, it has become a new prerequisite.

The Council Process

By Stephen Cheliotis
Chairman
Superbrands Councils UK

As the chairman of the Superbrands Council my role is to construct and oversee the council and manage the stage of the selection process involving their expert opinion. This phase of the process is however not the first step in the methodology; stage one involves a group of independent researchers, who compile a population list of brands operating in the business to business environment. These individuals are tasked with building the long list throughout the year and are constantly monitoring a range of trade media, consulting with experts in specific fields and reviewing relevant research, databases and a wide variety of other sources. The diversity of the brands and sectors considered is extensive and under regular review.

The size of the population list varies each year but invariably consists of between 5,000 and 10,000 brands. I first become involved when assisting the researchers to cut the list down to a manageable size that the council could go through. Using the information provided, which may reveal everything from revenues and profits to number of employees, and through our own specialist knowledge, we construct the 'short-list'. This has a tendency of closing at between 1,200 and 1,500 brands. Where there is a genuine possibility of the brand qualifying as a Business Superbrand we include it. We tend to edge on the side of caution in deleting any brands – indeed many council members consider that we are too conservative with our cutting policy but we prefer the council to confirm whether a brand is strong enough to be considered a Business Superbrand rather than make the decision ourselves. This year the list that the council scored consisted of 1,322 brands.

All members of the council are able to insert any brand that we have omitted – usually around a dozen brands are considered absent and subsequently added and scored by all council members. Of course, unlike almost every other 'award' scheme in the industry Superbrands do not invite brands to submit an entry or interest in the programme. The aim is to review everyone based on merit whether they wish to have a wider involvement with us or not – this seems to be a fairer and more holistic method.

The size of the council has historically been in the region of 12 members. This year I increased that number to 17 to include a wider range of experts from a variety of fields, enabling us to create a diverse collective of perspectives and experiences. Members tend to come from three categories; firstly senior figures from marketing services agencies, secondly senior practitioners at highly regarded and relevant brands and thirdly from the media and/or trade bodies and associations. In addition, we ensure that expertise from a range of marketing disciplines is covered. In this case we have highly experienced individuals in brand design and strategy, market research, direct marketing, public relations and advertising as well as more general marketing practitioners. We are likely to continue increasing the size and diversity of the council as we move forward and we are always open to recommendations.

No council member is paid by Superbrands and they all provide their time and expertise voluntarily. The decision on which council members are appointed lies with me and is not influenced by commercial consideration from anyone else within Superbrands. The council consists of a combination of new and existing members from the previous year, this is to ensure that the council is always fresh yet has some consistency – this gives us new perspectives but not a 100 per cent change from one year to the next year, enabling reasonable year on year comparisons of brand performance.

Council members score each brand on the presented short-list, giving each a rating from 1-10. The range was wider in the past but consulting research experts felt that this was too extensive. Council members are asked to score each brand instinctively. As we are considering overall brand image we do not want individuals to research the brand or think too long about each entity. We need their initial perception as other stakeholders also frequently make decisions on a brand from their intuitive observation of that brand.

Council members only consider each brand's status within the UK, although clearly a brand's international strength may constitute part of its make-up and improve the perception individuals may have of it overall. Individuals cannot score brands that they are involved with, i.e. that they work for or might be a client of their company. In addition, competitor brands are not to be scored. Equally, council members are asked not to score a brand that they have no knowledge of – we do not want them to fathom a ranking based on a glance at the brand's website or through second-hand opinion for example. Instead, we apply an average score to that brand based upon the ratings of the other council members.

Whilst council members are asked to consider their overall perception of the brand and its strength in the market, we do request that individuals consider three factors and keep these in mind when allocating their scores. These factors are:

Quality – does the brand represent quality products and services?

Reliability – can you trust the brand to deliver consistently against its promises and maintain product and service standards across all customer touch points?

Distinction – is the brand well known in its sector, is it suitably differentiated from its competitors and does it have a personality and values that make it unique within its market?

We believe that all three qualities are essential ingredients in any Business Superbrands. In addition all brands that are highly rated should be able to stand up against the following definition: "a Business Superbrand has established the finest reputation in its field. It offers customers significant emotional and or tangible advantages over its competitors, which (consciously or sub-consciously) customers want, recognise, and are confident about investing in. Business Superbrands are targeted at organisations (although not necessarily exclusively so)".

Finally council members score the brands in the context of the entire list. So Merrill Lynch are not scored compared to just Lehman Brothers or Goldman Sach but against the list generally. Inevitably psychologically some comparison is made but the key is not to weight the list to try to have brands from each field. The aim is to find the overall strongest brands and some sectors may find that all of its brands qualified with high scores whilst in other sectors no brands qualify.

My commercial involvement in Superbrands is on a part-time basis and I do not score the brands. This means that no commercial consideration unduly influences the process at any point.

The returned scores are collated and a league table is created. This league table is presented to the council members who have the opportunity to review and discuss it at a council meeting. This is the final opportunity they have to add any missing brands, note any mistakes, discuss any further brands' inclusion, examine the definition and the methodology and provide opinion on the next and final stage of the selection process, which is the consumer election (in this case the

business professionals' election). The number of brands awarded Business Superbrands status and invited by Superbrands to participate in the wider programme is also debated and agreed.

Council members are engaged throughout the year on an ad hoc basis and provide their feedback and thoughts on the process and programme as appropriate to ensure that we make continuous improvements. The redesign of the book and the introduction of the consumer/YouGov stage were as a result of council feedback and I act as a bridge in providing Superbrands comment from our expert group to ensure the programme moves forward. Now that Superbrands in the UK is an independent franchise its ability to make change quickly has been enhanced further.

The aim of Business Superbrands from the council perspective very much marries Superbrands' view, which is that the project will give people, not just in the marketing industry but more widely, a greater appreciation of the discipline of branding and a greater admiration for the brands that are performing well. As a subjective process

we appreciate that case studies featured in this book do not represent all of the brands awarded Business Superbrands status. Nevertheless all have qualified to be involved following the selection process and deserve recognition. Equally those that qualified, but have decided not to work with Superbrands, are included in a listing in this publication and will be recognised on our website and in related PR. Their reasons for not being involved may vary and range from a current rebranding exercise being underway through to not having time to work with Superbrands and its freelance journalists on the case study. Some brands choose to be involved every other year as their stories develop but all the brands involved are recognised and can claim to be Business Superbrands – something not possible in award schemes where brands submit an entry (and the vast bulk of brands do not of course).

If you have any questions, comments or thoughts on the programme and the process please do contact me on: stephen.cheliotis@superbrands.uk.com

Business Superbrands Council 2007

Stephen Cheliotis
Chairman
Superbrands Councils UK

Stephen attained a degree in PR & Marketing before joining global brand valuation and strategy consultancy, Brand Finance, where he helped to advise brands on maximising shareholder value through effective brand management. In addition he produced a range of significant reports, including comprehensive studies of global intangible assets. His annual study of City Analysts, which explored the City's need for marketing information, was vital in understanding the importance of marketing metrics in appreciating and forecasting companies' performance.

In 2001 Stephen joined Superbrands and in 2003 became UK Managing Director, overseeing two years of significant growth. He was given a European role in 2005 where his expertise was used across 20 countries. In late 2006 he set up his own business providing PR and Marketing advice to companies.

Stephen chairs the three independent Superbrands Councils in the UK. He speaks at conferences on branding and is a regular commentator for international media on the subject. He is a frequent guest on CNN, the BBC and Sky amongst others.

Anthony Carlisle
Executive Director
Citigate Dewe Rogerson

In his current role, Tony acts for companies such as T-Mobile, Yell, Legal&General, Carphone Warehouse, National Grid and Iberdrola. He is also a non-executive director of CSR, the global leaders in Bluetooth wireless.

Anthony began his career at Lintas Advertising, working on fmcg accounts. He helped found Dewe Rogerson, later becoming chief executive and then chairman, building it into a leading international marketing and communications group, before creating Citigate Dewe Rogerson, now part of Huntsworth Group. He led around 90 per cent by value of UK privatisation marketing and communications, pioneering wide share ownership.

Anthony has advised numerous companies in the UK and abroad on their marketing, branding and communications strategies; their positioning with corporate and investor audiences; and on capital raising and bid defence as well as acquisitions. He was also in the core adviser group in creating Orange.

He is married with two children.

Steve Cooke
Marketing Director
BMRB

For the past 10 years Steve's responsibilities have been in corporate and service marketing. In his current role he is responsible for developing communications strategy for BMRB and the KMR Group. Steve manages all central aspects of brand development which includes advertising, PR, corporate events, conferences, website, internal comms and marketing collateral. He recently headed up a rebranding programme, resulting in the launch of a new identity for BMRB.

Steve has a wealth of experience in business to business marketing and market research, gained from his current role and previous positions at television sales house TSMS and media independent BBJ. He holds a postgraduate diploma in marketing.

Jonathan Cummings
Marketing Director
Institute of Directors

As marketing director, Jonathan is responsible for marketing strategy and delivery across the diverse IoD range of activities, from top-end hospitality to publishing and from business information and advice to director-level training. He also has responsibility for all IoD events, along with the award winning business information and advisory services provided for members of the organisation.

Jonathan represents the IoD on various advisory boards and collaborative bodies. In addition, he presents regularly on e-business and marketing issues that affect businesses of all sizes. A key theme for Jonathan is to communicate to business leaders the benefits of a holistic brand engagement strategy, and the importance of ensuring that every stakeholder truly understands the brand and their influence on it.

Cherry DeGeer
Global Practice Leader – Communications
Rio Tinto

Cherry has responsibility for Rio Tinto's global communications activities and visual identity, promoting design, editorial and brand consistency across the company's business units worldwide. In her current position, Cherry's role includes accountability and strategic planning and development of all external, employee and shareholder communications through digital and multimedia, websites, intranet, video, advertising and printed literature. Cherry is also editor of Review, Rio Tinto's corporate magazine.

Her time at Rio Tinto builds on over a decade of communications experience gained working with or for some of the UK's top brands, in various design and communications consultancies or in corporate communications roles in FTSE100 companies and at the London Stock Exchange.

Marc Edney
Group Marketing Manager
BSI Group

Marc is responsible for BSI's brand and PR at the corporate level.

His career in marketing began with the John Lewis Partnership and progressed to publishers Reed Elsevier. In 2002, Marc joined BSI and was initially responsible for marketing the British Standards portfolio of publications and for developing the division's strategies for exhibitions and key third-party relationships.

Moving to his current role in 2005, Marc is now steward of the BSI brand. Work is always ongoing - strengthening and revitalising the brand and in 2006 one key task was rolling out a new strapline (raising standards worldwide™) across the 100 plus countries in which BSI operates.

Marc also handles BSI Group's sponsorship of the BSI Sustainability Design Awards in conjunction with the Royal College of Art, London, as well as publishing and promoting the Group's member and customer magazine Business Standards.

Gary Groenheim
Head of Marketing
CNBC Europe

In 2006 Gary joined CNBC Europe after five years at TIME where he marketed their magazine across Europe.

Gary oversees all marketing and advertising activity for CNBC in Europe, working closely with the sales teams across the region as well as with CNBC in the US and Asia. He has created campaigns targeting the channel's affluent and highly-valued business audience as well as launched CNBC's new digital offerings in Europe.

During his tenure at TIME, Gary created international multimedia marketing programmes that increased the magazine's brand profile and advertising revenues. Gary created TIME's highly acclaimed European Heroes Awards and established the magazine's exclusive media partnership with the World Economic Forum.

Before joining TIME, he had been an international account manager at advertising agency Wieden & Kennedy, working in both London and Amsterdam on pan-European and international accounts including Nike, Coca-Cola and Alta Vista.

Ruth Mortimer
Editor
Brand Strategy

Ruth Mortimer is editor of Brand Strategy magazine, the leading global business magazine for senior marketing executives. She is responsible for the title's print product, website, newletter and blog. In this role, she often appears on the BBC or Sky News to comment on branding issues. She was previously freelance, writing about business issues for a large number of magazines and newspapers in the UK and Australia. Prior to this, Ruth had a former existence as an archaeologist specialising in the Middle East and based in south east Turkey.

Marc Nohr
Managing Partner
Kitcatt Nohr Alexander Shaw

Marc is responsible for business development and client strategy at DM Agency of the Year, Kitcatt Nohr whose clients include Waitrose, Virgin, Citroën and Friends Reunited.

Marc is an honorary fellow of the Institute of Direct Marketing, and one of the Institute's most popular speakers. He has spoken at marketing conferences around the world, including South Africa, Canada and Korea, as well as in the UK at the London Business School and Institute of Directors, amongst others. He regularly contributes to debates on marketing in the media, having written for The Independent and The Guardian as well as the trade press and was one of the founding columnists in Financial Times Creative Business. He now has a column in the leading DM monthly title Marketing Direct and features highly in their DM Power 100.

Daniel Rogers
Editor
PRWeek

Danny Rogers has edited the communications industry bible PRWeek since 2004, making it more heavyweight, outward looking and brand focused in that time. He has been a marketing and media journalist for a decade, having spent stints as contributing editor to Financial Times Creative Business and Media Guardian, and previously as deputy editor on Marketing magazine. Danny is a columnist for Travel Weekly, a contributor to several hotel and travel guides, and a regular broadcast commentator on media issues.

Simon Gruselle
Corporate Marketing Director
Datamonitor

Simon was appointed Datamonitor's Corporate Marketing Director in 2002 with responsibility for the company's brand development. He has since overseen a number of rebranding projects for companies newly acquired by Datamonitor. He has also played a key role in the development of Datamonitor's latest brand values, in conjunction with the launch of the Knowledge Centers. Prior to this appointment, Simon ran a number of the business units within Datamonitor. Simon was one of the first people to join Datamonitor shortly after it was founded in 1989, starting his career in the information industry as an Analyst.

John Mathers
CEO
Enterprise IG, UK

John is the CEO of Enterprise IG in the UK. Part of WPP, Enterprise IG is one of the world's leading brand and design specialists. John has a broad mix of experience, on both the client and agency sides. On the client side, this ranges from relaunching Lyons Ground Coffee to a comprehensive rebranding of Safeway in the mid 1990s, which encompassed everything from the identity through to complete new store design as well as an internal brand engagement exercise with all 56,000 employees. On the agency front, John spearheaded the complete branding of the Sheffield Supertram system; helped to reposition BP as an energy organisation; and revamped the Belgian Post Office network.

John is also president of the Design Business Association.

David Mitchell
Ex Head of Brand Communication EMEA
Intel

David has recently left Intel after 10 years and is now looking at a number of business opportunities in the marketing field. For the last three years, he was responsible for Intel's advertising and media across EMEA; covering both business and consumer markets. In 2006, he led Intel's Interactive Marketing team and relaunched Intel's websites in Europe, driving substantially higher traffic through the sites. Brand strategy played a big part in David's Intel career, and in 2006, Intel underwent a global brand refresh under the tagline of 'Leap Ahead'. The refresh simplified a previously complex brand hierarchy and helped drive brand value back to the Intel masterbrand.

Prior to Intel, David worked for Dell and Compaq computers, and spent six years working in marketing agencies.

Graham Spencer
Director of Marketing, Europe
Towers Perrin

Graham is a principal and director of marketing for Towers Perrin in Europe. He joined Towers Perrin in 1989 and is responsible for leading the development and implementation of marketing strategy and plans across Europe.

On joining the Towers Perrin group, Graham was tasked with creating a marketing strategy to support the group's growth objectives. This involved opening seven new offices throughout Europe in just over a year. Using client research and a highly segmented marketing approach he has prime responsibility for growing the Towers Perrin brand in Europe.

Prior to joining Towers Perrin, Graham led the media relations function for the English Tourist Board, and subsequently for the combined British Tourist Authority. He was later recruited by Chesterton, a leading international firm of chartered surveyors, to lead its marketing and PR function. At Chesterton he provided external marketing consultancy to its clients.

Simon Woodroffe
Founder
YO!Company

Simon spent 30 years in the entertainment business. His production companies in London and Los Angeles designed and staged concerts for many artists during the 1970s and 1980s, including Madness, Stevie Wonder and George Michael.

In the 1990s, Simon spearheaded the development of television deals to show huge international rock concerts worldwide, including Nelson Mandela, Amnesty and the Prince's Trust concerts.

In 1997, Simon founded YO! Sushi. The concept was to make eating a complete entertainment experience and featured call buttons and robot drinks trolleys. The first restaurant opened in London and became an overnight phenomenon. Today it continues to expand both at home and abroad and Simon now heads up YO!Company, which is working on new YO! brands including YOTEL and YO! Zone.

In 1999 Simon won the Ernst & Young Entrepreneur of the Year Award and was awarded an OBE in the Queen's Birthday Honours list in 2006.

Simon Wylie
Founding Partner & Managing Director
Xtreme Information

Simon Wylie is a founding partner of Xtreme Information. Launched in 1983 as the TV Register, Xtreme Information is the leading media intelligence source of global TV, press, radio, cinema, outdoor and internet advertising. After graduating with a degree in History & French from Goldsmiths, Simon joined the TV Register in 1985. In 1989 he founded the company's first international office in Italy, returning to the UK in 1995. He became sales & marketing director in 1996 and then took on the same role in the newly formed Xtreme Information in 1997. He is currently managing director of the Advertising Division London HQ.

Panos Manolopoulos
Managing Director
YouGov plc

Panos Manolopoulos is responsible for business development and market research services. Panos is a client-focused market research professional, with an established track record in business development, key account and project management and team leadership. He has previously worked for NOP, Taylor Nelson Sofres (TNS) and set up Lightspeed Research – the WPP online research agency – in Europe. He has worked for clients in Telecoms, IT, Financial, Travel & Leisure, fmcg, Media/New Media, Utilities, Automotive and Consumer products verticals and has obtained an understanding of the business drivers in these industry sectors.

Panos has completed projects across a broad range of research types including advertising effectiveness research, customer satisfaction, usage and attitudes, brand awareness, concept testing, origin and destination, product testing and more. He has worked on both adhoc as well as continuous and tracking contracts in the UK and internationally. Panos has been involved in consumer and business research using a range of offline and online data collection methods.

Over the last four years, Panos has obtained an insight into online market research methods and has supported clients and research agencies in their understanding, adoption and use of the new methodologies and research platforms.

Panos completed his graduate studies at the London School of Economics and joined the market research industry in the late 1980s. He is a member of the MRS and has presented survey findings and research papers at seminars, conferences and other public platforms. His latest award was for the Best Presented Paper at the ESOMAR Technovate Conference, Berlin 2002.

Business Superbrands
YouGov Online Election

By Panos Manolopoulos
Managing Director
YouGov plc

About YouGov plc

YouGov plc is a full service online market research agency pioneering the use of the internet and information technology to collect higher quality in-depth data for market research and public consultation. YouGov operates a diverse panel of over 150,000 UK residents with similar operations in the US and the Middle East.

Based on its past record, YouGov is the UK's most accurate public opinion pollster and dominates Britain's media polling. YouGov is one of the most quoted agencies in Britain and has a well-documented and published track record illustrating the success of its survey methods and quality of its client service work. Based on its work in the consumer research and opinion polling sector, the agency has one of the fastest growth rates in the industry.

YouGov is a pioneer of online research and e-consultation, using its strong market research skill set and industry expertise to support its clients. The agency's full service work extends across industry sectors including consumer, financial, healthcare, media, new media and technology. A range of research types and data collection methods are used in survey designs tailored to individual client requirements. YouGov offer innovative and tailored market research

solutions, quality of service and insight that allow its clients to make effective decisions about their business.

YouGov plc and Business Superbrands

YouGov has worked with the Superbrands organisation over the past few years in providing comprehensive data which reflects the opinions of consumers and, in the case of Business Superbrands, business professionals.

The aim of the Business Superbrands Online Election was to establish which business to business brands respondents rated most highly. The survey results are reflective of industry in Great Britain and play a key role in the Business Superbrands selection process, which establishes the 500 strongest brands in Britain who are awarded Business Superbrands status. YouGov also conducts online elections for the organisation's other UK programmes – Superbrands and CoolBrands.

At the beginning of this publication you will find a step by step explanation of the Business Superbrands selection processes, however you will find to follow details of the methodology used by YouGov for the completion of the Business Superbrands Online Election.

The survey, which took place for Business Superbrands 2007, was conducted using an online interview system. This was administered to members of the YouGov plc GB panel of individuals who have previously agreed to take part in surveys for the company.

Online research has proved to be the best medium for quantifying the perception of Business Superbrands amongst business professionals. Its inherent qualities mean that extremely useful data can be delivered. This type of research has been found to be engaging and the questionnaire process stimulating. The process is intuitive, so it can be quick and enjoyable for participants. In addition, online research is non-intrusive as the questionnaires are completed by invitation. It is representative as there are sufficient numbers of individuals online to compensate for the biases in the online community when sampling. Furthermore, it is faster and more accurate than other conventional methodologies. Finally, online research is more cost effective than conventional approaches.

The sample of respondents was drawn from senior business professionals – defined as those individuals who are decision makers or have company purchasing responsibility – across a wide range of industry sectors and company sizes controlled by quota. The final responding sample was 1,420 individuals.

As business professionals have begun to take a more active interest in the brands they consume in recent years, they are inherently qualified to aid in the judging process. This allows brand owners a direct insight into consumer perspectives about their brands. Some further analysis of the data can also help brand owners to better understand some of the key demographics that play a role in driving perceptions of their brands as well as the market in which they operate, and how these perceptions compare with other brands in their competitive landscape.

An email was sent to the sample, inviting them to take part in the survey and providing a link to this. YouGov plc normally achieves a response rate of between 35 per cent and 50 per cent to surveys, however this varies depending upon the subject matter, complexity and length of the questionnaire.

Within a typical Business Superbrands election, business professionals are asked to choose the brands that they view as a Business Superbrand. The definition of a Business Superbrand that the respondents consider when scoring is: 'a brand that represents quality products and services, is

considered reliable, i.e. it delivers consistently against its promises, and is distinctive, i.e. well known in its sector, suitably differentiated from its competitors and has a personality and values that make it unique within the market place in which it operates'.

Sectors that are considered for Business Superbrands are wide ranging and include Utilities, General Financial, Healthcare Equipment, Insurance, Media, Pharmaceuticals, Support Services, Travel & Leisure, Automobiles, Mining and Computer Software.

When the online election has been completed the final scores are sent to Superbrands who incorporate the results together with the scores given to the brands by the council (see selection process details at the beginning of this publication)

The chart below shows the factors that are viewed as critical for a Business Superbrand, as voted for by business professionals from the Business Superbrands Online Election. Respondents were asked to select all factors that they viewed as being of greatest importance to a highly performing Business Superbrand.

One can clearly see that two thirds (66 per cent) of those surveyed believe that 'delivery of quality products/services' was the most important factor. Having an excellent

reputation was rated in second place, with more than a half (55 per cent) of respondents citing this factor. 'Innovative products and services' and 'financial stability' are rated as being comparably important, with just under half (46 per cent and 43 per cent respectively) of the votes.

YouGov plc operates under the MRS code of conduct and is a member of the British Polling Council. YouGov is also registered with the Information Commissioner.

www.yougov.com

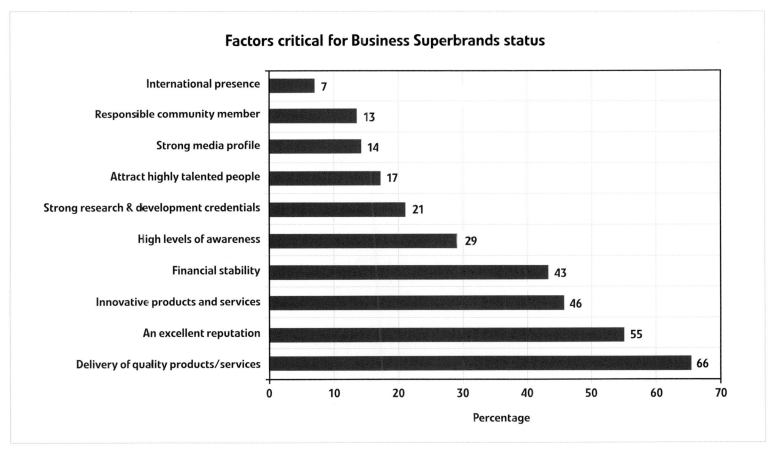

Factors critical for Business Superbrands status

Factor	Percentage
International presence	7
Responsible community member	13
Strong media profile	14
Attract highly talented people	17
Strong research & development credentials	21
High levels of awareness	29
Financial stability	43
Innovative products and services	46
An excellent reputation	55
Delivery of quality products/services	66

Percentage

Qualifying Business Superbrands 2007

3
3Com
3i
3M
AA Insurance
ABN AMRO
ABTA
Acas
Accountancy Age
Acer
ACNielsen
Adecco
Adobe
Aer Lingus
AIG
AIM
Air Miles
Airbus
Akzo Nobel
Alamo
Alfred Mcalpine
Allen & Overy
Alliance Unichem
Allianz
Allied Irish Bank (GB)
Alstom
Amec
American Airlines
American Express
Amicus
Amtrak
AMV BBDO
Anglo American
Apax Partners
Apple
Arriva
Ashridge
Associated British Ports
Association of British Insurers
AstraZeneca
Augusta Westland
Autocad
Avery
Avis
Aviva
AXA
Axa PPP Healthcare
BAA
Babcock
BACS
BAE Systems
Bain & Company
Baker & Mckenzie
Balfour Beatty
Banco Santander
Bank of America
Bank of Scotland
Barclaycard
Barclays
BASF
Basildon Bond

Bayer
BBC
BBH
BDO Stoy Hayward
Belkin
Bell Pottinger
BG Group
Bic
Big Yellow Storage
Blackberry
Bloomberg
Blue Circle
Bluetooth
Blu-Tack
BMI
BMRB
BNP Paribas
BOC
Boeing
Bombardier
Booker
Booz Allen Hamilton
Bosch
BP
British Airways
British Energy
British Gas
British Land
Brittany Ferries
Brook Street
Brother
Brunswick Group
BSI
BT
Bupa
Burson-Marsteller
Burtons Foods
Business Week
Cable & Wireless
Calor Gas
Campaign
Canon
Cap Gemini
Capita
Carat
Casio
Caterpillar
Cathay Pacific
Cazenove
CBI
Centaur Communications
Centrica
Chubb Security
CIM
CIMA
Cisco Systems
Citigate
Citigroup
Clifford Chance
CNBC Europe
CNN

Commerzbank
Compass Group
Conqueror
Continental Airlines
Corus
Costain
Coutts
Cranfield School Of
    Management
Credit Suisse
Crowne Plaza
D&B
Daewoo
Dairy Crest Group
Datamonitor
DC Thomson & Co
DDB London
De La Rue
Dell
Deloitte & Touche
Delta Airlines
Design Week
Deutsche Bank
Deutsche Post
DHL
Dolby
Dow Jones
Dreamweaver
Dresdner Kleinwort Wasserstein
Dunlop
Dupont
Earls Court and Olympia
Easycar
Easyjet
Eddie Stobart
EDF Energy
EDS
Eli Lilly
Emirates
Enterprise IG
Epson
Ericsson
Ernst & Young
Esso
Euro RSCG
Eurocar
Euromoney Publications
Eurostar
Eurotunnel
Eversheds
Excel London
Exel
Experian
Express Dairies
Exxon Mobil
FedEx Express
Fidelity Investments
First
First Direct
Fish4Jobs
Flybe

Forbes
Fortune Magazine
Four Seasons Hotels
Freshfields Bruckhaus Deringer
FSA
FT
FTSE Market Information Service
Fujitsu
FutureBrand
Gatwick Express
GE
Geest
General Dynamics UK
Getty Images
GKN
GlaxoSmithKline
GMB
G-Mex & Micc, Manchester
GNER
Goldman Sachs
Goodyear
Google
Grant Thornton
Grey Worldwide
Group 4 Securicor
Gulfstream
H.R. Owen
Halifax
Hanson
Haymarket Group
Hays Logistics
Hays Personnel Services
HBOS
Heathrow Express
Henley Management College
Hertz
Hill & Knowlton
Hilton
Hitachi
Hogg Robinson Group
Holiday Inn
Honeywell
HP
HSBC
HSS Hire
IATA
IBM
ICI
Imagination
IMG
Intel
Interbrand
Invensys
Investec
Investors in People
IoD
ISO 9000
ITV
Jarvis Hotels
JCB
Jewson

John Laing Plc
Johnson & Johnson
Johnson Matthey
Jones Lang LaSalle
JP Morgan
JWT
Kall Kwik
Kimberly-Clark Hygiene
KLM Royal Dutch Airlines
KPMG
Land Securities
Landor
Lazard
Le Meridien Hotels & Resorts
Legal & General
Lehman Brothers
Leo Burnett
Lex
Lexmark
Leyland Daf
LG
Liffe
Linklaters
Lloyd's
Lloyds TSB
Lockheed Martin
London Business School
London School of Economics
  and Political Science
Lotus
Lovells
Lowe
Lucent Technologies
Lufthansa
Lycra
Lynx Express
M&C Saatchi
Macromedia
Maersk
Maiden Group
Malaysian Airlines
Management Today
Manchester Business School
Manpower
Marconi Corporation
Marketing
Marketing Week
Massey Ferguson
Mastercard
MBNA
McAfee
McCann Erickson
McGraw-Hill
McKinsey & Co
Mediacom
Mediaedge:Cia
Mercedes Trucks
Merck
Merrill Lynch
Michael Page International
Michelin
Microsoft
Millenium & Copthorne
Millward Brown
Mindshare

Mintel
Moat House Hotels
Monster.co.uk
Moody's
Morgan Stanley
Mori
Mother
Motorola
Mowlem
Multimap
Naked
National Express
National Grid
Natwest
NEC Birmingham
Nectar
NFU
NHBC
NM Rothschild
Nokia
Nomura
Nortel
Northern Foods
Northwest Airlines
Norton Rose
Norton Symantec Corporation
Norwich Union
Novartis
Novell
Npower
NTL
NUT
O2
Office Angels
Ogilvy & Mather
Olivetti
OMD UK
Oracle
Orange
P&O
PA Consulting
Palgrave MacMillan
Palm
Papermate
Parcelforce
Parceline
PC World
Pearl & Dean
Pearson Education
Pfizer
Pickfords
Pilkington
Pirelli
Pitman Training
Pitney Bowes
Portman Travel
Posthouse Forte Hotels
Powergen
PR Newswire
Pratt & Whitney
Premier Travel Inn
Price Jamieson
PricewaterhouseCoopers
Pritt
Prontaprint

Prudential
Publicis
Qantas
Qinetiq
Quark
RAC
Radisson Edwardian Hotels
Rainey Kelly Campbell
  Roalfe/Y&R
Ramada Jarvis Hotels
Redwood Publishing
Reed
Reed Business Information
Reed Elsevier
Reg Vardy
Regus Group
Rentokil Initial
Retail Week
Reuters Group
Ricoh
Rio Tinto
Roche
Rolls-Royce Group
Royal & Sun Alliance
Royal Bank of Scotland
Royal Mail
Ryanair
Ryman
Saatchi & Saatchi
Sage
Sagem
Salvesen
Samsung
SAP
SAS
SAS Travel
Savills
Schering-Plough
Schroders
Scottish & Southern Energy
Scottish Power
Securitas
Sellotape
Severn Trent
Sharp
Shell
Siemens
Singapore Airlines
Sir Robert McAlpine
Sky
Skype
Slaughter & May
Smith & Nephew
Sony
Southern Water
St Lukes
Staedtler
Stagecoach
Standard & Poor's
Standard Life Healthcare
Stanley
Staples
Stena Line Ferries
Sun Microsystems
Swiss Re

T&G
Tarmac
Tate & Lyle
TBWA\London
TDK
Telewest
Thales
Thames Water
The Bank of New York
The Carbon Trust
The Economist
The Gallup Organization
The Grocer
The Guardian Media Group
The Lawyer
The London Stock Exchange
The Open University
The Press Association
The Priory Group
The Telegraph Group
Thistle Hotels
Thompson Financial
Thomson Directories
Thyssen Krupp
Ticketmaster
Time
Tippex
T-Mobile
TNT
Topps Tiles
Toshiba
Total
Trafficmaster
Travis Perkins
UBS
Unison
Unisys
United Airlines
United Business Media
Unix
UPS
Velux
Vent-Axia
Viacom Brand Solutions
Viking
Virgin Atlantic
Virgin Mobile
Virgin Money
Virgin Trains
Visa
VNU Business Publications
Vodafone
Warwick Business School
WCRS
Weber Shandwick
Wembley Exhibition &
  Conference Centre
Wickes
Wolff Olins
Xerox
Yahoo!
Yellow Pages
YouGov
Zenith-Optimedia
Zurich